The Will to Kill

The Will to Kill

Making Sense of Senseless Murder

SECOND EDITION

James Alan Fox

Northeastern University

Jack Levin

Northeastern University

Kenna Quinet

Indiana University–Purdue University Indianapolis

Boston • New York • San Francisco
Mexico City • Montreal • Toronto • London • Madrid • Munich • Paris
Hong Kong • Singapore • Tokyo • Cape Town • Sydney

Series Editor: *Jennifer Jacobson*
Editorial Assistant: *Emma Christensen*
Senior Marketing Manager: *Krista Groshong*
Editorial Production Service: *Whitney Acres Editorial*
Manufacturing Buyer: *JoAnne Sweeney*
Cover Administrator: *Joel Gendron*
Electronic Composition: *Omegatype Typography, Inc.*

For related titles and support materials, visit our online catalog
at www.ablongman.com

Between the time Website information is gathered and published, some sites may have closed.
Also, the transcription of URLs can result in typographical errors. The publisher would appreciate
being notified of any problems with URLs so that they may be corrected in subsequent editions.

Library of Congress Cataloging-in-Publication Data
Fox, James Alan.
   The will to kill : making sense of senseless murder / James Alan Fox, Jack Levin,
Kenna Quinet.
      p.   cm.
   Includes bibliographical references and index.
   ISBN 0-205-41880-5 (pbk.)
      1. Murder.   2. Homicide.   3. Criminal psychology.   4. Criminal justice, Administration
of.   I. Levin, Jack, 1941–   II. Quinet, Kenna.   III. Title.

HV6515.F69 2005
364.152'3—dc22
                                                                    2004044742

Printed in the United States of America
10 9 8 7 6 5 4 3 2 1   09 08 07 06 05 04

*To the Lipman and Brudnick families
for their affection and generosity*

Contents

Preface

The second edition of *The Will to Kill* has provided us with a welcome opportunity to improve on our original work. We have expanded and updated a number of topics presented in the earlier version of the book. Almost every chapter has undergone significant revision, but especially our discussion of theories in "Explaining Murder." We have added some new chapters—"Medical Murder" on homicides committed within health care settings and "Catching Killers" that reviews a wide variety of investigative approaches. Additionally, a new chapter on "Murderous Terror," which includes the tragic events of September 11th, discusses issues of homegrown forms of terrorism as well. Finally, a third scholar—Kenna Quinet—has joined the authorship team, broadening the perspective, particularly with respect to theory, and female and medical murderers.

Like the first edition, this book is about the circumstances in which people kill one another. In the pages that follow, we review homicide laws, present statistical data depicting patterns and trends in homicide, and introduce theories purporting to explain why murder occurs. Then, we cover a range of topics from domestic and workplace homicide to cult and hate killings; from murder committed by juveniles to serial slayings. In two closing chapters, we examine criminal justice responses to homicide, including the strategies and tactics employed to apprehend, prosecute, and punish killers. In particular, we focus on DNA testing, behavioral profiling, the death penalty, the insanity defense, and our changing juvenile justice system.

Notwithstanding its broad scope, this book is by design far from comprehensive. As our subtitle, *Making Sense of Senseless Murder* correctly indicates, we purposely concentrate on the extraordinary and seemingly inexplicable cases—those involving large body counts, bizarre crime scenes, elements of sadism, and irrational motivation. Thus, the reader will hardly find in the pages that follow detailed accounts explaining why a man who loses his temper impulsively shoots his spouse, why a barroom brawl results in a fatal stabbing, or why an impoverished out-of-work father robs a liquor store. The chapters focus much more on family annihilations, fatal romantic attractions, school shootings, mass poisonings by cultists or medical practitioners, serial killers who torture their victims, and disgruntled ex-workers who go on a rampage.

We have accepted the challenge to concentrate on homicides that don't make obvious sense. This is not to suggest, however, that *The Will to Kill* would not be useful for understanding a much broader range of murders. We believe, on the contrary, that the lessons to be learned from examining senseless and outrageous murders can be easily extrapolated to more ordinary and mundane homicides as well. By dissecting extreme cases, we derive a selection of "pure types" against which most murders can be compared and, hopefully, better understood.

The intriguing and sensational circumstances that surround most, if not all of, the cases of homicide presented throughout this book have made them inordinately important in a public policy sense. These are, after all, the murder cases that have typically made the headlines and the evening news; they are the examples that politicians refer to when they seek to change some aspect of criminal law or to secure funding for programs and policies to reduce violence. These are also the murder cases on which public opinion about homicide is often based.

A data file on homicides in the United States for the years 1976 through 2002 is used throughout the book. A note at the end of the book describes in detail the elements and contents of this data file. Analysis of these data was supported by grants from the U.S. Department of Justice, Bureau of Justice Statistics.

We owe a special debt of gratitude to the Lipman and Brudnick families for their generosity and encouragement of our work. We also benefited from the institutional support of Northeastern University, Indiana University–Purdue University Indianapolis, and Guardsmark, LLC. Finally, we wish to thank Jennifer Jacobson, our editor at Allyn & Bacon, for her continuing faith in us, as well as our spouses and children whose love is only equaled by their patience.

James Alan Fox
Jack Levin
Kenna Quinet

About the Authors

James Alan Fox is The Lipman Family Professor of Criminal Justice at Northeastern University in Boston. He has published 16 books and numerous journal articles and newspaper columns, primarily in the areas of multiple murder, juvenile crime, school violence, workplace violence, and capital punishment. As an authority on homicide, he has appeared on such national television programs as *The Today Show, Meet the Press,* and *Oprah* and is frequently interviewed by the national press. He has worked on several homicide cases as a consultant or expert witness, including serving as a member of the task force investigating the Gainesville student murders. He also served as a consulting contributor for Fox News following the 9/11 terrorist attacks and as an NBC News Analyst during the DC sniper investigation. Fox worked closely with the Clinton administration, advising the White House and the Office of the Attorney General in the area of youth violence and school shootings. Finally, he is a visiting fellow with the U.S. Department of Justice, Bureau of Justice Statistics specializing in the measurement of homicide trends.

Jack Levin is the Irving and Betty Brudnick Professor of Sociology and Criminology and Director of the Brudnick Center on Violence and Conflict at Northeastern University in Boston. He has published 25 books and numerous journal articles and newspaper columns, primarily in the areas of serial and mass murder, hate crimes, school violence, juvenile murder, and workplace violence. Levin has appeared on such national television programs as *48 Hours, 20/20, Dateline NBC, The Today Show, Good Morning America, Oprah, The O'Reilly Factor, Larry King Live,* and all network newscasts and is often interviewed by the national press. He has served as an expert witness or consultant in a number of cases involving murder, cults, hate crimes, and the death penalty and has been a speaker to a wide range of community, college, and professional groups including the Dallas Woman's Club, the International Association of Chiefs of Police, the American Psychological Association's Symposium on School Violence, the Academy of Psychiatry and the Law, the White House Conference on Hate Crimes, and the University of Paris Conference on "Killing the Other."

Kenna Quinet is an associate professor and chair of the faculty of Criminal Justice, Law and Public Safety in the School of Public and Environmental Affairs at Indiana University–Purdue University Indianapolis (IUPUI). She is also a Research Fellow at the Indianapolis-based Center for Urban Policy and the Environment. Her research interests include homicide, suicide, line of duty deaths and injuries to police, and the evaluation of police interdictions. She teaches classes in homicide and criminological theory and public policy.

The Will to Kill

1

The Lure and the Law
of Homicide

Homicide intrigues virtually all of us. From the sensational and historic double murder trial of ex-football star O. J. Simpson to the travails of the elusive yet fictional Hannibal Lector of Thomas Harris's *The Silence of the Lambs,* we are drawn irresistibly to the drama, mystery, intrigue, and power of murder and murderers, both real and invented.

It would hardly be an overstatement to suggest that within popular culture, murder has become a cottage industry. In bookstores across America, the "true-crime" section, new since the late 1980s, offers an expanding array of books primarily about serial killers, multiple murders, killer cults, and crimes involving celebrities. *People* magazine, a yardstick for America's enchantments, increasingly places killers on its front cover. Film, trading cards, action figures, even artwork center on murders and murderers, creating a cottage industry in "murderabilia."

Fascination with Murder

What is it about homicide that captures our attention? Or perhaps the more fitting question is, what is it about us that explains our captivation? And what kinds of killings are especially appealing to the general public, which seems to have an insatiable appetite for true-crime books and films. It is our obsession with murder both as news and as entertainment that prompts print and TV magazines to feature infamous killers of the day.

For most of us, a fascination with murder is entirely benign. Ironically, we are drawn to murder, and especially to its most grisly and grotesque examples, as an escape from the mundane problems we face in everyday life—how to pay the bills, how to avoid being mugged, how to get a long-awaited promotion at work, and so on. Paying the bills, avoiding a mugger, and waiting for an overdue promotion—these are all too real. By contrast, some homicides are so extraordinary that psychologically they might as well be fiction. The killers might as well be characters in a novel or a film. Because they are so unlikely—at least from the point of view of true-crime buffs—they are also a form of entertainment and enjoyment. Homicides yielding large body counts—a massacre in a shopping mall or at a law firm or in the family—may qualify as crossing the line into fantasy. But the most fascinating homicides are those involving extreme forms of sadism—crimes in which victims are tortured, raped, and dismembered. The more grotesque (and therefore removed from ordinary life) a particular killing spree, the more likely it is to entertain us.

A second source of fascination with murder is not so trivial. In fact, there are many people who feel intensely vulnerable to the effects of violence—so much so that they read true-crime stories and watch TV docudramas about murder, not because they seek to escape psychologically, but in order to learn how to avoid becoming victims of homicide. Going beyond their role as members of the audience for murder, some actually seek to overcome feelings of powerlessness, anxiety, and vulnerability by planning careers as crime investigators or forensic psychologists. They hope to learn the techniques of criminal profiling and DNA analysis. The better they understand the murdering mind and the process of criminal investigation, the more they are able to distance themselves psychologically from the killers they fear and to feel safe.

The third and final source of fascination is also the most troubling. There are some individuals—hopefully, few in number—who live vicariously through the exploits of sadistic killers. Fascinated with power but controlled by normal feelings of conscience, these individuals are psychologically incapable of murdering for pleasure, money, or protection. They can, however, learn every detail of a killer's biography, every detail of a killer's modus operandi, every detail of the investigation by which a killer is brought to justice.

The most infamous and celebrated killers sometimes attract fan clubs, complete with member organizations, newsletters, and even fund-raisers. At the extreme, we occasionally hear about a woman, a so-called killer groupie, who dates or even marries an incarcerated murderer. Among the many possible motivations for her attraction, she may regard her "man" as an important celebrity, a powerful figure worthy of respect and admiration.

The public preoccupation with murder apparently extends to the news media as well, both print and electronic. In a sense, the prime-time news is more like the "crime-time" news, and the events that are the least common in reality appear to be featured more than the rest. According to the Center for Media and Public Affairs, more than a third of the crime stories presented on the major network evening news broadcasts during 1998 concerned homicides.[1] By contrast, homicide, according to FBI tallies, accounts for only 1 percent of all violent offenses and 0.1 percent of all serious offenses. Furthermore, the murders that seem particularly exploited are those that involve sex, sadism, or celebrity, hardly the norm in stark reality.

The criminal trial of O. J. Simpson, who was accused of having stabbed to death his estranged wife and her companion, provides a major example of this excess. The case contained all of the elements required to gain the attention of the nation and achieve top TV ratings—a well-liked, even heroic, celebrity football player and his beautiful wife, an inter-racial romance gone bad, rumors of spouse abuse, and charges of police racism. Indeed, the television coverage of the trial was so excessive that someone unfamiliar with American popular culture might have thought that O. J. Simpson was a senator or that the trial was a congressional impeachment proceeding. For a period of time, regular television programming was pre-empted, so that Americans could get their daily dose of courtroom drama. In addition, periodic rundowns of trial proceedings were regularly featured on network newscasts, morning talk shows, and prime-time news magazines.

The advent of *Court TV* assured that the "O. J. Simpson phenomenon" would continue unabated into the foreseeable future. Television trials, while entertaining millions of Americans who subscribed to cable news channels, also gave them access to a non-degree education in the law.

Homicide Law

In everyday usage, the terms "murder," "homicide," "kill," plus a variety of more colorful synonyms such as "slaughter," "butcher," "massacre," "slay," or even slang terms like "knock off," "bump off," and "polish off" are often used somewhat interchangeably. This practice (except for the slang) will be followed throughout most of this book for the sake of convenience, if not readability. It is important nevertheless to understand the important distinctions among these concepts.

"Killing" represents the most general notion of extinguishing life. Although there is nothing inherent in the broad concept of killing that excludes suicide or even animal abuse, our attention shall be limited to homicidal acts, those specifically directed against other human beings. We shall discuss suicides, but only those which are coupled with a homicide. We shall also examine killers who train on animals, but only as a pathway to targeting human prey.

Not all acts of killing are illegal. Most societies authorize agents of the state—police officers and soldiers, for example—to kill under appropriate circumstances. Wartime aggression against an enemy nation as well as state-sanctioned executions of condemned prisoners are not violations of the law, although certain governmental acts of violence can be proscribed by international treaty (e.g., genocide—the attempt to exterminate a racial or ethnic group).

Criminal homicide refers to unlawful and unjustifiable actions or inactions that result in the death of other human beings. Homicidal acts include such clear-cut misdeeds as shooting a semi-automatic rifle at a crowd of people in a shopping mall or poisoning cold medications sold over the counter. As we shall see, stabbing an intruder to death during a burglary is also a homicide but may be legally justifiable (that is, non-criminal), depending on the particular circumstances.

Failures to act (known in the law as "omissions") can also result in criminal charges if such inactivity helps to precipitate a death. This is subtle yet nonetheless illegal, such as a landlord who disregards faulty wiring that causes a fatal blaze may be charged with homicide, or a parent who neglects a child to the point at which the youngster starves to death, even if the parent had not intended this tragic outcome.

These various situations may all constitute homicide, but they do so at varying levels of culpability or punishability. The criminal law recognizes types and degrees of homicide based on such notions as intent, premeditation, provocation, and foreseeability. The law of homicide is particularly complex and differs somewhat from jurisdiction to jurisdiction. State laws change frequently, moreover, as politically minded legislatures and constitutionally minded courts struggle to fine-tune the definitions and applications of criminal codes. Some fundamental commonalities do exist across the land, nevertheless, which guide the administration of justice in the area of homicide.

Murder

The first distinction among types of criminal homicide is that between murder and manslaughter. Murder requires malicious intent (or simply "malice"), an aim to cause death or great bodily harm. In addition, malicious intent can extend to acts that are reckless or show "depraved indifference" to human life, such as exploding a bomb inside a school, even if the perpetrator never meant to hurt anyone. Assaults not necessarily designed to be fatal can constitute murder so long as the deadly outcome is a reasonable or foreseeable possibility. Thus, if a victim of an unarmed assault—a blow to the chest—falls down, bangs his head on the sidewalk, and then dies three days later from the head injury, the assailant can be brought up on murder charges. A parent, distraught over a crying, colicky baby, who shakes the infant to silence her and does it so vigorously as to cause death can also be charged with murder, so long as the parent is aware that this rough form of treatment can be detrimental.

In early English common law, the root of the American legal system, murder was automatically punishable by death. In post-revolutionary America, however, legislatures, wishing to mitigate the law's inflexibility and excessive harshness, moved to limit capital punishment only to the most grievous acts of homicide, by establishing degrees of murder, typically first and second degrees for capital and non-capital murder.

In contemporary statutes, the degree of murder, first vs. second, essentially turns on whether or not the offender premeditated the act of violence. Premeditation entails some evidence of planning, deliberation, or scheming, although not necessarily over a prolonged time period. In fact, the extent of deliberation can be a matter of minutes or even seconds. A plan to kill one's spouse after doubling the size of her life insurance policy obviously reveals cunning and cold-blooded deliberation. Yet an act of road rage in which a motorist deliberately chases another vehicle, forcing it off the road into a fatal encounter with a concrete pole, can also reflect sufficient deliberation so as to constitute first-degree murder.

Many states also include as first-degree murder intentional acts of homicide that are especially brutal, cruel, or extreme, even if the crime is not premeditated. On the evening of August 28, 1995, for example, Richard Rosenthal and his wife, Laura Jane, argued heatedly in the backyard of their suburban Boston home. The fight began over a burned ziti dinner and escalated quickly. The 40-year-old insurance executive lost all control over his temper and started beating his wife repeatedly with a rock. He then cut open her chest with a six-inch kitchen knife and impaled her heart and lungs on a stake in the backyard. Although Rosenthal may not have planned the fatal attack, the jury convicted him of first-degree murder because of the "extreme atrocity and cruelty" of the crime.

The so-called felony-murder rule also grants murder status, typically in the first degree, for any death that results during the commission of a dangerous felony, such as a robbery or arson. Even though the felon may not have planned or intended for someone to die during the crime, the intent and planning surrounding the commission of a reckless crime are by law transferred to the homicide. If a robber fatally shoots a store clerk because the victim is too slow in handing over the contents of the cash register, the charge is "murder one." He may only have planned to use the gun to intimidate but not to fire it; however, the deliberation in committing a dangerous felony like robbery translates into premeditation for the homicide.

The felony-murder rule may even apply when the felon does not directly cause the death, so long as the fatality results from an act or conspiracy in which he or she is implicated. If, for example, the police shoot and mistakenly kill a hostage whom the robber has taken as a shield, the robber may be charged with first-degree murder.

Twenty-nine-year-old Aldrin Diaz was charged with murder following a January 28, 2000, disturbance outside a Providence, Rhode Island, restaurant, even though he never fired his weapon and dropped it when ordered to do so by the police. During the incident, an off-duty cop, rushing to assist fellow officers with his gun drawn, was fatally shot by a uniformed officer who had mistakenly identified the cop in street clothes as one of the combatants. Because Diaz's use of a gun precipitated the chain of events leading to the officer's death, he could have been held legally responsible under the felony-murder rule although the charge was ultimately dropped.

The felony-murder rule may appear unreasonably strict when, for example, the person charged with murder takes a fall for the one who directed the crime, or, as in the Diaz case, when a police action results in a death. In an attempt to address this concern, some courts have limited the application of the rule to deaths that were foreseeable during the commission of the dangerous felony.

Homicides that reflect malicious intent yet lack premeditation, that do not show extreme cruelty, and that are not committed during the course of a dangerous felony are considered murders in the second degree. For example, a man who impulsively stabs his teenage son to death during an argument over a football game has, given the spontaneity of the act, committed second-degree murder. Homicides committed under the influence of alcohol or drugs are also generally considered second-degree murders, if the intoxication is believed to have reduced the drunken person's capacity to act deliberately and premeditate the deadly assault.

Manslaughter

Homicides that lack malicious intent or reckless disregard for life are considered manslaughters, which in turn are divided into voluntary and involuntary forms. Voluntary manslaughter is the intentional killing of another person but under extenuating circumstances, such as provocation or emotional duress (the so-called heat of passion) without time or opportunity for cooling off. A woman who kills her husband upon finding him sexually molesting their daughter has committed voluntary manslaughter. If, on the other hand, she deliberately seeks him out in order to avenge his act of incest, she could be charged with murder, although most juries would likely respond sympathetically.

Also considered manslaughter are deaths that result from fistfights, barroom brawls, or similar conflicts between equal combatants. Of course, picking a fight with someone who is less than your size can easily be considered murder if the disadvantaged victim dies. Voluntary manslaughter also applies when a person uses excessive force in self-defense or wrongly but honestly perceives that self-defense is required given the situation. Thus, for example, shooting a neighbor under a genuine yet mistaken belief that he was a burglar is not murder, but neither is it accidental in the eyes of the law.

In the crime of manslaughter, it is the heat of passion, intense fear, or provocation that negates the malice required for murder. Malicious intent is presumed absent when the killer reacts, understandably yet unjustifiably, to some provocation (such as the discovery of an unfaithful lover or the attack by an inebriated drinking buddy) or duress (such as cannibalizing another human being in order to stay alive while lost in the wilderness). While one may use deadly force in self-defense or to survive a perilous attack, the use of excessive force (e.g., shooting an unarmed attacker) also constitutes manslaughter.

There are limits to the levels of provocation that can reduce murder to manslaughter. Words, slogans, insults, gestures, or style of dress and appearance may be socially provocative, yet not so in a legal sense. A hot-tempered individual who fatally attacks someone for uttering a racial slur and a homophobic man who kills in reaction to a proposition from another man have committed murder, even though in both cases the victims may have precipitated their own demise. Jonathan Schmitz of Lake Orion, Michigan, for example, was convicted of second-degree murder after he shot to death his friend and neighbor Scott Amedure. Amedure, age 32, had revealed his secret crush on Schmitz during a 1995 taped episode of the Jenny Jones television talk show. Because of the three-day time span separating the defendant's public embarrassment from the subsequent murder, the jury rejected Schmitz's claim that he killed during an insane rage provoked by his victim's public admission.

In recent years, homicides inspired by a victim's sexual orientation, race, religion, or gender have come under particular scrutiny in both the criminal court as well as the court of public opinion. Known as bias or hate crimes, such offenses are typically dealt with at the state level by enhancing the defendant's sentence—that is, by increasing his prison time over what he would have received had he not selected his victim based on a protected characteristic like race or sexual orientation. In addition, as a violation of the victim's civil rights, bias-motivated offenses may also result in additional charges under federal hate crime statutes. Thus, a perpetrator who commits a hate-inspired manslaughter might spend as much time incarcerated as someone who commits second-degree murder.

A death resulting from negligence is considered involuntary manslaughter. Following the February 29, 2000, fatal shooting of a 6-year-old girl by her first-grade classmate in Mount Morris Township, Michigan, 19-year-old Jamelle James, who lived with the young perpetrator, was charged with involuntary manslaughter. Although he was not present at the scene of the shooting, court papers alleged that James had carelessly left the murder weapon, a loaded 32-caliber semi-automatic, within easy reach of the 6-year-old shooter. It is also involuntary manslaughter if a physician carelessly writes out a prescription for the wrong medication or the improper dosage, thereby causing the death of a patient.

Like the felony-murder doctrine, the misdemeanor-manslaughter rule applies if a death occurs while the offender is engaged in a misdemeanor, an act less serious than a felony. In Worcester, Massachusetts, for example, a homeless man and woman were charged with involuntary manslaughter following an abandoned 1999 warehouse blaze in which six firefighters perished. Not only had the homeless squatters caused the fire with careless burning of a candle, but they apparently failed to report the fire as it spread rapidly. In many states, moreover, deaths resulting from motor vehicle infractions—such as speeding or failure to stop at a red light—are considered involuntary manslaughter and are assigned the special category of "vehicular homicide." States have also passed special laws for drunken driving deaths, upgrading them to voluntary manslaughter or even second-degree murder.

Defenses to Criminal Homicide

The law recognizes both *defenses* and *excuses* which exclude or limit an individual's criminal responsibility for committing homicide. In defenses (sometimes referred to as justifications), defendants admit having carried out the killing but maintain that under the circumstances (e.g., the exercise of police powers or citizen use of self-defense) what they did was proper under the law and therefore non-criminal. Thus, a claim of self-defense would suggest that an individual committed the act but was justified in doing so. In excuses, by contrast, defendants admit what they did was wrong but maintain that under the circumstances (duress, mistake, entrapment, insanity, intoxication, extreme youth or senility, diminished capacity, or various psychiatric syndromes), they were not fully responsible for the criminal act they perpetrated.

In July 2003, a motorist, 86-year-old George Russell Weller hit the gas pedal instead of the brake and careened into a crowded farmer's market, in Los Angeles, killing 10 people ranging in age from 7 months to 78 years. In addition, he injured more than 50 pedestrians. Although Weller had tested negative for drugs and alcohol and had passed a vision and written driving exam three years earlier, evidence came to light that his driving skills had for some time been impaired. Ten years earlier, Weller had crashed his car into a retaining wall. More recently, he damaged his own garage on at least two occasions. Weller's horrendous accident brought the issue of elderly drivers and the law to the forefront of public debate. Despite his age, Weller was charged with 10 counts of vehicular homicide. In all likelihood, the final disposition will take into account the advanced age and competence of the defendant.

Killings by public officials in the course of executing their duties and job responsibilities are generally considered justifiable, although in reaction to recent abuses of power the police have been restricted from using deadly force against unarmed, non-dangerous suspects fleeing the scene of a felony. Four white New York City police officers were charged with but acquitted of second-degree murder after firing a 41-shot barrage of bullets at an unarmed West African immigrant, 22-year-old Amadou Diallo, on February 4, 1999, during an anti-crime sweep through the Bronx. The jury felt that the officers were justified in using deadly force when they mistakenly yet reasonably believed Diallo had reached for a gun. The victim was actually reaching for his wallet presumably in order to produce some identification.

Homicides are considered justifiable if they are in reaction to a level of provocation so great that deadly force is necessitated to defend oneself, other innocent people, or even one's home and property. To constitute self-defense, however, only that amount of force sufficient to repel an attack or intrusion is permitted by law. Generally, one cannot fend off a fist with a gun, unless the weapon is required to balance off any disadvantage in size or strength. Thus, a child or diminutive adult may be justified when using a gun to defend against a knife assault by a larger assailant. However, if excessive force is in fact used in defense of self or others, then manslaughter charges may result.

In general, self-defense is only justified if no other reasonable means of escape or retreat exists. If the victim of an attack can safely flee, rather than use lethal force, then this opportunity must be taken. However, some states allow homeowners to defend their "castle" by using deadly force, and juries have typically been sympathetic to the "castle doctrine" over the retreat requirement.

Many states allow deadly force if a resident reasonably believes it is needed to protect self or others from harm or to prevent a suspect from committing a violent crime. Once the threat is over, the resident must allow the police to take control. The citizen cannot keep a would-be robber or rapist in the basement to mete out his or her own form of justice and in most cases cannot pursue the assailant beyond the reasonable "curtilage" area surrounding the home. In December of 2001, Indianapolis homeowner Michael Clements pursued an intruder, Leon Williams Jr., who had entered Clement's home to burglarize it. Clements chased Williams down the street away from the house and shot him in the back. A jury convicted Clements of aggravated battery and carrying a weapon without a license, and he was sentenced to six years in prison. In pursuing the intruder beyond his home, Clements had changed roles from that of victim to that of assailant.

Even though the law generally permits individuals to use force in the defense of property, it is the element of personal danger (not property rights) that underlies this prescription. Thus, a resident or retailer is not permitted to set a death trap in order to catch a burglar or some other intruder. Even so, the sympathies of jurors often run contrary to the law. In 1986, Prentice Rasheed, a store owner in the Liberty City section of Miami, set a makeshift booby trap to ward off burglars, resulting in the electrocution of a drug-addicted intruder. The grand jury, seeing him more as hero than villain, elected not to indict Rasheed for manslaughter.

Obviously people sometimes perceive personal danger where there is none. A 16-year-old Japanese exchange student, Yoshihiro Hattori, was shot and killed by Rodney Peairs in Louisiana in 1994. Dressed up like John Travolta in the film *Saturday Night Fever,* Hattori went to the wrong address looking for a Halloween party to which he had been invited. As Mrs. Peairs saw him approach their house she told her husband to get his gun. Hattori was gesturing wildly and had a camera in his hand, trying to explain to Mr. Peairs that he was there for a party. The Japanese exchange student likely did not understand Mr. Peairs' demand to "Freeze!" Although the case prompted local petitions for tighter gun control and sparked public outcry in the victim's home country of Japan, a jury acquitted Mr. Peairs. It seems that his wife panicked and he feared for her safety and the safety of their three children. The jury thought this was a reasonable response to a perceived threat, even if the perception was incorrect.

The legitimate use of deadly force as self-defense is also limited to the immediate time frame when danger is imminent. An attempt to fight back, for example, following an assault that had occurred the previous day becomes an act of aggression or vengeance and can be punishable as murder.

In such instances, we might sympathize with the avenger. We may feel that his or her culpability is limited, even though the act of revenge cannot be tolerated or legitimated in a civilized society. Thus, the law provides a range of excuses that reduce the wrongfulness of the act. Contrary to justifiable homicide in which the claim is "I killed him, but it was my responsibility, right, or duty," in excusable killings, the reasoning is "I did it, but I couldn't help myself."

Historically, mental illness (being too confused), intoxication (being too drunk), and age (being too young) have been used to negate or reduce culpability, the logic being that these conditions limit or even eliminate criminal responsibility or punishability. More recently, legislatures and courts have grappled with novel theories of how free will may be restricted, including defenses based on such conditions as battered woman syndrome (BWS), premenstrual syndrome (PMS), postpartum depression (PPD), and posttraumatic stress disorder (PTSD). The list of potential defenses is seemingly endless. In recent years, even some sociological defenses, such as black rage, urban survivor syndrome, and gay panic, have been raised in attempts to excuse criminal responsibility, although with very little success.

Forty-four-year-old Scott Falater of Phoenix, Arizona, raised a somnambulism (sleepwalking) defense as an excuse for his rather bad night in January 1997 when he stabbed his wife of 20 years with a hunting knife 44 times before holding her head under water until she drowned. The defense argued that lack of consciousness would fail to meet the intent requirement of the law. The jury rejected entirely his explanation and excuse.

Defendants have also raised cultural customs and religious beliefs as excuses for criminal conduct, but also with mixed success. The First Amendment of the Constitution protects the free exercise of religion, yet this right can sometimes come in conflict with another person's rights, including the right to life. Laurie Grouard Walker, a practicing Christian Scientist from Sacramento, California, for example, was convicted of involuntary manslaughter following the 1984 death of her 4-year-old daughter, Shauntay, from meningitis. Consistent with her religious beliefs, Walker had chosen prayer—rather than medicine—as a means of treating her daughter's flu-like symptoms. Although California, like many other states, provides a statutory exemption to criminal prosecution in the practice of religion, the California Supreme Court held that the rights of the child preempted the exemption. A federal judge later overturned Walker's conviction, but on procedural, not religious, grounds. By contrast, in a similar case in Massachusetts (the home of the Christian Science Church), the state's Supreme Judicial Court, citing religious freedom as a basis, overturned the manslaughter convictions of David and Ginger Twitchell who also had relied unsuccessfully on faith healing to treat their 2-year-old son, Robyn.

Law and culture sometimes come in conflict, forcing an individual to make a very difficult choice. In January 1985, after learning of her husband's adultery, Fumiko Kimura, a 33-year-old Japanese immigrant, walked with her 4-year-old son and infant daughter into the Pacific Ocean off Santa Monica to save them from the shame that her husband had brought upon the family. Kimura was pulled to safety and charged in the deaths of her two children. Although customs of her cultural heritage could not excuse her actions entirely, her lack of malice did result in a light sentence of one year in jail and five years' probation.

Homicide Law in Practice

The levels and types of homicide are summarized in Table 1.1. When homicide cases come to trial, however, the jury is typically offered a range of possible verdicts. If a defendant is charged with first-degree murder, for example, jurors are typically presented with the option of convicting on a lesser charge—second-degree murder, manslaughter, or possibly

TABLE 1.1   *Types of Homicide*

Classification	Elements	Example
First degree murder	Homicide with malicious intent and with premeditation or extreme cruelty	A man decides to kill his wife, rather than divorce her, to ensure that he maintains sole custody of their children.
Second degree murder	Homicide with malicious intent but without premeditation or extreme cruelty	A man kills his wife during an argument over how best to discipline their children.
Felony murder	Homicide during the course of a dangerous felony	A man commits arson in order to collect insurance, not knowing that his wife is home and dies from smoke inhalation.
Voluntary manslaughter	Willful homicide with provocation or from excessive force	A man kills his wife when he finds her spanking their child with a belt.
Involuntary manslaughter	Non-willful homicide resulting from negligence	Driving while dialing his cell phone, a man slams into a tree, killing his wife who is seated next to him.
Misdemeanor Manslaughter	Homicide during the course of a misdemeanor	As a prank, a man yells "fire" in a crowded theater, and his wife dies in the subsequent rush to escape.
Justifiable Homicide	Killing a fleeing felon or in self-defense	A man kills his wife as she attempts to strangle their child.
Excusable Homicide	Homicide with diminished capacity based on mental illness, age, and other conditions	A man kills his wife under a delusion that she is demonically possessed.

even assault with a deadly weapon. On many occasions a jury will find a defendant guilty of a lesser charge than the facts would dictate or even not guilty altogether because of their sympathies surrounding the case.

Jury nullification, as it is called, is particularly common when smaller or weaker victims are charged with using excessive force to kill an abusive partner or a feared predator. Even if the facts fall short of self-defense, the jury can still choose to excuse. The infamous subway vigilante Bernhard Goetz was cleared by a New York City jury of homicide charges for his December 22, 1984, shooting of several black youngsters who had accosted him on the train. Even though the teens were unarmed, the jurors apparently identified with Goetz's fear in the situation and excused his quick-on-the-trigger response. Goetz was acquitted of all charges except a minor gun offense.

In the vast majority of criminal prosecutions, the case never reaches a jury. The charges may be dropped without a trial because of insufficient evidence, or the case may be decided by a trial judge. But most often, the defendant accepts a negotiated guilty plea. In such instances, the charge may be reduced from what the facts would indicate in exchange for the defendant's plea. Also, in crimes involving two or more accomplices, one defendant will often plead out to a lesser charge in exchange for giving testimony against his or her accomplices.

The physician's prescription blunder, which as noted earlier would constitute involuntary manslaughter, may also result in a civil action—a malpractice claim or even a wrongful death suit. In fact, virtually all criminal homicides can result in two kinds of trials, which can proceed in succession—civil suits brought by families of the victims to recover financial damages as well as criminal prosecutions leading to prison time. Unlike the criminal proceedings, moreover, the burden of proof in the civil action is far less demanding—guilt shown by a preponderance of evidence rather than beyond a reasonable doubt. Thus, for example, it is not inconsistent or even uncommon to encounter defendants like ex-football star O. J. Simpson being found not guilty criminally but responsible civilly.

The criminal prosecution of O. J. Simpson, the most watched trial in American history, provides an important lesson for understanding the application of homicide law to real-world cases. As critical as were the eyewitness testimony, the DNA evidence, and the credibility of the defendant's alibi in shaping opinion inside and outside the courtroom, issues of race, class, and gender also had an impact. Some observers speculated that the jury, in acquitting Simpson, had sought to send a message about racism and police misconduct. Others argued that the defendant's wealth had bought him the best defense—"The Dream Team"—that money could buy; still others claimed that Simpson's celebrity earned him special treatment.

Notwithstanding the actual rule of law, the political context surrounding a homicide—issues of race, gender, class, among others—ultimately determines, as University of Southern California Law Professor Susan Estrich persuasively argues, how the criminal law is applied to the facts, how a case is charged by a prosecutor, how a jury responds to a defendant's strategy, and how an appellate court considers procedural challenges.[2] For these many reasons, therefore, the punishment may not exactly fit the crime.

Endnotes

1. Center for Media and Public Affairs, *Media Monitor,* Vol. 8, January/February 1999, Washington, D.C.

2. Susan Estrich, *Getting Away With Murder.* Cambridge, MA: Harvard University Press, 1998.

2

Explaining Murder

While legal scholars debate issues of intent and criminal responsibility in homicide cases, criminologists tend to take a different approach. They seek to answer the question: Why do people kill one another?

The major schools of thought regarding the causes of crime, and thus the causes of homicide, have included supernatural, free will, biological, psychological, and sociological explanations. Is violence an inherent aspect of human nature? Or, do we learn it from others? Is it simply the result of a choice made by the murderer? Is it the result of poor parenting or inferior schooling?

Society cannot make informed policy decisions and create successful intervention and prevention programs without attempting to understand the causes of violent behavior. If homicidal acts are learned and reinforced in social settings such as the family or schools, prevention policies would be very different from those that would be appropriate if the primary causes of violence are biological.

Once we begin to explain acts of murder, it leads us to some inevitable questions: Does explanation translate to justification? At what point, if ever, does the cause of a behavior become an excuse? At what point does, for example, abuse or neglect actually reduce criminal responsibility? The Supreme Court of the United States recently overturned the death sentence of Kevin Wiggins due to the incompetence of his lawyers (*Wiggins vs. Smith,* 2003). The justices felt that competent attorneys would have presented information regarding Wiggins' "excruciating" childhood. They felt that if the lawyers had properly included this information in his defense, Wiggins might not have received a death sentence for his crimes. So even if an explanation of an individual's behavior does not affect the decision of guilt or innocence, it may still be relevant in determining the severity of the punishment.

The Devil Made Me Do It

Only since the late 1800s has our approach to criminal violence been informed by scientific criminological theories. Before that, there were two major schools of thought about the causes of criminal behavior. For most of human history, society accepted supernatural or spiritual explanations.[1] Whether the crime was stealing a goat or murdering a neighbor, the explanation was the same—demonic possession.

The supernatural phase of explanation left a legacy of irrationality and thousands of executions. Some sources report that by the end of the 1600s, hundreds of thousands of people were executed throughout the world because they were believed to be inhabited by evil spirits. Often these executions included torture, such as burning at the stake or boiling in oil, in part to extract a confession or an admission of consorting with the devil.

By the mid-18th century, the supernatural phase of explanation and its history of chaos, injustice, and torture gave way to the classical school of thought. Yet the devil or other "evil spirit" explanations of homicidal behavior are still with us. In May of 1993, three 8-year-old boys were murdered in West Memphis, Arkansas. Three local teenagers were convicted of these murders under a cloud of rumors about satanic sacrifices, rituals, and cults. When the three young defendants appeared outside the courthouse, local residents threw rocks at them, reminiscent of witch burnings in 15th-century Europe. More recently, the defense team for Scott Peterson, a Modesto, California, man accused of the December 2002 death and dismemberment of his wife Laci and her unborn child, suggested that satanic cults might be responsible for the murder. Satanic influence—"the devil made me do it"—remains a convenient explanation for what we do not understand.

Back to the Classics

In response to the irrationality, anarchy, and injustice of the supernatural phase of explanation and its harsh punishment methods, a school of thought emerged in the 18th century that viewed criminal behavior, including homicide, as a product of free will, a rational choice. Marking a return to the principles of early Greek philosophers, the writings of Cesare Beccaria (1738–1794) and Jeremy Bentham (1748–1833) shaped the foundations of the second phase of explanation—classical criminology.[2]

Although the classical school included a number of complexities, its fundamental premise about the cause of criminal behavior was simple: Crime is a rational choice made by the offender, who chooses to kill with free will. Rather than believing that the murderer was a witch or possessed by a demon, classical criminology viewed human beings as possessing small mental calculators that they could use to determine, "Is this murder worth it? What do I have to lose? And what are the costs versus the gains?" Thus, a murderer would strike when, after evaluating all other options, killing seemed to be the best possible solution. In other words, the killer decided that the crime was worth the risk. Government officials believed that in order to prevent crime, criminal codes, laws, and punishments should be created so that each person, knowing the risks, would decide that crime does not pay. For each offense, therefore, there would be a fitting and proportional punishment.

Obviously, many factors such as alcohol, drugs, anger, and mental illness can affect our decisions and choices. The classical school lost favor in part because of its rigid orientation toward punishing the crime and ignoring these individual circumstances. But it also lost momentum when immigration, industrialization, and urbanization during the late 1800s drove crime levels upward. The prevailing view in society was that the classical notions about criminal behavior and punishment were failing.

Although proponents of the scientific method rejected the philosophical approach, classical ideas are still detectable in contemporary explanations of homicidal behavior, re-tooled as rational choice theory.[3] Are murderers rational? In 1990, 22-year-old Pamela Smart, a media services director at a New Hampshire high school, hired three students (including one who was her lover) to kill her husband, Greg. She was convicted and sentenced to life in prison for his calculated murder. Pamela Smart planned her husband's death in great detail. Her scheme included an affair with a teenage student, a staged burglary, an un-locked front door, disguises, and the decision to use a gun instead of a knife so there would be less blood on her white leather furniture. She even instructed the boys not to kill her husband in front of her beloved Shih Tzu, Van Halen, for fear that it would traumatize the lit-tle dog. From Smart's perspective, the murder of her husband was worth about $140,000 in life insurance and the couple's personal property.

For 42-year-old Wanda Holloway of Houston, Texas, a murder was worth planning if it meant that her eighth-grade daughter Shanna would get to become a high school cheer-leader. Holloway hired her former brother-in-law to kill another girl's mother so that Shanna's chief rival would be too emotionally distraught to try out for the cheerleading squad. Holloway would have paid to have both mother and daughter eliminated, but could not come up with enough money for two victims. For Holloway, a human life was worth trading for a cheerleading spot for her daughter. The "cheerleader mom" was convicted of attempted murder-for-hire but only served 6 months of her 10-year sentence.

Using Science to Explain Violence

Emerging in the late 19th century, positivism—as reflected in biology, psychology, sociol-ogy, and economics—employed scientific observation and measurement to explain crimi-nal behavior. This approach was a shift away from free will and rational choice toward determinism. Why do people commit murder? Positivists believe that external factors cause criminal behavior. The first positivistic criminological theories were biological, and these were quickly followed by psychological and sociological explanations.

Most of the criminological explanations of homicide are not theories specific to homicide—they are broader, more general explanations of crimes ranging from shoplift-ing, drug use, and exam cheating to rape and murder. Moreover, even theories that try to explain why people kill aim to address the whole class of events, not just one case. Thus, we do not have a theory about why Ted Bundy was a serial killer (since theories are not designed to explain single cases), but a theory about serial killers or perhaps, even more broadly, murderers in general.

It is sometimes frustrating that we cannot definitively state what causes crime or vi-olence. Criminology is a "soft" science; there are no certainties, but only likelihoods and probabilities. It is not a certainty that severe child abuse will create a murderer, but abuse is one of many factors that may increase the likelihood that someone will behave criminally.

Biology Then and Now

The earliest biological theories of criminal behavior focused on body constitution, heredity, and intelligence. As early as the 18th century, scientific researchers were applying the techniques of physiognomy (the study of facial features) and phrenology (the study of bumps on the head) in search of clues to criminal behavior. Although not noted at the time, phrenology or "skull feeling" presents an interesting causal order problem: Did the bumps on the head cause the homicidal behavior? Or did a history of violent behavior leave the offender with bumps on the head? This "which came first" causal order dilemma haunts a number of biological theories, including theories about a possible link between violence and testosterone levels, head trauma, and premenstrual syndrome (PMS).

The apparent breakthrough to uncovering the secrets of criminal conduct came, in 1876, when an Italian physician, Cesare Lombroso, published his famous volume, *The Criminal Man,* advancing the premise of a "born criminal." Lombroso suggested that criminals are *atavistic*—they are a throwback to an earlier, more primitive evolutionary stage of human development, a notion influenced heavily by Charles Darwin's 1871 treatise, *The Origins of Man.* Lombroso, in his detailed empirical study of Italian prisoners, noted that criminals show outward signs of their differentness (known as *stigmata*), such as long arms, large ears, and sloping foreheads.

Although the theory has long since been discredited, Lombroso's work in criminal anthropology spirited a new tradition of empirical research, both in Europe and the United States, earning him the undisputed title as the "father of modern criminology." Many followed Lombroso's lead in trying to expand or refute his theories. Richard Dugdale's study of the Jukes family and Henry Goddard's report on the Kallikak clan both suggested that criminal tendency, although not necessarily visible from physical characteristics, is an inherited condition that persists through generations of offspring. Even though the work of both Dugdale and Goddard has been rejected as unscientific, the idea that some people "look" like criminals (e.g., profiling) or that some families are genetically predisposed to violence is still part of contemporary thinking about the origin of criminal behavior.

Ernst Kretschmer and William Sheldon both attempted to use somatotyping or constitutionalism (i.e., classification of body and physique to understand criminality). As late as the 1950s, Harvard University researchers Sheldon and Eleanor Glueck were including various body measurements in their multi-disciplinary studies of the biological, psychological, and social factors distinguishing delinquents and non-delinquents.[4] Although at the time social scientists sharply criticized the Gluecks for including biological traits among the thousands of variables they examined, years later their work was praised as one of the most significant multidisciplinary efforts to explain crime ever undertaken.[5]

Whatever momentum the biological school of criminological theory had retained went on life support during the sociologically-dominated, humanistic climate of the 1960s. In more contemporary times, however, the biological approach (not nearly as dogmatic and narrow as in Lombroso's day) appears to have been resuscitated with the aid of new ideas and new technologies, allowing us to probe deeply into the bodies and brains of violent criminals. Modern biosocial theories of crime place biological variables such as learning disabilities, food allergies, neurological problems and genetics within a social context of family structure, childrearing, abuse, and other factors.

One of the more recent biosocial approaches is the link between aggression and various biochemical factors, including food allergies, hormones, sugar, fluorescent lighting, lead exposure and other environmental contaminants, as well as the psychopharmacological effects of alcohol and drugs. Presenting a new twist to the "drugs cause crime" argument, various psychiatric drugs widely prescribed to treat depression and attention deficit disorder have recently been suspected of triggering murderous behavior. Joseph Wesbecker, on the morning of September 14, 1989, went on a 20-minute rampage at the Standard Gravure printing plant in Louisville, Kentucky, where he had worked as a pressman for over two decades. Opening fire with an AK-47 assault weapon, Wesbecker shot to death eight of his co-workers and then took his own life. Some people tried to blame Wesbecker's deadly outburst on his longstanding struggle with depression. Others placed the blame squarely on the anti-depressant Prozac that he had been taking for several weeks prior to the massacre.

Besides Wesbecker, there is a long list of other high-profile killers who were treated with psychiatric medications just before they committed senseless murders. On September 27, 1997, Sam Manzie, a 15-year-old boy from Freehold, New Jersey, who was being treated with the antidepressant Paxil, raped and strangled to death an 11-year-old boy in his neighborhood. On May 20, 1999, T. J. Solomon, a 15-year-old student at Heritage High School in Georgia who was taking Ritalin, opened fire on his classmates, wounding six of them. On May 21, 1998, Kip Kinkel, a 14-year-old boy from Springfield, Oregon, who took both Ritalin and Prozac, killed his parents and then launched a shooting spree through his high school. On April 20, 1999, 18-year-old Eric Harris of Littleton, Colorado, who was taking the anti-depressant Luvox, teamed up with his friend Dylan Klebold to perpetrate a horrific rampage at Columbine High School, killing 12 students and a teacher.

The case against psychiatric medications might be stronger if it were not for the fact that killers who were being treated at the time they committed murder typically had many of the usual warning signs associated with such crimes. In almost every case, there was good reason why a psychiatrist had prescribed a psychotropic drug: The killer had been profoundly depressed, disappointed, and discouraged about the future. Moreover, the actions of killers who commit a rampage are typically neither episodic nor spontaneous. Whatever role Prozac may have had in lifting the weight of depression and enabling him to take action, Wesbecker began preparing for mass murder, purchasing guns and making hit lists, six months before starting the medication. At most, the drug may have reduced his inhibitions, but hardly inspired him to kill. The Prozac controversy surrounding cases like Wesbecker's shooting spree affirms the importance of establishing causal order when attempting to explain how various factors may "cause" a murder.

In a four-year longitudinal study of antisocial boys, researchers at the University of Chicago Medical School discovered a biological propensity for violence.[6] Boys with histories of starting fights, stealing, carrying weapons, and engaging in forced sexual acts had lower-than-expected levels of the stress hormone cortisol (a hormone typically released in response to fear) in their saliva. More than one-third of the boys with low cortisol levels were identified by their peers as the "meanest in their class." Some researchers have also connected antisocial criminal behavior with high levels of the male hormone testosterone. Though studies have frequently confirmed this relationship, there is little evidence yet of a strong causal effect of testosterone on the propensity to commit criminal violence.[7]

If the findings about testosterone, cortisol, or other important hormones are valid, then at least some violent children may have a biological predisposition for antisocial behavior, even youngsters who grow up in healthy, non-threatening families. This predisposition may make them less fearful of the possible punishments for their antisocial behavior and also less amenable to counseling or therapy. At the extreme, some of these violent children may be inclined to commit homicide, regardless of the punishment they anticipate. Even if hormones do not have a profound influence on homicidal behavior, there is growing evidence of a biological basis for differences in the propensity for violence. Researchers have shown, for example, that animals become more or less aggressive depending on changes in their level of the neurotransmitter serotonin. There is some evidence that the same effect can be achieved in humans.

In another controversial area of biology, researchers in the 1960s purported to demonstrate that inmates in institutions for the criminally insane were significantly more likely to possess the "XYY syndrome." That is, they believed that as many as 100,000 men—so-called "Super Males"—were inclined to violence by virtue of an extra Y or male sex chromosome.[8] Punishment would do little, if anything, to discourage those bearing this genetic abnormality from committing violent acts. It was, after all, a matter of genetic destiny.

The XYY anomaly for a while became a popular explanation for extreme forms of violence after it was erroneously reported that mass murderer Richard Speck possessed the extra-Y chromosome. In July, 1966, Speck had committed the "crime of the century" when he murdered eight student nurses in their Chicago apartment. Newspaper articles and even some scientific accounts reported that Speck's XYY constitution was apparent in such phenotypical characteristics as facial acne, tallness, long extremities, mild mental retardation, and a history of mental illness.

To this day, high school science teachers occasionally repeat the Richard Speck as "Super Male" mythology. However, we now know that very few violent criminals possess an extra Y chromosome. Those who actually have this genetic abnormality may be treated more harshly and be more likely institutionalized, often simply because of their abnormally awkward and substantial physical features.[9] Thus, the disproportionate presence of XYYs in institutions for the criminally insane may be more a function of the way they look than the way they act.

This is not to say that chromosomes are unimportant in explaining differences in homicidal proneness. Clearly, males have a far greater propensity for committing senseless and extreme acts of violence than do females, a fact which seems to hold true almost universally, across virtually all cultures and time periods. Thus, it is more accurately the normal Y chromosome (the 46th or male chromosome), not the extra Y (the 47th or "Super Male" chromosome) that might make the vital difference.

Even if the XYY anomaly has been overgeneralized, present-day researchers continue to search the biology of human beings in order to explain and predict homicidal behavior. At every turn, another variable is offered as an explanation—or excuse—for someone who has committed a senseless act of murder.

Millions of Americans are the victims of some form of brain dysfunction involving epilepsy, mental retardation, attention deficit disorder (ADD), hyperkinesis, minimal brain disorder, strokes, brain tumors, head injuries, or malnutrition. Clinical studies suggest that certain brain diseases or injuries can result in outbursts of anger and occasionally in episodes of violent behavior. In a Polish study, for example, researchers discovered an organic lesion to the central nervous system in 14 of 24 killers. Mortimer Gross and William Wilson similarly concluded that a large body of evidence points to an association between organic brain disorder and impulsive violence.[10] Generally, brain disorder cannot fully explain why a vengeful husband methodically plans the murder of his wife or why the members of an organized hate group commit a series of murders and robberies in the hope of inciting a race war; however, it may help to explain their predisposition toward pursuing violent solutions.

The policy implications of biological sources of crime can be frightening. The early Lombrosion and inheritance theorists recommended eugenics—the idea that some people would need to be sterilized or even euthanized because of their biological deficiencies. Although modern day biological policy responses to aggression include less offensive treatments including drugs and even vitamins, the dangerous notions of preventing violence by selective breeding, sterilization, castration, or euthanasia emphasize the importance of linking theory with sensible public policy.

Another critical policy question spawned by biological theories of violence is that if the offender is a victim of a biological abnormality, to what extent should he or she be held accountable for criminal acts? Although the public may recognize the facilitating role played by various biological predispositions toward aggression, most people still want the offender to be punished, and they still believe the offender made a choice. Recent integrated theories of crime are sensitive to these issues by blending various biological, psychological, and sociological variables along with a component of individual choice.[11]

Psychological Causes of Violence

Biological, psychological, and sociological theories can be difficult to disentangle. For example, what causes someone to be a sociopath, a person who acts completely without conscience or remorse? While the biologist might point to the role of testosterone, cortisol, or adrenalin in the development of the antisocial personality disorder (i.e., sociopathy), some psychologists have long argued instead that antisocial behavior, and especially homicidal proneness, has its roots in early childhood.[12] In particular, some youngsters are so brutalized—physically or sexually abused, neglected, abandoned, or adopted under extremely harsh circumstances—that they fail to develop a capacity to bond with other human beings.[13]

Illustrating another perspective that is both biological and psychological, Freud embraced the human nature viewpoint when he proposed that people have "an active instinct for hatred and destruction."[14] He argued that two opposing instincts motivate human behavior: the life instinct called "Eros" and the death instinct known as "Thanatos." In the Freudian view, Eros is a positive force in our behavior, responsible for all actions aimed at furthering and enhancing life. By contrast, Thanatos has as its central aim the ruin and destruction of human life. When externalized and turned on other people, Thanatos is, according to Freud, the source of all aggression in human beings, including war and murder. This psychoanalytic view of human nature suggests that all human beings are predisposed, given particular circumstances, to lash out at other people. Of course, most individuals never succumb to the temptation, especially not in the extreme case of committing murder.

Although few practicing criminologists adhere to Freudian traditions, Freudian theory in the form of "bonding" or "attachment therapy" is still a respected treatment method for troubled children.[15] As is the case with many therapies, positive outcomes are not always the result. In April 2000, 10-year-old Candace Newmaker was smothered during a "rebirthing" session conducted by therapists and her mother. The Freudian-based therapy was intended to give the troubled child a new bond and new beginning with her adoptive mother via the new birth—in this case, a child was suffocated and asphyxiated by five adults who were acting as a quasi-birth canal by crushing the girl with pillows. So far, two of Candace's "therapists" have been convicted of reckless child abuse in her death, and her mother is awaiting trial.

Freudians are not alone in their emphasis on inborn, biological traits in explaining the will to kill. Proponents of the field of ethology (the study of animals in their natural environment) also support the existence of an aggressive instinct—a natural urge to be violent and commit murder. Prominent ethologist and Nobel Prize winner Konrad Lorenz presented a large amount of evidence that animals are aggressive by nature.[16] He described, for example, the battles between male animals as they compete for females and the defensive behavior of a group of animals whose territory is invaded by another creature of the same species. He described the massacre that ensues when different colonies of insects or rodents are mixed together: They literally tear one another apart.

Lorenz argued that because humans evolve from violent animals, they must have inherited their destructive dispositions. Denying the possibility that behavior is primarily a reaction to environmental conditions, he asserted instead that it results from internal and spontaneous forces. External stimulation is often unnecessary. Lorenz assumed that aggression gives animals an advantage in the struggle for survival. He assumed further that human violence could be explained in the same way. There is little doubt that animals do in fact engage in the kinds of aggressive behavior that ethologists have reported. The question is whether Lorenz and others who hold this view are correct in the meaning they attribute to some of this behavior.

Since the theory proposed by Lorenz, a wealth of research has illustrated the critical importance of external, sociological variables. The frustration-aggression hypothesis suggests that some sort of frustration precedes a natural response of aggression. But clearly, most frustration is not followed by aggression (or none of us would make it home each day). When is frustration followed by aggression? When people think they can get away with it, when there are no police around, when they don't care what parents, teachers, or significant others think, when they are drinking, or when the frustration is extreme. All of these examples illustrate the obvious contextual factors that facilitate or limit how the psychological state of frustration manifests itself. Thus, although humans may descend from a long line of aggressors, societal pressures or controls can increase or decrease those instincts.

Erich Fromm suggested that Lorenz may have been only half right.[17] Fromm argued that instrumental aggression—violence as a means to an end—may indeed have roots in our biological heritage, being necessary for our survival as individuals and as a species. Instrumental aggression is self-defensive, protective, and therefore necessary. Expressive aggression—violence for its own sake—is, in Fromm's view, another story altogether. What Fromm called human destructiveness—sadistic aggressive behavior as an end in itself—is not instinctual, but completely learned in response to society's failure to satisfy the basic human needs of its members. According to Fromm, destructive aggression increases to the extent that society becomes "civilized" and therefore more out of touch with the basic human needs of its citizens. This theory loses its strength, of course, when we consider the highly violent nature of many past and present "less civilized" societies.

Fromm reminded us that instrumental aggression is found among all primates, not just human beings. The great apes are extremely violent toward one another in the interest of securing food or maintaining dominance. In sharp contrast, however, Fromm also claimed that only human beings engage in destructive aggression. We are the only primates (but not the only mammals) who, sadly enough, kill one another for the sheer pleasure of it. You won't find a Ted Bundy among the great apes!

The work of evolutionary psychologists Daly and Wilson, also blends biological and psychological factors. For these researchers, the psychological processes involved in the homicidal act are so much choice as they are a matter of thousands of years of experiences in human decision-making. Why do we like sweets? Because thousands of years ago, our ancestors found out that foods with a sweet taste were rich in nutrients. Why are we so threatened by the infidelity of our mate? Is it perhaps because we don't want to spend our time caring for someone else's gene pool? Humans with a common goal of survival of their genetic heritage make decisions that they believe will support their own self-interests.[18]

Basing their conclusions about human behavior on animal studies, evolutionary psychologists have similarly contended that human violence is triggered by so-called "selfish genes," which are propelled by a biological need to perpetuate themselves in one's offspring. If true, an individual would be less likely to eliminate people who are closely related by heredity—less likely to murder siblings than cousins, and less likely to kill cousins than unrelated strangers. It is self-defeating, according to the evolutionary psychology perspective, for individuals to murder those who share their genetic makeup.

Some researchers have used the sociobiological perspective to explain violence in stepfamilies. Stepparents have absolutely no biological investment in their spouses' children—even if they love them. Thus, we might expect parents to murder their stepchildren at a greater rate than they kill their biological offspring. If the sociobiologists are right, then stepfamilies should be at greater risk of violence than blood relatives. According to the research of Daly and Wilson, the incidence of violence is indeed far greater in stepfamilies than in traditional families where the children are genetically related both to parents and to one another.[19] For example, Daly and Wilson determined that the rate of infanticide (the killing of young children) is 60 times higher in stepfamilies than in biologically-connected families.

Daly and Wilson also suggested that homicides perpetrated by stepfathers differ from those by biological fathers not only quantitatively, but qualitatively. Unlike the large number of despondent fathers who slay their genetic offspring as a desperate act of twisted love before committing suicide, stepfathers virtually never kill their children in this manner. Moreover, stepfathers are much more likely to beat their young stepchildren to death, while biological fathers are more likely to kill their youngsters with guns or asphyxiation, methods that do not require brute force.

We should keep in mind that murder is a rare phenomenon, of course, and the members of most stepfamilies do not harm one another. The theoretical task is to pinpoint the factors that increase the probability that rare instances of deadly violence are more likely to occur. Moreover, as is the case with all of our biological and psychological variables, there are social and environmental contexts that might explain differences in infanticide between biological and stepfamilies.

Is there a violent personality? The psychological perspective considers the relationship between various personality traits and aggressive behavior. Many people have taken the MMPI (Minnesota Multiphasic Personality Inventory) or other personality tests that attempt to measure traits such as introversion, hostility, suspicion, assertiveness, and impulsiveness. There should be no surprise that comparisons of inmate and student population personality inventories often show no significant differences since these are not mutually exclusive categories of people (students can become inmates, and vice versa). Although some researchers, such as the Gluecks, found significant personality differences between offenders and non-offenders, most research has been far less definitive regarding the violent personality. Some recent research has found that a set of personality traits may cluster together to create "negative emotionality," and this cluster of traits is more likely to be present in juvenile offenders. These traits include stress, excessive control, cowardice or bullying, approval seeking, jealousy, low self-esteem, fears of abandonment, moodiness, anger, immaturity, and suspicion.[20]

As we have seen, certain personality traits may manifest themselves, at least in part, in the social context. While one person who is an aggressive risk-taker grows up in a loving home, another person born with a similar set of personality characteristics may be raised in conditions of abuse or neglect. Additionally, if individuals with a personality or genetic predisposition toward risk taking are born into prosperous families, they may have legitimate ways to satisfy their need for thrill and excitement, for example by engaging in certain high-risk sports like skydiving. But if these same people are instead born into poor or dysfunctional families with no legitimate avenues to exercise risk-taking, the outcomes could be deadly and criminal.

Are most murderers mentally ill? If so, what kinds of mental illnesses do they tend to have? And what are the causes of these illnesses? There is some empirical connection between various mental illnesses and criminal behaviors, but the association is rather weak. Obviously, most mentally ill people never hurt or kill anyone. Furthermore, the link between mental illness and crime may be indirect. If people suffering from mental illness are more likely to self-medicate with drugs and alcohol, it could be that substance abuse is the key to their violent behavior rather than the mental illness itself. Also, to the extent that violent behavior and mental illness are both linked to such background factors as child abuse, trauma, and neglect, then the apparent association between homicide and mental illness may be spurious or misleading.

Finally, if mental illness were determined to be a strong predictor of violent behavior, then what should our policy response be? Should it be mandatory psychiatric treatment and medication (e.g., chemical lobotomies) for violent offenders? Should these perpetrators be institutionalized in mental hospitals rather than prisons?

A psychological dimension that does appear to be associated with at least one type of murderer, the serial killer, is the presence of various paraphilias—sexual attractions to unusual or bizarre objects. Obviously, not all paraphilias are linked to murder (e.g., exhibitionism, cross-dressing, or foot fetishes). However, several sexual proclivities, such as pedophilia and necrophilia, necessitate some level of criminal behavior that may in some cases also lead to murder. Because of his sexual craving for corpses, Jeffrey Dahmer committed a string of brutal murders, lobotomizing his victims to create zombie-like sex partners. Although necrophilia is obviously a mental disorder, the State of Wisconsin did not believe that Dahmer's necrophilia was so incapacitating to sustain his insanity plea. While paraphilias represent distortions in what a person perceives to be sexually arousing, they are generally not the kind of profound distortions in thinking or perception that would mitigate criminal responsibility.

One of the most hotly debated topics related to criminality is whether low intelligence predicts criminal and violent behavior. As early as the 1920s, Goddard and several other psychologists were applying the new Simon-Binet intelligence quotient (IQ) in their studies of criminal populations.[21] In Congressional testimony, they argued that Americans needed protection from the "worthless" Eastern and Southern European immigrants who scored lower on intelligence tests than their counterparts from Western and Northern Europe. This work sparked a history of feeblemindedness profiling that lasted at least from 1900 through the 1930s. In 1907, Indiana passed the first eugenics law allowing for state-authorized sterilizations and many other states followed with their own, sometimes even more aggressive, laws. Lasting until the 1960s, many states had mandatory sterilization laws for residents of mental institutions, welfare moms, the retarded, and epileptics. Not until 2003, did the state of North Carolina abolish its 74-year-old eugenics law that allowed them (among other things) to sterilize a woman without her consent based on the conclusion that she was feebleminded. Thus, the IQ debate and the frightful social policy that flows from it have a long checkered past in the annals of criminological theory.

Notwithstanding the questionable policy responses, quality scientific research, such as the work of Sheldon and Eleanor Glueck in *Unraveling Juvenile Delinquency* (1950), has indeed found IQ to be a significant predictor of delinquency. As recently as 1977, criminologists Travis Hirschi and Michael Hindelang observed IQ to be a stronger predictor of delinquency than either social class or race.[22] It is in large part because of racial differences in IQ that the relationship between intelligence and crime is so politically volatile. Some research speculated that IQ differences between whites and blacks could be genetic, and that the genetic "inferiority" of blacks, in turn, is related to their higher rates of poverty and criminality.[23] In 1969, educational psychologist Arthur Jenson hypothesized that "genetic factors are strongly implicated in the average Negro-white intelligence difference."[24]

While many critics viewed this type of work as misguided and reflective of political ideologies, the publication in 1994 of *The Bell Curve* by two respected Harvard researchers, Charles Murray and Richard Herrnstein, kept the IQ issue alive, at least in the public mind.[25] Murray and Herrnstein reported significant differences in intelligence among races, but they were unable, like their predecessors, to rule out important educational differences and racism as factors that could account for these disparities.

The controversy surrounding whether IQ is a significant predictor of violent crime as well as the debate about the factors influencing IQ remain unresolved, even after a half-century of research. Why would we expect IQ to predict violence? Do we believe that people with a low IQ could be more easily convinced by others to kill someone, or that they are too unintelligent to see viable solutions other than murder? Does low IQ leave people with such limited means of earning money that they kill because of the frustration of being poor or as part of their menial job? Perhaps the strongest possible link between IQ and violence would be in the extent to which IQ affects a person's ability to perceive consequences and make informed choices.[26] As with many other biological and psychological variables, IQ also fails to account for significant gender, seasonal, regional and age variations in homicide.

Obviously, very low intelligence can restrict a person's ability to understand right from wrong, but the association between low IQ and the will to kill remains dubious. Studies of IQ and crime are generally performed on convicted offenders. And since more than one-third of murders are unsolved, perhaps it is the more intelligent offenders who are less likely to be caught, convicted and therefore studied.

Whether Freudian theory, personality traits, mental illness, natural aggression or IQ, the psychological variables reviewed here are characteristics of individuals. Thus, to some extent, criminal justice responses and punishments need to be individually tailored as well. Yet many citizens and policymakers are not comfortable with therapies or sanctions that vary from individual offender to individual offender. However, based on what we know about individual biological and psychological predispositions toward violence, overly rigid punishment responses that treat all offenders the same may be questionable in terms of their fairness or appropriateness.

The Social Sources of Murder

Rather than the individual-specific variables of biological and psychological positivism, sociologists look for the origins of crime and violence in the external world. Characteristics of neighborhoods, poverty, subcultural value systems, learning, and lack of social bonds to others reflect the important variables of 20th-century criminology. Sociological positivism began with theories that attempted to explain the high crime rates in lower-class urban areas. From the early 1900s through the 1950s, criminological theory operated on the assumption that crime is predominantly a problem of lower-class areas and its residents. While these early theories may have been useful in explaining the activities of lower-class boys who joined urban gangs, they were obviously inadequate to explain homicides that did not involve offenders from a lower economic class.

Social disorganization theory focused on the factors that weaken communities—mobility, heterogeneity, and poverty—rather than biological or psychological deficiencies in the residents of those communities. Transiency and poverty combine to create conditions such that no matter who lives there, those areas will have higher crime rates.[27] In social disorganization theory, the causes of violent behavior are the very factors that lead to social disorganization. Clearly, this sort of theory would be most useful for explaining felony murders or even homicides that result from an argument on the street corner, but would fail to explain murder committed by middle- and upper-class offenders.

Some researchers have retooled social disorganization theory to incorporate many area-level variables other than mobility, poverty, and heterogeneity. These so-called "social ecology theories" still focus on the characteristics of areas and how some areas may be particularly fertile ground for crime and violence. For example, the recent "broken windows" approach to policing—cleaning up the neighborhood to eradicate conditions that breed lawlessness and disorder—is based in part on ideas from social disorganization theory.[28] These types of community-level explanations are particularly helpful in understanding why certain areas of cities have a disproportionate share of homicides.

Strain, Frustration, and Murder

In 1998, Robert Cleaves, a retired actor who played a minor role in "Dragnet" and other popular television shows during the 1950s and 1960s, killed 38-year-old Arnold Guerreiro in an extreme episode of what has in recent years been termed "road rage." Cleaves and Guerreiro had exchanged words after a near collision. Guerreiro attempted to return to his car, but Cleaves wasn't through venting his frustration and anger over the incident. Cleaves ran over the victim twice, dragged him along the street under the car and then backed over him once again. After the victim died in the hospital from the injuries, Cleaves was charged and eventually convicted of second-degree murder and was sentenced in a Los Angeles court to 16 years to life in prison. The tragic events of that day may have been out of character for Robert Cleaves, but not necessarily for human behavior. Frustration often brings out the worst in us—loss of temper, anger, and even violence.

The concept of frustration-aggression has had a powerful influence on the field of criminology. In 1939, a group of Yale University psychologists (Dollard, Doob, Miller, Mowrer, and Sears) focused on the effects of frustration—an unpleasant psychological state resulting from the failure to satisfy some need or desire—on aggressive behavior.[29] They suggested that frustration and aggression are inextricably connected. In what became famous as the "frustration-aggression hypothesis," they argued that frustration always causes some form of aggression, and that aggression is always preceded by frustration. Thus, anything that interferes with an individual's movement toward a goal—whether it is as minor as waiting for a long red light to change or as major as failing to earn enough money to feed one's children—will inevitably lead to the expression of aggression, including murder.

Though the original frustration-aggression hypothesis may have been overstated, it is not without some validity. Aggressive behavior does tend to increase when people are prevented from reaching a goal they expect to attain. There are people who yell at their children after a bad day at the office; there are men who punch the wall after being dumped by a girlfriend. At the extreme, some individuals have annihilated their ex-spouse and children because of a nasty divorce and custody battle. Others have murdered their supervisor after being fired from a job. A few students have been so frustrated with school that they have gunned down their teachers and classmates.

Clearly, we now know that the progression from frustration to aggression is not inevitable. For a variety of reasons other than biology, many people deal with the frustrations of daily life without harming or killing others. Indeed, commuters are much more likely to wait patiently for a long light to change or seek a faster route home than to shout obscenities or shoot another driver, even though some motorists do vent their feelings of road rage. People are more likely to change jobs or seek training for higher paying work than to stab their boss or a family member. Frustration does not always lead to aggression. More likely, people learn to develop coping skills in responding to the frustrations of everyday life.

Not only does aggression not follow every frustrating episode, but just as clearly, frustration does not precede every aggressive action. There are countless examples of violence that occur in the absence of any especially frustrating circumstances. For example, a soldier engages in combat because he is ordered to do so by his commanding officer. A young child shoots his playmate after seeing a gunfight on television. A hit man for the mob eliminates the leader of a rival "family" because he was paid to do so.

The tendency for frustration to lead to aggression is greatest when the frustration is severe and unexpected—that is, if people are deprived of something important that they were certain of getting such as a promised promotion that falls through at the last moment. The tendency is also greater when people believe they can get away with being aggressive— when they do not anticipate being punished in return or being rejected by their friends and associates. For example, a child is more likely to bully his playmates if he thinks none of them will stand up to him and that his parents will not find out.[30]

Animals certainly tend to respond aggressively after they are deprived of a reward that they are accustomed to receiving. In 1966, Azrin and his associates published the results of an experiment in which pigeons received food every time they pecked at a key. Once the birds had learned this behavior, the experimenters suddenly withdrew their reward: no more food was administered even if the birds pecked appropriately. As expected, the birds responded by attacking other pigeons in the experimental chamber.

Of course, pigeon behavior is quite different from human behavior. Do people attack one another when their goals are blocked and they cannot get what they want? In 1960, Stuart Palmer studied 51 convicted murderers to determine whether severe frustrations suffered during childhood might have led them to commit murder later in their lives.[31] To provide a comparison group of similar men who had not killed anyone, Palmer also studied the nearest-in-age brother of each murderer. He found that the 51 convicted killers had indeed experienced more intense frustrations than had their brothers who were not convicted of murder. Specifically, the convicted murderers were more likely to have been dissatisfied with their prestige or status, to have suffered physical defects, to have done poorly in school, and to have had fewer friends. In short, they had led "dismal, unprestigious, frustrating lives." An extremely deadly response to frustration, a number of the more infamous mass murderers— including Mark Barton who slaughtered nine and injured a dozen others at two Atlanta investment offices in 1999, had recently suffered "reward withdrawal" or status loss before their violent rampages.

Building on the social psychological view of strain, Robert Agnew's recent general strain theory (GST) transformed the frustration-aggression hypothesis into a much broader concept.[32] Criminal violence, Agnew proposed, is a result of strain—frustration, anger, disappointment, fear, or depression—that originates in destructive social ties. Agnew identified four important sources of strain: a) the presence of negative stimuli (e.g., child abuse, peer rejection, school failure, and physical punishment); b) the removal of positive stimuli (e.g., death of a loved one, parents' divorce, and residential mobility); c) perception of inequity (e.g., peers who make more money or get better grades because they have "connections"); and d) failure to achieve desired goals (e.g., missing out on success because of a lack of educational opportunities).

One important advantage of Agnew's general strain theory over the earlier frustration-aggression hypothesis is its emphasis on more than just absolute levels of deprivation. In focusing on the gap between expectations and achievements and between the successes of individuals and their peers, Agnew incorporated what sociologists have called "relative deprivation."

Social scientists have long recognized that absolute levels of unemployment or income do not necessarily translate into a subjective feeling of misery. The impact of economic variables on feelings of deprivation or frustration—especially at levels that promote murder—depends at least to some extent on an individual's standards of comparison. On both individual and aggregate levels, criminologists focus on perceptions of relative deprivation by asking: How much status and salary do individuals enjoy relative to the amount of prestige and money they had five or ten years earlier? How much money do they earn relative to their friends, neighbors, and other significant people in their lives? To what extent has the unemployment rate risen or fallen over time? How wide is the income gap between rich and poor, and how does income inequality across countries and over time correlate with rates of murder?

Downward mobility—the very process of losing economic ground—may contribute to individuals' feelings of deprivation, even if they are millionaires.[33] As a cohort, those baby boomers who entered the labor force during the late sixties and seventies may experience a sense of losing economic ground even at a time when the unemployment rate is very low. Since the early 1970s, the income gap between the haves and the have-nots has continued to widen, resulting in a shrinking middle class. At the bottom of the socio-economic ladder, the level of permanent, inter-generational poverty in major American cities, often referred to as the underclass and the "truly disadvantaged," has not abated.[34]

According to a recent study by the Economic Policy Institute and the Center on Budget and Policy Priorities, income inequality has been on the rise. During the late 1970s, in not one state did the wealthiest 20 percent earn 9.5 times more than the poorest 20 percent. At this juncture, however, the "top to bottom ratio" exceeds 9.5 in nearly half the states and continues to rise in all states but Alaska, Louisiana, and Tennessee. It seems that prosperity has not had the same impact throughout the class structure. Instead, it has pushed rich and poor Americans further and further apart. Downward mobility has been particularly steep for displaced manufacturing workers, who, since the 1970s, have found themselves stuck in service-sector jobs that pay less and have fewer fringe benefits. More recently, a bull market made the wealthy even wealthier and further widened the disparity between rich and poor. The median income of families in the top 20 percent of income distribution is now more than 10 times as large as the median income of the poorest 20 percent.[35]

Cross-national comparisons have often failed to uncover any relationship between aggregate rates of unemployment and homicide. At least at the national level, the unemployment rate seems to have little if anything to do with differences in murder rates across countries. Comparing income inequality across nations yields quite a different result, however. Specifically, countries with high levels of income inequality, such as the United States, also tend to have high rates of homicide.[36] Still, as income inequality has continued to increase over the past decade in the United States, homicide rates have declined. Thus, income inequality may help explain cross-national differences in homicide rates but does not seem to be a reliable tool for explaining recent fluctuations of homicide rates within the United States.

Principles of psychology and sociology, rather than economics, might explain the differential impact of unemployment vs. income inequality on murder rates. When joblessness prevails, many citizens feel that everyone is in the same sinking boat. Economic misery may therefore not be tied to feelings of inequity or unfairness (i.e., things are bad, but they are bad for everyone). Under conditions of income inequality, however, citizens find themselves in different boats, some much larger and more lavish than others. A few even own luxury yachts while many others have merely rowboats that are rapidly taking on water. Those individuals who are left behind—even if their boats are bigger than ever before—feel as though they are victims of economic injustice. Compared with wealthy segments of their society, they are losing ground and feel relatively deprived.

A sense of relative deprivation seems to increase among the impoverished members of communities where rich and poor live in close proximity. For the same reason, perhaps, rioting is more likely to occur in areas of a city where strict segregation gives way to close interaction between groups whose members reside together in the same neighborhoods.

Strain theory was originally an attempt to explain why certain areas have higher crime rates.[37] In his classic analysis, Robert Merton recognized that strain can be institutionalized in the misalignment of institutionalized goals and culturally prescribed means. According to American cultural values learned from an early age, all members of society are expected to strive for economic success. Yet, there is far less emphasis in American society on providing the structural opportunities for achieving that success. This disparity invites what Merton refers to as "innovation": an individual accepts the cultural emphasis on the success goal, but rejects the socially acceptable means for its attainment. In some cases, an individual will substitute illegitimate (often illegal) but more effective methods of securing wealth and power. For middle-class deviants, the pressure to innovate might take the form of unethical business practices and white-collar crime. But for members of society lacking in education and economic resources, innovation more frequently becomes street crime including gang membership, drug dealing, property offenses, and violence.

In the spirit of strain theory, Steve Messner and Richard Rosenfeld's recent work, *Crime and the American Dream,* suggested that the breakdown of social institutions regulating behavior (churches, schools, and families) has contributed to elevated levels of crime in the United States. For Messner and Rosenfeld, the economy has become the dominant force controlling behavior and has dwarfed any other institution's ability to curb crime. Families are run like a business, and roles that don't generate income (e.g., stay-at-home moms) are not valued. In a society where the pursuit of material success is valued above all else, we should not be surprised to witness a crime wave like the crack-related homicide epidemic of the late-1980s.[38]

Cultural Deviance

Cultural deviance theories (also called subcultural theories) do not contend that criminals are necessarily strained, but that they obey the norms they were taught—rules of behavior that just happen to differ from those of the law. In other words, criminals learn different codes of right and wrong. Wolfgang and Ferracuti long ago proposed that higher homicide rates among young men, in the lower classes, among blacks, and in the South may have a cultural basis. They are a result of a "subculture of violence," in which violent behavior, even murder, is regarded as an appropriate and rewarded response to a menacing situation (for example, a threatening glance, a jostle, an insulting comment, or the presence of a weapon).[39] In this subculture, violence is a norm to which everyone is expected to comply, and those who do so are accorded high status and respect. According to subculture of violence theorists, under such cultural conditions, murder becomes more likely.[40]

The subcultural explanation for southern homicide patterns is supported by evidence showing that murders occurring in the South are more likely than those in other regions to arise from arguments between people who know each other.[41] These confrontations typically escalate when the reputation or honor of an individual is impugned by an insulting remark. Also supporting the subcultural perspective is evidence that southerners, more than residents of other regions, approve of using defensive violence against people who pose a serious threat to their personal safety, rather than seeking non-violent alternatives.[42]

There are many different versions of cultural deviance theory, but they all embrace the argument that homicide offenders have learned a set of values and beliefs that promote the use of violence.[43] Although most of the fundamental premises of subcultural theory make sense, these theories have received little empirical support, as the variables associated with violence are more likely to be structural or situational than cultural. Rather than a "southern subculture of violence," the source of higher homicide rates in the South could just as likely result from such factors as poverty, income inequality, racial segregation, weather, alcohol and drug use, and gun ownership.

Learning to Kill

Some criminologists would argue that it is not primarily the area, strain, or exposure to a subculture that creates the propensity for violence, but rather that people learn to kill one another. Forms of violence vary tremendously from culture to culture, and violent behavior does not occur at all in some, although these instances are more of an anomaly. No one suggests that the propensity to kill is totally inborn, and criminologists recognize the occasional but rare instance of a group that has very little, if any, violence.

In the tradition of the "potlatch," for example, the Kwakiuti Indians conquer their opponents, not with physical confrontation, but by giving away or destroying more of their own personal property (for a people to whom spirituality is paramount, material possessions only increase one's vulnerability). Among the Indians of Santa Marta, contestants fight by striking a rock or tree with a stick until it breaks. In Eskimo culture, arguments are resolved through a contest in which opponents sing nasty songs about one another.[44] The Arapesh of New Guinea, the pygmies of the Ituri rain forest, the Lepchas of Sikkim, and the Australian Aborigines apparently display few if any signs of violence. They live for long periods at peace with one another, lacking everyday expressions of anger or even words in their language for weaponry or defense. For these groups, murder is virtually non-existent.

Human beings may have some instinctual tendencies toward violence, but levels and types of violence vary considerably depending upon contextual effects such as learning. For example, the southern states have traditionally had more than their share of single-victim homicides, but less than their share of mass murders. By contrast, California, Texas, Alaska, and New York have experienced a disproportionate number of multiple murders, including the grisly killings by the Hillside Stranglers, the Night Stalker, Joel Rifkin, Robert Hanson, and Henry Lee Lucas. In addition, murder is much more likely to be committed by men than women, and by young people than their elders. Furthermore, the murder rate varies over time.

Social learning theory offers another approach to explaining individual and social differences in the propensity to commit acts of extreme violence. According to this theory, most aggressive behavior involves skills that we must learn from others.[45] We learn to be violent not only through rewards and punishments, but also through the role models we imitate. Clearly, significant people around us may serve as models of learning in many other areas of life—for example, in acquiring language, using facial expressions, and dressing for various occasions. In a similar fashion, imitation may also occur in learning violent behavior, even behavior as violent as homicide.

Albert Bandura suggested that the mass media generally, and television in particular, provide powerful models for aggressive conduct. Findings obtained in a large number of studies over several decades on the effects of television on behavior support this argument. These studies show that television may serve as a tutor in teaching violent behavior. However, Bandura's research suffers from the same methodological and ethical problems that haunt much of the research on the link between violent media and violent behavior. Most of these studies exposed white male college students to violent media to assess attitudinal shifts, not behavioral shifts.

Research by David Phillips strongly suggests that media images can teach even the most violent acts.[46] Philips examined the homicide rate in America immediately following televised heavyweight prizefights, and found a brief but sharp rise in homicides, an overall increase of 13 percent. This effect seemed to peak on the third day after the bouts, especially following most heavily publicized fights. Like Bandura's work, Phillips' findings are far from definitive regarding a casual link between violent media and violent behavior. The increase in homicide may not have been due to mimicking the aggression displayed in prizefights, but due to alcohol consumption, hangovers, lost money from gambling, lack of sleep, and missed work/wages associated with the event. Obviously, the vast majority of people exposed to violent media do not behave violently at all. There are clearly some people who seize upon this sort of media as a model for their own behavior, yet there are likely a number of other stronger causal factors at work for these people.

The latest technology in the violent media debate is the video game. Whereas television involves one-way interaction, a passive form of potential learning, video games are active and interactional—players get in on the action. Games like *Postal, Doom,* and *Kingpin* reward players for killing scores of people; and with advanced graphics and multi-media sound, the line between virtual reality and stark reality can become rather thin, particularly to an impressionable youngster. Several of the recent school shooters were known to have had an affinity for video games, a fact that became the focus of lawsuits against the gaming industry.

Obviously, many murders were committed long before Nintendo, PS2, and Xbox games existed. Homicide rates were skyrocketing during the era of Atari and Pacman when games were more the arcade variety, so we can hardly blame violent video games as one of the primary sources of homicidal behavior. However, if an already troubled youngster—someone with a history of abuse, neglect, personality and adjustment problems, substance abuse, or other risk factors—is exposed daily to violent entertainment, the result may be tragic. Violent media may facilitate homicidal behavior, even if not the primary cause.

Rather than the media, many learning theories have focused on arguably the stronger influence of the day-to-day interactions that we all have with others. Models for murder can be located in the groups to which an individual belongs. Edwin Sutherland's differential association theory contends that criminal behavior is learned during adolescence from an individual's most intimate social relations—his peers, family, and friends. In addition to learning attitudes supporting violence, individuals acquire criminal skills through these associations (no one is born knowing how to roll a joint, hotwire a car, make a bomb, or use a gun). In addition, individuals learn by observing group members who violate the law, from shoplifting and taking illicit drugs to armed robbery and murder. To the extent that people associate with others who regard criminal behavior in a positive light, they are also excluded from associating with those who reject the criminal lifestyle. Just as they learn a host of important values, individuals adopt the criminal attitudes and behavior of their intimate associates.[47]

In a more recent version of social learning theory, Akers blended differential association with conditioning effects of rewards and punishments to explain the development of criminality.[48] In his differential reinforcement theory, Akers suggests that the acceptance of violence does not come merely from associating with a particular group of intimates, but from associating with a group whose members reinforce violent behavior and punish law-abiding behavior. According to Akers, offenders learn violence in several different ways from group members—by observing and imitating the deviant behavior of others, by being rewarded and praised by group members for engaging in deviant behavior, and by acquiring attitudes from group members that support and stimulate deviant behavior. The significant level of empirical support for learning theories should give us pause about the criminogenic effects of incarceration—if prisons aren't schools for crime, then perhaps they are at least study halls.

Self-Control, Social Control, and Murder

Still another theoretical perspective hypothesizes that criminal behavior is a result of a lack of control rather than a function of learning. Control theories envision a set of controls or bonds that work to limit involvement in criminal behavior. But control theory also takes account of the fact that not everyone's moral sense prevents them from committing acts of criminal violence. Hirschi argued that criminality is often controlled by an individual's commitments and attachments to conventional institutions, beliefs, activities, and groups.[49] Many people refrain from engaging in violent behavior because they fear losing their relationships with significant others—with family, friends, and peers. However, members of society who lack strong social ties may also lack the motivation to become law-abiding citizens. In this theory, a person would commit violence or murder when he or she had no controlling influence from attachments to others, commitments to conventional behavior, involvements in conventional activities and belief in the morality of the law—in a sense, nothing left to lose.

Similarly, Sampson and Laub suggested that the ability of people to form bonds and connections through stable relationships and job and career opportunities may protect them from committing criminal acts.[50] Furthermore, Gottfredson and Hirschi, in their book *A General Theory of Crime,* pointed to the importance of parental love, supervision, and consistent discipline in the formation of self-control. This theory not only seeks to explain why someone might be a shoplifter or serial killer (both would primarily be a function of low self-control and opportunity), but can also be used to explain a host of other maladaptive behaviors such as gambling, alcohol and drug use, financial irresponsibility, interpersonal relationship problems, smoking, and eating disorders. Part of the appeal of the Gottfredson and Hirschi perspective is that the theory incorporates biological, psychological, and sociological variables within a context of opportunities.

An important insight provided by control theory is that commitment or attachment to conventional individuals and institutions inoculates human beings from committing violent offenses. Regrettably, in recent years Americans have suffered a sharp decline in close bonds with others in their communities, particularly in some regions of the country. Those geographic areas that attract large numbers of individuals lacking in social bonds—drifters, transients, migrants, and newcomers—also tend to have high rates of crime, including murder. The eclipse of community can be seen most clearly in states like California, Alaska (beware of the person who wants to get away from it all), Florida, and Texas—states that are known for providing the opportunity for a new beginning or a last resort.

Years ago, in an early version of control theory, Walter Reckless described the factors that encourage criminal behavior as a set of "pushes and pulls."[51] Adapting Reckless's perspective, we have discussed in this chapter a number of conditions that can pull an individual away from conventional society—for example, being a victim of frustration or disappointment that results from not "measuring up," in the conventional sense; having a personality disorder characterized by lack of remorse and empathy; feeling distant from conventional beliefs, institutions, or individuals; or suffering from repeated head traumas, a disorder that can make everyday functioning difficult. Other factors reviewed in this chapter push individuals toward murderous behavior—for example, growing up in a subculture in which violence is seen as a virtue; finding social support with a group of friends who engage in criminal behavior; or finding models (fictional or factual) whose murderous behavior is rewarded. In explaining the will to kill, we might then search for the presence of the forces that both pull individuals away from conventional society and push them toward the crime of murder.

A Word of Caution about Cause

Having reviewed in this chapter a wide range of theories, summarized in Table 2.1, all purporting to explain murderous intentions and other violent behavior, we may have left a rather confusing image of the variables responsible for murder. Certainly, each theory has limitations. Most have been criticized if not condemned for their shortcomings and flaws.

It is wise to keep in mind that even good theories that have been tested and validated with empirical research cannot account for the full variety of human behavior. Good theories can explain some cases of homicide, but not all forms of homicidal proneness, no matter which variables are used.

The important notion that correlation does not imply causation is virtually a mantra of social science research. For example, blacks have significantly higher rates of committing murder than do whites, but this correlation is not necessarily the impact of race itself; instead, it is likely a result of a host of socio-economic conditions associated with race.

In addition, correlation also does not guarantee predictability. Men have rates of committing homicide many times higher than women. Yet, though most killers are male, most

TABLE 2.1 *Selected Theories of Violence and Homicide*

Theory and Dates	*Selected Proponents*	*Key Concepts*	*Policy Implications*
Supernatural Through the late 1600s		Demonic possession, evil spirits, witchcraft and the Devil cause crime	Torture and execution drive out evil; chaos, cruelty and anarchy characterize punishments for crime
Classical Mid 1700s–late 1800s	Beccaria and Bentham	Violent behavior is a result of choice and free will, reasoning, decision making, and assessment of pain versus gain	Deterrence through certain, swift and pro-portional punishment; utilitarian-based notion of justice
Biological Late 1800s–1960s	Lombroso, Garafalo, Goddard, Dugdale and Sheldon	Criminals have a physical and/or genetic inferiority that predisposes them to criminal behaviors; includes atavism, criminal anthropol-ogy, genetics, body types, and XYY chromosome	Eugenics; sterilization; feeblemindedness profiling; psychosurgery
Psychoanalytic 1920s–present	Freud	Unconscious motives and repression drive criminal behavior; deviant behavior is linked to inadequate devel-opment of personality com-ponents in early childhood as a result of abuse, neglect, extreme permissiveness, or unconditional love	Psychoanalysis to relieve overactive id, neurosis, and psychosis
Psychological and Psychiatric Early 1900s–present	Lorenz, Fromm, Skinner, Bandura, Eysenck, and Herrnstein & Murray	Aggression is a response to frustration; aggression is a result of imitation, modeling and rewards for violence; violence is linked to mental illness, personality disorders or low IQ	Counseling, drug therapy, and behavior modification to treat violence as an individual-level phenomenon
Rational Choice Mid 1970s–present	Clarke & Cornish	Classical notions of free will combined with positivistic variables; offenders choose to be violent but certain variables influence the ability to make reasoned choices	Target hardening; situa-tional crime prevention; displacement; classical punishment responses with more focus on severe punishments
Social Disorganization and Social Ecology 1920s–present	Shaw & McKay, Bursik, and Sampson	Disorganized areas breed criminal influences	Employment and edu-cational opportunities; neighborhood revitali-zation; positive role models; strong families and schools

(continued)

TABLE 2.1 *Continued*

Theory and Dates	*Selected Proponents*	*Key Concepts*	*Policy Implications*
Cultural Deviance 1920s–present	Wolfgang & Ferracuti, Cohen, Miller, and Cloward & Ohlin	Some groups/individuals have different value systems; different socialization forms the foundation for subculture or gang support for violence	Positive role models; legitimate educational and economic opportunities
Strain 1930s–present	Merton, Agnew, and Messner & Rosenfeld	Frustration results from blocked legitimate opportunities; crime and delinquency is an individual adaptation or coping mechanism in response to strain; economic success is a primary form of institutional control	Focus on values and institutions other than financial success (family, church and school); provide psychological and structural opportunities for success
Social Learning 1930s–present	Sutherland, Burgess, Akers, and Phillips	People learn to commit violent acts; violence continues if reinforced; peer groups influence modeling; highlights copycat offending and media influences	Positive role models and relearning non-criminal values and strategies
Social and Self Control 1950s–present	Reckless, Hirschi, Gottfredson & Hirschi, and Grasmik	People must be socialized to resist pushes and pulls towards crime; delinquency as a result of weakened bonds to society; proper parental supervision, love and discipline develops self-control in children; self-control as the ability to control natural tendencies	Encourage bonding and attachment to conventional others; increase individual stakes in conformity
Integrated 1950s–present	Gluecks, Daly & Wilson, Murray & Herrnstein, Fishbein, Gottfredson & Hirschi, and Sampson & Laub	Biological predispositions create conditional free will; unchangeable latent traits; malleable developmental and life-course approaches	Combined modalities (drugs, counseling, family intervention); educational opportunities; possibilities for marriage, family and career to redirect criminals

males do not kill. Theories that reduce a murderous response to the impact of a single variable fail to recognize the complexity of the will to kill. Even elaborate models that predict murder based on demographics, family patterns, peer groups, and other factors fail more than they succeed in identifying killers. The best they can do is to pinpoint those at greatest risk, usually *after* they have already committed serious crimes. What society would do with these high-risk individuals if we could predict their future behavior then becomes an important ethical and policy question.

In this chapter, we have offered a taste of the many perspectives and theoretical traditions that have been invoked in attempts to explain and predict violence, in general, and homicide, in particular. Any effort to survey completely and in depth the broad array of theories for homicidal proneness would likely fill volumes, and already has. In 1988, the National Academy of Sciences commissioned an expert panel on violence to describe in some detail the multitude of causal theories.[52] Even after the publication of the panel's four volumes of research findings, our understanding and ability to predict, much less explain, extreme violence is still quite limited. Human behavior is complex, and the linkages between biological, psychological, and sociological stimuli and the subsequent homicidal response are much more complicated and difficult to identify than the movements of laboratory mice in search of a piece of Velveeta at the finish line of a circuitous maze.

After all that has been researched and written on the topic of homicide, which disciplinary tradition has the most to contribute in explaining why some people kill and others do not? Does the abnormal psychology of the murderer or his physical constitution hold greater insights into the mystery of murder? Are the bad schools, bad parents and/or bad peers more telling?

The simple answer to these difficult questions is: It depends. It is likely that all of these notions have some merit—not to understand all kinds of murder, but perhaps some discrete subset. A focus on head trauma or environmental toxins may help us to comprehend sudden and uncharacteristic outbursts of murderous rage, but will do little to account for cold-blooded acts of murder for hire. Learning theories of social psychology and sociological hypotheses pertaining to social class and social structure are valuable for understanding serious gang violence, but inadequate for interpreting infanticide.

Regardless of the theoretical approach, we often think of causation in terms of some form of deficiency, deviation, or defect. A "bad seed," diseased brain, poor parenting, maltreatment, drug side effect, running with a bad crowd, exposure to harmful media, poor opportunities, bad days, and bad breaks are all valuable notions, but none alone is generally sufficient to drive a person to kill. Even a person struggling with a combination of biological, psychological, or sociological abnormalities (such as a learning-disabled child raised by an impoverished and unconcerned single parent and who plays violent video games with his delinquent buddies) has an ability to make a choice, though it may be limited by his various handicaps. While our options and opportunities in life are impacted by a host of advantages and disadvantages, virtually all of us have some degree of free will. Unlike Azrin's pigeons, human beings have choices in how to respond when the rewards we have come to expect are suddenly withdrawn or unavailable. By nature of heredity and nurture of environment, some individuals are more prone to violence than others, yet free will still exists. The will to kill, though governed by numerous internal and external forces, still includes choice and human decision-making, and thus accountability and culpability.

Endnotes

1. George B. Vold, Thomas J. Bernard, and Jeffrey B. Snipes, *Theoretical Criminology.* New York: Oxford University Press, 2002.

2. Cesare Beccaria, *On Crimes and Punishments,* translated by Henry Paolucci. Indianapolis: Bobbs-Merrill, 1963. Jeremy Bentham, *A Fragment on Government and*

an Introduction to the Principles of Morals and Legislation, ed. Wilfred Harrison. New York: Oxford University Press, 1967.

3. Derek Cornish and Ronald Clarke, eds., *The Reasoning Criminal: Rational Choice Perspectives on Offending.* New York: Springer-Verlag, 1986.

4. See George B. Vold and Thomas J. Bernard, *Theoretical Criminology.* New York: Oxford University Press, 1986. Stephen Schaefer, *Theories in Criminology.* New York: Random House, 1969.

5. Robert Sampson and John Laub, *Crime in the Making: Pathways and Turning Points Through Life.* Cambridge: Harvard University Press, 1993. Sheldon Glueck and Eleanor Glueck, *Unraveling Juvenile Delinquency.* Cambridge: Harvard University Press, 1950. Sheldon Glueck and Eleanor Glueck, *Predicting Delinquency and Crime.* Cambridge: Harvard University Press, 1967.

6. Keith McBurnett, Benjamin B. Lahey, Paul J. Rathouz, and Rolf Loeber, "Low Salivary Cortisol and Persistent Aggression in Boys Referred for Disruptive Behavior," *Archives of General Psychiatry* 57 (January 2000): 21–27.

7. Alan Booth and D. Wayne Osgood, "The Influence of Testosterone on Deviance in Adulthood," *Criminology* 31 (1993): 93–117.

8. Saleem Shah, "The 47, XYY Chromosomal Abnormality: A Critical Appraisal with Respect to Antisocial and Violent Behavior," in W. Lynn Smith and Arthur Kling, eds., *Issues in Brain/Behavior Control.* New York: Spectrum Publications, 1976. See also Lawrence Taylor, *Born to Crime: The Genetic Causes of Criminal Behavior.* Westport, CT: Greenwood Press, 1984.

9. Edward Green, *The Intent to Kill: Making Sense of Murder.* Baltimore: Clevedon Books, 1993.

10. Mortimer D. Gross and William C. Wilson, *Minimal Brain Dysfunction.* New York: Brunner/Mazel, 1974.

11. Diana H. Fishbein, Biological Perspectives in Criminology. *Criminology* 28 (1990): 27–72. James Q. Wilson and Richard J. Herrnstein, *Crime and Human Nature.* New York: Simon Schuster, 1985.

12. Eric Fidler, "Hormone Level Linked to Antisocial Behavior in Boys," *The Boston Globe,* January 14, 2000, p. A16.

13. K. Magid and C. A. McKelvey, *High Risk: Children Without a Conscience.* New York: Bantam Books, 1988. Robert D. Hare, *Without Conscience: The Disturbing World of the Psychopaths Among Us.* New York: Guilford Publications, 1997.

14. Sigmund Freud, *New Introductory Lectures on Psychoanalysis.* London: Hogarth Press, 1949.

15. See *www.therapyinla.com* for discussions of successful Attachment Therapy.

16. Konrad Lorenz, *On Aggression.* New York: Harcourt, Brace and World, 1966.

17. Erich Fromm, *The Anatomy of Human Destructiveness.* New York: Holt, Rinehart, and Winston, 1973.

18. Martin Daly and Margo Wilson, "An Evolutionary Psychological Perspective on Homicide," in M. Dwayne Smith and Margaret A. Zahn, eds., *Homicide: A Sourcebook of Social Research.* Thousand Oaks, CA: Sage Publications, 1999.

19. Daly and Wilson, op. cit.

20. Avshalom Caspi, Terrie Moffitt, Phil Silva, Magda Stouthamer-Loeber, Robert Krueger, and Pamela Schmutte, "Are Some People Crime Prone? Replications of the Personality-Crime Relationship Across Countries, Genders, Races and Methods," *Criminology* 32 (1994): 163–195.

21. Vold and Bernard, 1986, op. cit.

22. Travis Hirschi and Michael Hindelang, "Intelligence and Delinquency: A Revisionist Review," *American Sociological Review* 42 (1977): 471–586.

23. William Shockley, "A 'Try Simplest Cases' Approach to the Heredity—Poverty—Crime Problem," *Proceedings of the National Academy of Sciences* 57 (6): 1767–1774, 1967.

24. Authur R. Jenson, *"How Much Can We Boost IQ and Scholastic Achievement?"* Harvard Educational Review Reprint Series 2 (1969): 1–123.

25. Charles A. Murray and Richard J. Herrnstein, *The Bell Curve: Intelligence and Class Structure in American Life.* New York: Free Press, 1994.

26. Fishbein, op. cit.

27. Clifford R. Shaw and Henry D. McKay, *Juvenile Delinquency and Urban Areas.* Chicago: University of Chicago Press, 1972.

28. George L. Kelling and Catherine M. Coles, *Fixing Broken Windows: Restoring Order and Reducing Crime and Communities.* New York: Simon and Schuster, 1996.

29. John Dollard, Leonard W. Doob, Neal E. Miller, O. H. Mowrer, and Robert R. Sears, *Frustration and Aggression.* New Haven, CT: Yale University Press, 1939.

30. Jeffrey H. Goldstein, *Aggression and Crimes of Violence.* New York: Oxford University Press, 1986.

31. Stuart H. Palmer, *The Psychology of Murder.* New York: Crowell, 1960.

32. Robert Agnew, "Foundation for a General Strain Theory of Crime and Delinquency," *Criminology* 30 (1992): 47–88.

33. Katherine S. Newman, *Falling From Grace.* New York: Free Press, 1988.

34. William Julius Wilson, *The Truly Disadvantaged: The Inner City, the Underclass and Public Policy.* Chicago: University of Chicago Press, 1987.

35. Shannon McCaffrey, "Bull Market Leaving Poorest Way Behind, Report Says," *The Boston Globe,* January 18, 2000.

36. Gary LaFree, "A Summary and Review of Cross-National Comparative Studies of Homicide," in M. Dwayne Smith and Margaret Zahn, eds., *Homicide: A Sourcebook of Social Research.* Thousand Oaks, CA: Sage Publications, 1999.

37. Robert K. Merton, *Social Theory and Social Structure.* Glencoe, IL: Free Press, 1957.

38. Steven F. Messner and Richard Rosenfeld, *Crime and the American Dream.* Belmont, CA: Wadsworth Publishing Company, 2001.

39. Marvin E. Wolfgang and Franco Ferracuti, *The Subculture of Violence: Towards an Integrated Theory in Criminology.* London: Tavistock Publications, 1967.

40. Richard. E. Nisbett, "Violence and U.S. Regional Culture," *American Psychologist* (1993): 441–449.

41. T. W. Rice and C. R. Goldman, "Another Look at the Subculture of Violence Thesis: Who Murders Whom and Under What Circumstances," *Sociological Spectrum* 14 (1994): 371–384.

42. Christopher G. Ellison, "Southern Culture and Firearms Ownership," *Social Science Quarterly* 72 (1991): 267–283. Jay Corzine, Lin Huff-Corzine, and Hugh P. Whitt, "Cultural And Subcultural Theories of Homicide," in M. Dwayne Smith and Margaret Z. Zahn, eds., *Homicide: A Sourcebook of Social Research.* Thousand Oaks, CA: Sage Publications, 1999.

43. The major cultural deviance theories developed in the 1950s and 1960s were Albert Cohen, *Delinquent Boys: The Culture of the Gang.* Glencoe, IL: Free Press. R. A. Cloward and Lloyd E. Ohlin, *Delinquency and Opportunity: A Theory of Delinquent Gangs.* New York: Free Press. Walter Miller, "Lower Class Culture as Generating Milieu of gang Delinquency," *Journal of Social Issues* 14 (1958): 5–19. Wolfgang and Ferracuti, op. cit.

44. Edwin G. Boring, Herbert S. Langfeld, and H. P. Weld, *Introduction to Psychology.* New York: Wiley, 1939.

45. Albert Bandura, *Social Learning Theory.* Englewood Cliffs, NJ: Prentice Hall, 1977.

46. David P. Phillips, "The Impact of Mass Media Violence of Homicide," *American Sociological Review* 48 (1983): 560–568.

47. Edwin H. Sutherland, *Principles of Criminology,* Fourth Edition. Philadelphia: J. B. Lippincott, 1947.

48. Ronald L. Akers, *Criminological Theories: Introduction, Evaluation and Application.* Los Angeles, CA: Roxbury Publishing, 2000.

49. Travis Hirschi, *Causes of Delinquency.* Berkeley, CA: University of California Press, 1969. Michael Gottfredson and Travis Hirschi, *A General Theory of Crime.* Stanford, CA: Stanford University Press, 1990.

50. Sampson and Laub, op. cit.

51. Walter C. Reckless, "A New Theory of Delinquency and Crime," *Federal Probation* 25 (1961): 42–46.

52. Albert J. Reiss, Jr., and Jeffrey A. Roth, eds., *Understanding and Preventing Violence: Panel on the Understanding and Control of Violent Behavior.* Washington, DC: National Academy of Science, 1993.

3

The Killers and Their Victims

Unlike television where the frequency of murders seems to increase unabated, the rate of murder in America is actually on the decline. As shown in Figure 3.1, during the 1990s, the nation enjoyed a steady drop in homicide. In fact, the rate of murder—the number of homicide victims per 100,000 population—has sunk below 6.0, a level not seen in this country for 30 years, ever since 1967 to be precise. With the new millenium, the homicide rate leveled off. From 2000–2002, the murder rate was stable.

Even the relatively low murder rate in recent years is, of course, still too high, particularly when contrasted with those of earlier times as well as those of other developed nations. Although the 2002 homicide rate of 5.6 may be a welcome change from the national experience of just a decade earlier (when the rate flirted with the 10.0 mark), it hardly can compare with the relative calm of the years prior to the mid-1960s. Thus, although the rate of murder may be at a 30-year low, it will have to drop more to set a 40- or 50-year record for lawfulness.

Also sobering is the nation's standing in relation to other countries around the globe. Table 3.1 displays homicide rates—for 38 nations around the world. Although these kinds of comparisons can be affected by variations in the quality of data collection procedures by

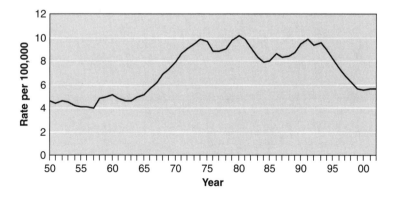

FIGURE 3.1   *U.S. Homicide Rate, 1950–2002*

39

TABLE 3.1 *Homicide Rates for Selected Countries in 2000*

Country	Homicide Count	Population	Homicide Rate per 100,000
South Africa	21,683	43,243,000	50.1
Russia[1] (1999 data)	31,140	145,500,000	21.4
Lithuania	370	3,699,000	10.0
Estonia[2]	143	1,439,000	9.9
Latvia	150	2,410,000	6.2
U.S.A.	15,586	281,422,000	5.5
Spain	1,192	40,500,000	2.9
Finland	148	5,181,000	2.9
Northern Ireland	48	1,692,000	2.8
Czech Republic	279	10,267,000	2.7
Slovakia	143	5,403,000	2.6
New Zealand	99	3,843,000	2.6
Romania[1]	560	22,400,000	2.5
Turkey	1,541	66,600,000	2.3
Poland	854	38,364,000	2.2
Scotland[3]	108	5,115,000	2.1
Hungary	205	10,043,000	2.0
Sweden[4]	175	8,883,000	2.0
Australia	346	19,157,000	1.8
France	1,051	58,747,000	1.8
Canada[5]	542	30,770,000	1.8
England & Wales	850	52,939,000	1.6
Belgium	158	10,239,000	1.5
Greece	158	10,522,000	1.5
Ireland (Eire)	56	3,790,000	1.5
Italy[5]	818	57,680,000	1.4
Netherlands[6]	226	15,941,000	1.4
Slovenia	28	1,990,000	1.4
Portugal	127	10,243,000	1.2
Germany	961	82,143,000	1.2
Japan[1]	1,391	126,862,000	1.1
Norway	49	4,478,000	1.1
Denmark[3]	58	5,330,000	1.1
Malta	4	378,000	1.1
Austria	82	8,127,000	1.0
Switzerland	69	7,210,000	1.0
Cyprus	4	671,000	0.6
Luxembourg	1	436,000	0.2

Notes:
1. Includes attempts
2. Excludes assaults leading to death
3. Includes all deaths initially reported as homicide
4. Includes all deaths initially reported as homicide and assisted suicides
5. Includes murder, manslaughter, and infanticide
6. Excludes euthanasia

country, the table does provide a fairly clear sense of the poor ranking of the United States among reporting nations.

As shown, the United States, even following its 1990s crime drop, has the sixth highest homicide rate and the absolute highest among industrialized nations. Heading the list, South Africa endures high levels of political turmoil and bloodshed (comparable in the United States only in extraordinary and rare cases such as the 1995 Oklahoma City bombing). America's homicide problem is more a matter of interpersonal rather than political conflict.

A popular explanation for the United States's dubious distinction among nations surrounds the easy availability of firearms and lax gun laws. There are some 250 million firearms in the United States, almost as many as there are citizens. While this may be true, the non–gun homicide rate for the United States (3.7) is still higher than the overall murder rate for Canada (1.8), England/Wales (1.6), Germany (1.2), France (1.8), and Japan (1.1), among others. Thus, guns may be part of the problem, but they are not the entire problem. Since many other countries have relatively high levels of gun ownership and low levels of gun homicide, it seems to be more a function of an American willingness to *use* a firearm, thus requiring a mindset change rather than just an access change.

Regardless of weaponry, American society is deeply rooted in violence. From the days of the American Revolution to the Wild, Wild West, the country was developed as a consequence of violent conquests. In modern-day America, moreover, the society applauds and rewards the victor, almost without regard for who is victimized in the relentless pursuit of success, profit, and power. This selfish drive for personal gain has led some social critics to label American culture as "sociopathic."[1] In popular culture as well, movies, music, and even fashion glorify and glamorize violence of all forms. It is often said that America has a love affair with violence, but it may be more like a marriage.

At the same time that many conditions of American culture and society have encouraged violence, the traditional institutions of social control—family, community, schools, religion—have grown particularly weak. In their place, we have invested heavily in formal institutions of social control, most notably prisons. With prison and jail populations pushing the 2 million mark, many times greater than even two decades ago, more dangerous felons are being incarcerated for longer periods of time. Undoubtedly, the downturn in murder rates is partially a result of increased punitiveness for all crimes, yet at a significant price. Each year, approximately 600,000 offenders are released from U.S. prisons. Unless their incarceration reformed them and their transition back into society is positive, much of the crime reduction gained during the 1990s could be lost.

The most significant drops in homicide during recent years have come in the large cities of America, the very locales that had experienced the most precipitous increases in murder during the late 1980s. To borrow on Newton's law of physics, what goes up generally comes down; and the steeper the rise is, the steeper the subsequent descent. In fact, as shown in Figure 3.2, most of the change, upward and downward, in U.S. homicide rates during the past two decades can be traced to the largest cities—cities such as New York, Chicago, and Los Angeles, which were overrun by crack cocaine markets during the late 1980s and responded with smart policing strategies in the 1990s to help reverse the trend.

Even though the rate of killing has moved downward throughout the 1990s, the American public apparently is not fully convinced. In fact, an October 1998 Gallup survey of over 1,000 Americans found, for example, that a slight majority of respondents still maintained that crime is on the rise, despite the compelling statistics showing otherwise.[2]

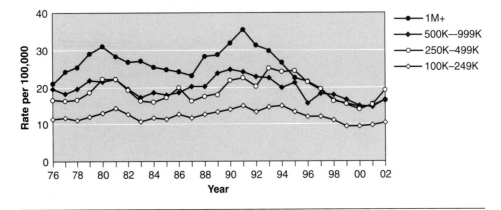

FIGURE 3.2 *Homicide Rate by City Size, 1976–2002*

The media obsession with crime as news and entertainment likely is responsible for this disconnect between perception and reality. Public perceptions of crime trends are based much more on media crime reports than the FBI's *Uniform Crime Reports.* Seeing is believing, it is said, and images of cold and lifeless bodies at a blood-splattered crime scene shown on the nightly news are far more persuasive in shaping public opinion than are cold and lifeless statistics presented in a newspaper report or a government document. Furthermore, news about crime rates coming down simply is not highlighted in the same way as are stories of mini-epidemics in carjackings, hate crimes, child abductions, school shootings, or whatever the journalist's crime *du jour* may be. In terms of the mass media, the popular idiom is reversed, "good news is no news," and turned inside out, "bad news is big news."

Because of fast-advancing telecommunications technology, news coverage of crime has become more immediate, more graphic, and more pervasive. Even if there are fewer homicides available to reporters today than in the early 1990s, there are still plenty to lead off the news. Furthermore, should a news station not have a nearby tragedy to feature, satellite feeds from other corners of the nation can easily fill the local news void. More than anything else, the national news picture is about violence, except of course when some other catastrophe like a plane crash or tornado demands center stage.

The evolution of all-news cable channels, such as MSNBC, CNN, and FOX News, among others, has also altered the way in which homicide and other crime stories are covered. In earlier years, when major television networks controlled most of the programming, affiliates would not normally interrupt the viewing schedule for anything other than a major breaking story of national significance (e.g., an assassination attempt on a top political figure) or a local matter of great importance. But by today's practices, the usually low-rated cable news channels are drawn to continuing coverage of crimes, investigations, or trials to fill their vacuum of airtime. Thus, events such as the Columbine school shooting or even the O. J. Simpson trial, if they had occurred ten years earlier, would not have been covered live by the major networks. Yet, given that the cable news channels now feature continuing coverage of breaking crime news (with music and graphics fitting the big event), the networks feel pressure to follow suit so as not to lose their audience.

Race Differences

More than just exaggerating the risk of murder, television portrayals of homicide also distort the characteristics of killers and their victims. Fabianic, for example, analyzed the content of two months of crime drama programming in 1995 (including episodes of *NYPD Blue, Murder She Wrote,* and *Law and Order,* among others) and found that whites constituted nine out of ten offenders and victims.[3] Motivated by ratings, television dramas feature white victims and perpetrators to appeal to a predominantly white audience. If they were driven more by a desire for realism, homicide offenders and victims would be roughly equally spread between whites and blacks.

As shown in Table 3.2, slightly more than half of homicide offenders are black, and slightly less than half the victims are black. Because, of course, the nation's white and black populations are quite different in size (over the two decades represented in the table, 84 percent of the population was white, 12 percent was black, and 4 percent other races), the rates of offending and victimization diverge. As indicated in the table, the rate of homicide (per 100,000 population) committed by blacks (38.4) is about eight times that of whites (4.9), and the rate of victimization is about six times higher for blacks (30.9) than for whites (4.9).

The large race difference among homicide victims and perpetrators has much to do with the kinds of killing in which blacks predominate. Table 3.3 shows the racial split among both victims and offenders in various homicide subtypes. At the extreme, blacks are greatly overrepresented among those who commit felony-related homicides (59.1 percent

TABLE 3.2 *Homicide Victims and Offenders by Demographic Group, 1976–2002*

	Victims	*Offenders*	*Population*	*Victims per 100,000*	*Offenders per 100,000*
Overall	100.0%	100.0%	100.0%	8.1	9.0
Race					
White	51.1%	46.0%	84.0%	4.9	4.9
Black	46.8%	52.1%	12.2%	30.9	38.4
Other	2.1%	2.0%	3.8%	4.4	4.7
Gender					
Male	76.4%	88.6%	48.8%	12.7	16.4
Female	23.6%	11.4%	51.2%	3.7	2.0
Age					
Under 14	4.7%	.5%	20.6%	1.8	0.2
14–17	5.1%	10.6%	6.1%	6.7	15.6
18–24	23.7%	36.2%	11.0%	17.2	29.7
25–34	29.0%	28.7%	16.0%	14.5	16.1
35–49	22.7%	17.2%	20.2%	9.0	7.7
50–64	9.3%	5.1%	13.9%	5.4	3.3
65+	5.4%	1.7%	12.2%	3.5	1.3

TABLE 3.3   *Race Differences by Homicide Type, 1976–2002*

	Victims			Offenders		
	White	**Black**	**Other**	**White**	**Black**	**Other**
All homicides	51.1%	46.8%	2.1%	46.0%	52.1%	2.0%
Intimate	56.2%	41.7%	2.2%	54.0%	43.9%	2.1%
Family	60.2%	37.5%	2.3%	58.8%	38.9%	2.3%
Infanticide	55.6%	41.9%	2.5%	55.0%	42.5%	2.5%
Eldercide	68.8%	29.7%	1.5%	53.8%	44.6%	1.6%
Felony murder	55.0%	42.5%	2.5%	39.3%	59.1%	1.6%
Sex related	67.1%	30.5%	2.4%	55.2%	42.9%	1.9%
Drug related	36.9%	62.2%	.9%	33.5%	65.5%	1.1%
Gang related	57.8%	38.7%	3.4%	54.3%	41.5%	4.2%
Argument	48.3%	49.7%	2.1%	46.5%	51.4%	2.1%
Workplace	85.1%	11.6%	3.3%	69.6%	27.4%	3.0%
Gun homicide	47.6%	50.6%	1.8%	42.3%	56.0%	1.7%
Arson	59.4%	37.7%	2.9%	55.6%	42.2%	2.2%
Poison	80.4%	17.1%	2.5%	78.7%	19.4%	1.9%
Multiple victims	64.2%	32.4%	3.3%	56.7%	39.9%	3.3%
Multiple offenders	55.4%	42.0%	2.7%	45.1%	52.5%	2.3%

of offenders) such as robbery, as well as those involved in drug-related incidents (62.2 percent and 65.5 percent of victims and perpetrators, respectively). Much of this extreme overrepresentation is related to the geography of homicide, in that violent crime is associated with the heavy concentration of blacks in urban underclasses. Blacks are also more than half the participants in argument-related killings. The link between race and conflict-based homicide has been traced to socio-economic factors such as low income, poor education, and inadequate employment opportunities.[4]

At the other extreme, blacks are far less overrepresented in domestic homicide—those involving intimates, infanticides, and family killings generally, as well as in sex-related murders. Also noteworthy is the limited representation of blacks as perpetrators of workplace homicides. Employee disgruntlement is not necessarily correlated with race. The limited representation of blacks as perpetrators of workplace homicide may be in part a function of higher black unemployment rates, particularly in the age categories most likely to perpetrate workplace violence. No job means no opportunity for killing co-workers. Since many of the workplace shootings have involved civil service positions (e.g., government and post office workers), it may also reflect the greater number of whites holding these jobs. Actually, the representation of blacks in workplace homicide is proportional to their share of the population—about 12 percent.

In recent years, hate crimes motivated by racial bias have received much attention. More than any, the 1991 beating of motorist Rodney King by a group of Los Angeles police officers stirred America's concern for racial violence. Although this incident was fortunately not a homicide, the fact that it was captured on video and replayed countless times on television made this case a particularly important event, if not a turning point, in American race relations. Seeing the videotaped episode provoked many otherwise skeptical Americans into believing, for the first time, the bitter complaints of black Americans that they were being singled out by the police for brutal treatment. Later in the decade, a national discussion of police brutality and excessive force was broadened to include the use of racial profiling as police policy for determining who is regarded as a suspect and who is not.

Other well-publicized atrocities have reinforced public concern for inter-racial violence. On June 7, 1998, for example, James Byrd, Jr., a 49-year-old black man from Jasper, Texas, was chained to the back of a pickup truck and dragged to his death by a group of three white supremacists. In New York City, white police officers dragged a black suspect into a precinct men's room, where they sodomized him with a broomstick. Such events have encouraged legislatures to consider new approaches for dealing with this insidious mistreatment of minority citizens.

Despite the increased concern with hate crimes inspired by racism and prejudice, most homicides are actually intra-racial rather than inter-racial. As shown in Figure 3.3, approximately 86 percent of white homicide victims are killed by white assailants, and a somewhat greater percentage of blacks (94 percent) are killed by members of their own race (the small handful of crimes involving races other than whites and blacks is excluded).

This pattern of similarity between victim and offender race, by far one of the most consistent patterns over the years, should not be surprising. Because homicides typically involve a victim and offender who know each other—often on intimate terms—the similarity of race between homicide participants follows from the similarity of race between individuals in most interpersonal relationships. This likeness of victim and offender race holds, moreover, even for relationships that are more distant than family. As shown, among homicides involving friends and acquaintances, 90 percent of white victims and 95 percent of black victims are slain by someone of the same race. Because of the racial homogeneity of most neighborhoods, moreover, it is even true that most stranger killings are intra-racial—68 percent for white victims and 87 percent for blacks.

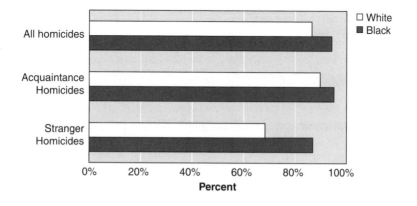

FIGURE 3.3 *Percent Intra-Racial Homicide by Relationship and Victim Race, 1976–2002 Combined*

The higher prevalence of blacks killing whites over whites killing blacks should not necessarily be interpreted as a greater propensity toward inter-racial attacks instigated by blacks. Even if the victim were chosen randomly, blacks would victimize whites more than whites would blacks simply because of the predominance of whites among the potential targets. After all, because the U.S. population is primarily white, it is easier for a black assailant to run across a potential white victim than it is for a white assailant to encounter a black target.

Despite the tendency for most homicides, even those involving strangers, to be intra-racial, it is important not to minimize the concern for fatal inter-racial attacks. The percentage of homicides that do cross race lines has increased from about 5 percent of the total two decades ago to nearly 10 percent of the total at present. This increase may not reflect just growing levels of racial hostility but also greater contact between black and white Americans in everyday activities, including work, school, and romantic relationships.

Gender Differences

In addition to race, media images of gender are also frequently distorted. Pritchard and Hughes, for example, examined the factors that affect four measures of print newsworthiness of homicide cases—frequency of coverage, average story length, proportion of front-page placement, and the use of photographs.[5] Overall, they found that homicides involving male offenders and female victims receive the most intense coverage. In most actual homicide cases, the offenders are indeed men. Contrary to the media emphasis on crimes against women, however, most murder victims are in reality also men.

As was shown in Table 3.2 on page 43, men are far more likely than women to kill (88.6 percent of offenders are men) and to be killed (76.4 percent of victims are men). Despite changing gender roles that have led to greater involvement of women in violent crimes generally, murder remains a male preoccupation. If anything, the gender ratio among perpetrators has widened in recent years to nine male killers for every female murderer.

As with race, most homicides occur in same-sex pairs; over two-thirds of all murders are men killing men. Overall, for the years 1976–2002, 89 percent of offenders were male, and 77 percent of their victims were also male, typically killed in disputes over money, drugs, turf, honor, or pride. Cross-sex homicides only predominate when women kill. That is, not only do most male murderers kill men, but most female murderers (81 percent) also kill men.

It is important not to lose sight of the particular physical and situational vulnerability of women in dealings with men. Moreover, the statistical predominance of male victims likely stems from issues of victim precipitation. That is, men are far more likely to start a fight or to place themselves in dangerous or volatile situations resulting in their own death. Yet, the common media focus on "femicide"—female victims of male killers—does not reflect the norm in actual patterns of murder.

When women do in fact commit homicide, the nature of the offense is sharply different from those perpetrated by men. Women tend to kill close intimates (husbands, boyfriends, sons, or daughters), while men often attack strangers or mere acquaintances. As shown in Table 3.4, the gender ratio among murderers narrows considerably in family homicides (29.7 percent of offenders are female) and especially infanticides (38.4 percent female

TABLE 3.4　*Gender Differences by Homicide Type, 1976–2002*

Homicide Type	Victims		Offenders	
	Male	*Female*	*Male*	*Female*
All homicides	76.4%	23.6%	88.6%	11.4%
Intimate	37.2%	62.8%	64.8%	35.2%
Family	52.0%	48.0%	70.3%	29.7%
Infanticide	54.5%	45.5%	61.6%	38.4%
Eldercide	58.2%	41.8%	85.5%	14.5%
Felony murder	78.1%	21.9%	93.3%	6.7%
Sex related	18.9%	81.1%	93.5%	6.5%
Drug related	90.1%	9.9%	95.7%	4.3%
Gang related	94.5%	5.5%	98.4%	1.6%
Argument	78.1%	21.9%	85.3%	14.7%
Workplace	78.5%	21.5%	91.5%	8.5%
Gun homicide	82.5%	17.5%	91.1%	8.9%
Arson	56.5%	43.5%	79.5%	20.5%
Poison	54.2%	45.8%	63.6%	36.4%
Multiple victims	62.8%	37.2%	93.6%	6.4%
Multiple offenders	85.6%	14.4%	91.8%	8.2%

offenders). Homicides by women often result from turmoil or stress that may build up over time. Men, by contrast, are often quick to respond violently, killing an acquaintance in a bar who challenges them or even a stranger on the street who insults them. Also shown in Table 3.4, predatory incidents, such as felony-murders, stranger killings, and especially sexual homicides, are overwhelmingly the province of men. Homicides within the family, by contrast, are somewhat more "equal opportunity" by gender.

The instruments of murder selected by men and women are also very different. Men are better trained in the use of firearms, often feel comfortable with them, and therefore favor a gun when there is some murdering to do. By contrast, women prefer methods that are cleaner and more distant. Whereas less than 10 percent of gun killings are committed by women, almost 20 percent of homicides by arson and more than a third of murders by poison involve female offenders. Also, women often choose poison or suffocation in cases of family murder, including infanticide.

Unlike guns or brute force, women have more equal access to fire or poison as a means of committing homicide. In fact, because of their traditional role as homemakers and caretakers, women are often better acquainted than men with the harmful effects of various drugs and poisons. It was not difficult, for example, for 64-year-old Sacramento landlady Dorothea Montalvo Puente to poison her elderly boarders in order to cash in their social security checks. It was also not difficult for Puente to cover up the crimes by burying her victims in the yard of her rooming house . . . until 1988, that is, when a local social worker discovered that her missing clients' social security checks were being cashed.

Over the past two decades, the country has endured several instances of product tampering, which not only scared the America public but also brought about major changes in the packaging of consumer goods. In 1982, seven Chicago-area residents were fatally poisoned when they unknowingly ingested cyanide-laced Extra-Strength Tylenol capsules. The killer responsible for placing the poisoned analgesics on the shelves of area drug stores and supermarkets was never apprehended, which led to some speculation, based at least on statistical patterns, that the murderer was a woman.

Regardless of the Tylenol poisoner's identity and gender, the case no doubt influenced the thinking of Stella M. Nickell of Auburn, Washington, when she conceived a plan to kill her husband, Bruce, in order to collect the proceeds of a $176,000 life insurance policy. In June 1986, 52-year-old Bruce Nickell died after swallowing a poisoned Extra-Strength Excedrin capsule. Susan Snow, age 40, also of Auburn but unknown to Nickell, died after purchasing a contaminated bottle from a local store. She was the unfortunate victim of Stella Nickell's scheme to make the deaths appear like the work of a random killer.

Murders for hire are also especially appealing for women who may see the deaths of their spouses as distasteful but necessary steps to resolve a difficult situation. By the spring of 1990, 22-year-old Pamela Smart of Derry, New Hampshire, had grown tired of her marriage of less than a year to her 24-year-old husband, Greg. Or maybe it was her affair with a 15-year-old student at the high school where she worked as media services director that had helped Pam sour on matrimony. She wanted to end the marriage but didn't want the stress and complications of a divorce, not to mention the possibility that her adulterous affair with a minor might come to light in the process. Murder would be quicker.

Pam Smart, always concerned about neatness, abhorred the idea of having to perform the unpleasant and messy task herself. Instead, she convinced her young lover that Greg would have to be eliminated for their relationship to continue, and that it was up to him to carry it out. The teen, infatuated and feeling special because of the attention he received from the attractive "older woman," persuaded two of his friends to serve as accomplices. Pam Smart made sure that she wasn't home when the shooting took place, her only requirement for the three young conspirators that they not kill her husband in front of the dog. She didn't want her "best friend" traumatized.

Reflecting recent thinking in criminology about female offenders, Patricia Pearson's book, *When She Was Bad,* argues that women are far more violent than most people assume. Much of this violence is explained away by portraying murdering women as mentally ill, hormonally unstable, or as victims whose actions are driven by forces beyond their control. But Pearson argues that this is a particularly unfeminist view of females. She discusses how indirect female aggression may look different than direct male aggression, but is deadly just the same. In school, girls engage in rumor-mongering and character assassination and provoking boys to beat up (or kill) other boys or their female rivals through social manipulation. Or they nonchalantly murder newborns and then go about their social lives of attending proms and parties with their dying babies abandoned in trash bins, coolers, and closets. Women assault and kill their ex- and current boyfriends and husbands rather than face being dumped for another woman. A scorned woman may run over her husband with his car, abuse her stepchildren as surrogates for her hostility toward her mate, or poison elderly men and women for profit.

When women do engage in direct aggression such as hitting, we refer to it in humorous, non-serious, trivial terms like "catfight" or "hair pulling contests" and we make jokes about aggressive women with PMS. Some people laughed when Clara Harris ran over and murdered her husband in front of his hysterical daughter. Others joked about Lorena Bobbitt excising her cheating husband's penis.

The time may have come to avoid being so quick to portray violent women as helpless or confused "children" rather than the cold, calculated killers they can be. Women may just be better than men at hiding their aggression, getting others to do their dirty work, or engaging in less brutal forms of lethal violence.

Certainly Karla Homolka, arrested in Canada in 1993, was convincing as the victim of a battering spouse rather than as a sexual predator. Along with her husband, Paul Bernardo, she participated in the brutal rapes and sadistic murders of three teenage girls—one of whom was her own sister. When police questioned Homolka about Bernardo's possible involvement in the death of one of the girls they offered her a "sweetheart deal" to talk. What the authorities did not realize was that Karla herself (who admits to performing oral sex on her own unconscious sister and wanting to give her husband her sister's virginity as a Christmas present) is a dangerous sexual sadist who played much more than an ancillary role in the rapes and murders. The deal had already been confirmed by the time police and prosecutors saw videotapes of the murders and heard other evidence about her involvement. Because of this premature negotiation, Homolka is scheduled to be freed in July 2005 at the end of her 12-year prison sentence.

Age Differences

A crime time capsule of the 1990s would likely be decidedly slanted toward murders committed by juveniles. In recent years, the mass media have focused heavily on homicides committed by teenagers—not just the most sensationalistic crimes like the April 1999 Columbine High School massacre, but also the general problem of armed and dangerous youngsters. On March 25, 1996, the usually understated cover of *U.S. News & World Report,* screamed "Teenage Time Bombs: Violent Juvenile Crime Is Soaring and It's Going to Get Worse." Even *People* magazine devoted its June 23, 1997, issue to the rhetorical query, "Kids Without a Conscience?" The report examined a variety of senseless homicides, including the case of a 15-year-old couple who murdered and disemboweled a 44-year-old drinking buddy in Manhattan's Central Park and the story of an 18-year-old New Jersey girl who delivered a baby in the bathroom during her senior prom, dumped the child in the trash, and then returned to dance with her prom date.

Despite the intense attention given to juvenile offenders, as was shown in Table 3.2 on page 43, only about 10 percent of murderers and victims are under 18 years old. By contrast, young adults, ages 18 to 24, represent over a third of the offenders and about a quarter of the victims.

The disconnect between media hype and statistical reality in regard to juvenile homicide has led some observers to allege that journalists as well as politicians have exploited a few highly publicized cases for their own ends. According to attorney and author Peter Elikann, a whole generation of teenagers has been demonized in media and political circles by casting them as ruthless superpredators.[6] The "superpredator" concept was conceived by William J. Bennett, John J. DiIulio, Jr., and John P. Walters. They wrote in their book *Body Count,* "America is now home to thickening ranks of juvenile 'superpredators'—radically impulsive, brutally remorseless youngsters, including ever more pre-teenage boys, who murder, assault, rape, rob, burglarize, deal deadly drugs, join gun-toting gangs, and create serious communal disorders."[7]

The term "superpredator" may indeed have been inflammatory and unduly sensationalistic. It may even be technically inaccurate, because juvenile violence is typically impulsive rather than predatory (the true superpredators are more accurately serial killers who prey on scores of innocent victims). Notwithstanding such caveats, the frequent attention given to youth violence and especially murder may have had much to do with the special character—the unmitigated senselessness—of youthful killings. When adults kill, it often involves rather commonplace motivations—jealousy, revenge, and greed. When kids kill, the reasons are often as trivial as a pair of sneakers or even the ownership of a Pokemon card.

Juvenile homicides are quite different from adult killings in several other respects. As shown in Table 3.5, the involvement of youngsters is far greater in gang killings (juveniles are implicated in a third of gang-related murders). Although less dramatic, homicides that involve multiple offenders (two or more accomplices working together), that are drug-related, or that involve arson, guns, or a felony also have a higher-than-average percentage of offenders under age 18.

Much more than their older counterparts, juveniles tend to travel and kill in groups, sometimes tightly organized gangs with a well-defined hierarchy of authority, but much more often just informal clichés or bands. It is often the strong influence of peers that motivates murder, rather than any particular burning desire of the perpetrator to kill. It is easier psychologically to participate in a horrible crime "because your friends are doing it, too."

TABLE 3.5 *Age Differences by Homicide Type, 1976–2002*

	Victims				Offenders			
Homicide Type	**Under 18**	**18–34**	**35–49**	**50+**	**Under 18**	**18–34**	**35–49**	**50+**
All homicides	9.8%	52.7%	22.7%	14.7%	11.1%	64.9%	17.2%	6.9%
Intimate	2.3%	46.9%	33.6%	17.2%	1.1%	47.0%	34.3%	17.6%
Family	19.2%	32.6%	26.5%	21.7%	6.1%	49.5%	27.8%	16.6%
Infanticide	100.0%				8.3%	81.3%	9.4%	1.1%
Eldercide				100.0%	10.5%	50.3%	18.3%	20.9%
Felony murder	7.7%	46.5%	21.6%	24.2%	15.1%	72.9%	10.1%	2.0%
Sex related	19.8%	45.2%	16.2%	18.8%	10.8%	74.1%	13.1%	2.1%
Drug related	5.5%	71.8%	19.6%	3.2%	10.9%	76.6%	11.3%	1.2%
Gang related	25.3%	67.5%	5.9%	1.3%	30.3%	67.8%	1.6%	.3%
Argument	5.4%	56.4%	26.1%	12.0%	6.9%	60.2%	23.1%	9.7%
Workplace	2.1%	28.6%	30.6%	38.6%	4.8%	53.6%	26.4%	15.2%
Gun homicide	7.5%	59.0%	22.5%	11.0%	12.1%	64.1%	16.1%	7.7%
Arson	28.5%	27.1%	19.0%	25.4%	11.7%	58.5%	22.7%	7.1%
Poison	26.7%	23.8%	16.3%	33.2%	3.7%	51.9%	26.5%	17.9%
Multiple victims	18.6%	45.9%	19.0%	16.4%	9.7%	65.8%	18.6%	5.9%
Multiple offenders	11.3%	55.2%	19.7%	13.7%	18.7%	72.8%	7.3%	1.1%

Despite the limited involvement overall of juveniles in homicide, the intensive focus on young killers can also be justified based on patterns of growth. Whereas 7.5 percent of murders during the mid-1980s were committed by offenders under age 18, juveniles during the mid-1990s were implicated in 15 percent of the killings. Correspondingly, as shown in Figure 3.4, the average (mean) age of murderers dropped over this time period, from about 31 years old on average in the mid-1980s, down to nearly 27 years old on average in the mid-1990s trending upward slightly since. A similar pattern of youth movement has occurred among victims with an average age in the mid-1980s of nearly 35 years old down to an average victim age of just over 31 years old in the mid-1990s. The parallel trends in the average ages of offenders and victims are understandable because offenders tend to murder victims close to their own age.

The younger the killer, it seems, the greater the shock. Over the past several years, the nation was clearly shaken when, for example, two boys, ages 10 and 11, dropped a 5-year-old out of a 14th-story window in a Chicago housing project in retaliation for tattling on them; when an 11-year-old and a 13-year-old killed four students and one teacher at their middle school in Jonesboro, Arkansas; and even when a 6-year-old Michigan boy shot and killed his first-grade classmate. Though little consolation for the rise in adolescent homicide over the past 15 years, murder at the hands of younger children—those under age 14—has remained especially rare. On average, about 50 children age 13 and younger, and fewer than 10 children age 10 and younger, commit homicide each year nationwide, and neither tally has shown any indication of increasing. Thus, despite the special senselessness of "kiddie murder," it remains little more than a horrifying aberration.

Homicide is intra-generational. Adults tend to target other adults (husband-wife, co-workers, friends), and adolescents tend to target their contemporaries as well. The major exception, of course, is in cases of infanticide (victims under the age of five), in which the perpetrator tends to be a parent or some other caretaker (e.g., babysitter), but certainly not a playmate. Figure 3.5 gives another view of the match between victim age and offender age. In this plot depicting homicides in 2002, the greater the density of points (each representing a separate murder), the more commonplace the victim-offender age combination.

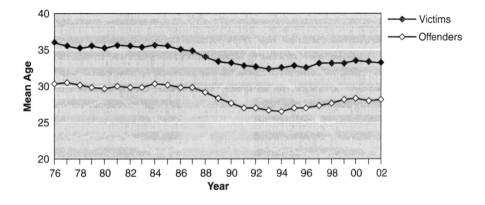

FIGURE 3.4 *Mean Age of Homicide Victims and Offenders, 1976–2002*

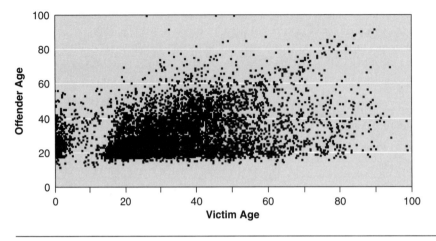

FIGURE 3.5   *Age of Homicide Victims and Offenders in 2002*

Aside from the sizable left-hand cluster of children killed by adults (infanticides) and a few elders killed (eldercides) by younger offenders, the plot thickens along the diagonal showing that most offenders and their victims are similar in age.

As frequently described by social scientists, numerous characteristics of lifestyle tend to change dramatically as a person moves through the life course from infancy into adolescence, and from adulthood into retirement age. The same can be said for styles of death by homicide. Figure 3.6 shows how three key homicide characteristics—whether a gun is used, whether the offender is known to the victim, and whether the homicide is felony-related— vary by the age of victims.

Firearms are rarely needed in murders of young children, but gun use increases steadily throughout the teenage years, peaks at nearly 80 percent for older adolescents, and then declines steadily with advancing victim age. The vulnerability of elders, as with young

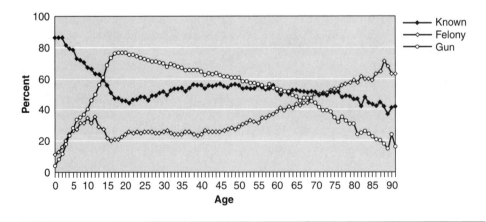

FIGURE 3.6   *Homicide Characteristics by Victim Age, 1976–2002 Combined*

children, produces a large proportion of deaths with weapons other than a gun. Also, children are almost always murdered by someone known to them, in contrast to victims of older ages who, nearly half the time, are killed by strangers or unidentified assailants. For elders, the percentage of known perpetrators is particularly low, which has much to do with the unusually high percentage of older victims who are killed during the course of a felony, such as a holdup. For victims beginning at age 50 and continuing forward, the proportion of murders resulting from robberies and other attacks by strangers increases while those resulting from interpersonal disputes declines.

Some criminologists have noted that the elderly have the highest levels of fear of violence yet the lowest risk of victimization. Their low victimization rate results, however, from the fact that senior citizens are rarely killed by family members or friends and often live alone with few occasions for deadly conflict. By contrast, elders have relatively high rates of felony-murder victimization and homicides by strangers, often dying in an attack that younger victims would survive. Thus, the fears of elders may not be as irrational as many observers have suggested.[8]

Differences by Location

Besides patterns by race, sex, and age, homicides also vary considerably by location—specifically urbanness and geographic region. As noted earlier, most of the recent shifts in homicide rates occurred in larger American cities, rather than small cities, suburbs, or rural communities. Table 3.6 shows that urban areas also tend to be overrepresented in homicides

TABLE 3.6 *Location Differences by Homicide Type, 1976–2002*

Homicide Type	Location Type			
	Large City	**Small City**	**Suburban**	**Rural**
All homicides	57.4%	11.4%	20.8%	10.3%
Intimate	41.0%	14.5%	27.6%	16.9%
Family	39.0%	13.1%	28.7%	19.2%
Infanticide	48.1%	14.9%	25.4%	11.5%
Eldercide	47.7%	13.4%	23.6%	15.3%
Felony murder	61.4%	10.9%	20.0%	7.6%
Sex related	48.4%	12.1%	27.2%	12.2%
Drug related	68.2%	9.7%	17.9%	4.3%
Gang related	69.8%	12.9%	16.6%	.8%
Argument	53.5%	12.6%	20.8%	13.1%
Workplace	32.0%	13.8%	37.0%	17.2%
Gun homicide	59.2%	10.5%	19.7%	10.7%
Arson	55.2%	12.9%	21.6%	10.2%
Poison	40.1%	15.2%	28.4%	16.3%
Multiple victims	47.5%	11.7%	27.1%	13.8%
Multiple offenders	62.4%	9.9%	18.8%	8.9%

that are gang-related, drug-related, and felony-related. By contrast, homicides in the family—including infanticides and killings by romantic intimates—as well as murders on the job are spread more evenly across location types, with particular prevalence in the suburbs.

Given the recent explosion in crystal methamphetamine (i.e., "crank") use in rural areas of the United States, rural America may soon witness an increase in drug-related crimes, including homicide, similar to the urban crack crime waves of the late 1980s and early 1990s. In fact, while the percentage of urban homicides classified as drug-related dropped from 10% to under 6% during the 1990s, the percentage of rural murders that were drug-related increased from about 2% to 3% over the same time span.

Crystal meth has already taken a terrible toll as homemade labs have exploded, killing and burning the cookers, family, friends and neighbors. Indiana, for example, a rural state where the number of meth labs has doubled every year since 1997, had approximately 980 lab busts in 2002. Officials estimated this figure would reach at least 1,500 in 2003.[9]

There have also been deaths associated with the noxious effects of the chemicals used in producing crystal meth (e.g., anhydrous ammonia) as well as drug overdoses. Not unlike the consequences of crack, the growing popularity of crystal meth has created "parentless" children living with drug addicted adults or residing in foster care as the adults go to prison or die. We may also see increasing violence related to the business of selling crank, similar to the territorial and money disputes associated with other drug crazes.

Figure 3.2 revealed earlier that by the late 1990s, after the crack epidemic had subsided, there was no longer a discernible difference by city size in the rate of homicide. That is, the aggregate rate of murder in cities over 1 million population was virtually the same as in medium-sized cities (those with populations between 250,000 and 1 million). This does not mean, of course, that all cities within these categories are on par with each other in terms of their murder rates.

As shown in Table 3.7, the 2002 homicide rates for the 40 largest cities vary widely, from a high of 53.1 per 100,000 for New Orleans to a low of 0.7 per 100,000 for Virginia Beach. Together these "Top 40" (all with populations over 400,000) represent less than 20 percent of the U.S. population yet accounted for 40 percent of the nation's murders in 2002. Given the extent of variability, many analysts have been tempted to treat these rankings as measures of comparative safety/danger. The news media, in particular, often attempt to approach these city-by-city rates as indicators of relative security and quality of life. Using homicide rates in this manner, however, is as tricky as it is enticing. These 40 cities vary considerably in terms of both demography (i.e., population characteristics) and geography, which cause any move to anoint America's safest or deadliest cities problematic at best.

The most difficult aspect of making sense of city homicide rankings involves the extent to which the municipalities include or exclude suburban communities. New York City, for example, consists of much more than the Manhattan downtown areas and also encompasses residential neighborhoods in Queens and Staten Island. The population in a city like San Antonio may have boomed in recent years, but the million plus population count is in large part a result of sprawling city limits. Cities such as Seattle and Boston are densely populated and urbanized, compared with, for example, Virginia Beach. Quite

TABLE 3.7 *Homicide Rates for 40 Largest Cities, 2002*

City	Homicides	Population	Homicide Rate
New Orleans	258	486,157	53.1
Washington, DC	264	570,898	46.2
Detroit	402	961,987	41.8
Baltimore	253	671,028	37.7
Atlanta	152	435,594	34.9
Memphis	151	662,441	22.8
Chicago	648	2,938,299	22.1
Philadelphia	288	1,524,226	18.9
Kansas City	83	447,650	18.5
Milwaukee	111	605,600	18.3
Los Angeles	654	3,830,561	17.1
Cleveland	80	481,274	16.6
Dallas	196	1,241,481	15.8
Long Beach	67	478,478	14.0
Indianapolis	112	804,034	13.9
Phoenix	177	1,404,938	12.6
Houston	256	2,040,583	12.5
Las Vegas	137	1,153,546	11.9
Jacksonville	90	769,253	11.7
Columbus	81	715,739	11.3
Albuquerque	51	457,488	11.1
Nashville	61	560,596	10.9
Charlotte	67	646,864	10.4
Boston	60	596,444	10.1
Fort Worth	53	558,493	9.5
Fresno	42	443,363	9.5
Tucson	47	517,607	9.1
Denver	51	581,105	8.8
San Francisco	68	805,269	8.4
San Antonio	100	1,195,592	8.4
Oklahoma City	38	512,448	7.4
New York	587	8,084,693	7.3
Seattle	26	580,089	4.5
San Diego	47	1,268,346	3.7
Portland	20	544,604	3.7
Austin	25	685,784	3.6
San Jose	26	927,821	2.8
El Paso	14	588,750	2.4
Honolulu	20	885,605	2.3
Virginia Beach	3	438,175	0.7

Source: Federal Bureau of Investigation, *Crime in the United States—2002* Washington, DC, 2003.

clearly, density and urbanness tend to correlate with crime levels, regardless of overall population count.

In addition to the issue of population density, the use of residential population figures may, in certain cases, distort the homicide victimization rates. Many cities contain large numbers of non-residents (for example, commuters, tourists, seasonal visitors, out-of-state college students, among others) who may be at some risk of homicide for certain periods of time yet are excluded from the population base used in calculating the city's homicide rate.

In addition to these qualifications, an unusual demographic distribution (by race, sex, or age) can impact a city's murder rate. Most notably, the top five cities in Table 3.7 (New Orleans, Washington, D.C., Detroit, Baltimore, and Atlanta) all have high concentrations of black residents, as do the next five cities.

It is not race itself that accounts for this pattern but the socio-economic conditions that tend to be associated with a sizable minority population. In a study of crime rates in the largest American cities, Cohen, Fox, and Wolfgang found that the strong statistical correlation between violent crime rates and the percentage of blacks in the population vanishes when controlling for the percentage of families below the poverty line, the percentage of children in broken homes, and other dimensions of social disorganization.[10]

Another common approach to analyzing murder rates is to examine variations among states. As shown in Table 3.8, state homicide rates for 2002 ranged from a high of 13.2 (per 100,000 population) in Louisiana to a low of 0.8 in North Dakota. As with the city tabulations, these state differences to some extent reflect the degree of urbanness and population density. For example, the bottom five states (New Hampshire, Maine, South Dakota, Iowa, and North Dakota) are especially rural and sparsely populated. At the same time, some regional differences are fairly significant and hard to miss. For example, six of the ten highest murder-rate states are within the southern region of the nation. As illustrated in Figure 3.7, there are some clearly defined clusters of low and high homicide rate areas within the nation. Specifically, in 2002, the New England, northwest, and north central regions generally had rates under 3.0 per 100,000, while the southern states were all within the higher two rate categories.

Homicide patterns among states translate, of course, into overall regional differences, as shown in Table 3.9. In relation to population share, homicides are more prevalent in the South, even though the region is not as urbanized as are others. The southern pattern is especially pronounced in gun homicides, incidents involving an argument, and murder within the family (see also Figure 3.8). Doerner has applied the subculture of violence theory described earlier to account for the elevated southern murder rates.[11] That is, in the South where rates of gun ownership are relatively high, violence is often seen as an acceptable way to resolve disagreements. Rather than taking it to court, southern combatants often take it outside, in the long-standing tradition of a duel.

Despite all the tendencies in murder victimization and offending described in this chapter, many homicides still run counter to the norm. For example, Aileen Wuornos was executed in October 2002 by the state of Florida because she killed seven total strangers in the style of male serial killers such as Theodore Bundy. In the small town of Plainfield, Wisconsin, Edward Gein was in his fifties when he began committing a hideous series of crimes including murder, cannibalism, grave robbing, and necrophilia. Almost all of the recent multiple shootings in schools around the country have been committed by white youngsters in

TABLE 3.8 State Homicide Rates, 2002

State	Homicides	Population	Homicide Rate	State	Homicides	Population	Homicide Rate
Louisiana	593	4,482,646	13.2	Kentucky	184	4,092,891	4.5
Maryland	513	5,458,137	9.4	Colorado	179	4,506,542	4.0
Mississippi	264	2,871,782	9.2	New Jersey	337	8,590,300	3.9
Nevada	181	2,173,491	8.3	Rhode Island	41	1,069,725	3.8
New Mexico	152	1,855,059	8.2	Delaware	26	807,385	3.2
Illinois	949	12,600,620	7.5	West Virginia	57	1,801,873	3.2
South Carolina	298	4,107,183	7.3	Washington	184	6,068,996	3.0
Tennessee	420	5,797,289	7.2	Wyoming	15	498,703	3.0
Arizona	387	5,456,453	7.1	Kansas	78	2,715,884	2.9
Georgia	606	8,560,310	7.1	Wisconsin	154	5,441,196	2.8
California	2,395	35,116,033	6.8	Nebraska	48	1,729,180	2.8
Alabama	303	4,486,508	6.8	Massachusetts	173	6,427,801	2.7
Michigan	678	10,050,446	6.7	Idaho	36	1,341,131	2.7
North Carolina	548	8,320,146	6.6	Connecticut	80	3,460,503	2.3
Texas	1,302	21,779,893	6.0	Minnesota	112	5,019,720	2.2
Indiana	362	6,159,068	5.9	Vermont	13	616,592	2.1
Missouri	331	5,672,579	5.8	Oregon	72	3,521,515	2.0
Florida	911	16,713,149	5.5	Utah	47	2,316,256	2.0
Virginia	388	7,293,542	5.3	Hawaii	24	1,244,898	1.9
Arkansas	142	2,710,079	5.2	Montana	16	909,453	1.8
Alaska	33	643,786	5.1	Iowa	44	2,936,760	1.5
Pennsylvania	624	12,335,091	5.1	South Dakota	11	761,063	1.4
New York	909	19,157,532	4.7	Maine	14	1,294,464	1.1
Oklahoma	163	3,493,714	4.7	New Hampshire	12	1,275,056	0.9
Ohio	526	11,421,267	4.6	North Dakota	5	634,110	0.8

Source: Federal Bureau of Investigation, *Crime in the United States—2002* Washington, DC, 2003.

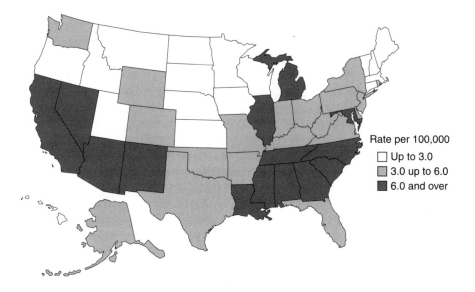

FIGURE 3.7 *State Homicide Rates, 2002*

TABLE 3.9 *Regional Differences by Homicide Type, 1976–2002*

	Region			
Homicide Type	*Northeast*	*Midwest*	*South*	*West*
All homicides	17.1%	19.1%	41.0%	22.8%
Intimate	12.3%	17.7%	49.0%	20.9%
Family	13.0%	18.1%	48.2%	20.6%
Infanticide	18.7%	22.4%	33.8%	25.1%
Eldercide	17.2%	19.7%	41.6%	21.5%
Felony murder	17.9%	19.6%	37.4%	25.1%
Sex related	12.3%	19.8%	35.8%	32.2%
Drug related	18.0%	16.3%	40.2%	25.6%
Gang related	3.3%	15.4%	6.1%	75.3%
Argument	14.0%	17.2%	45.8%	23.0%
Workplace	9.9%	22.0%	38.1%	30.0%
Gun homicide	15.5%	19.1%	43.1%	22.2%
Arson	31.9%	24.5%	27.2%	16.3%
Poison	16.6%	22.7%	31.3%	29.3%
Multiple victims	16.8%	20.2%	36.3%	26.7%
Multiple offenders	17.5%	19.3%	36.7%	26.5%

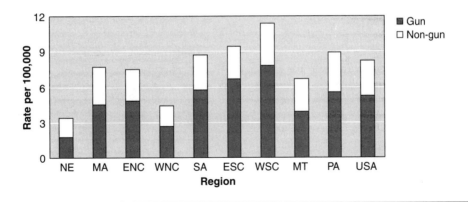

FIGURE 3.8   *Homicide Offending Rates by Region and Weapon, 1976–2002 Combined*

suburban or small towns. Incidents like these help to make the study of homicide ever fascinating and challenging to explain. The challenge is to make sense out of seemingly senseless acts of murder.

Endnotes

1. See Charles Derber, *The Wilding of America: How Greed and Violence Are Eroding Our Nation's Character.* New York: St. Martin's Press, 1996.

2. P. O'Driscoll, "Poll: Media Distort Public Perception," *USA Today,* November 19, 1998.

3. David Fabianic, "Television Dramas and Homicide Causation," *Journal of Criminal Justice* 25 (1997): 195–203.

4. William Julius Wilson, *The Truly Disadvantaged: The Inner-City, the Underclass and Public Policy.* Chicago: University of Chicago Press, 1987.

5. David Pritchard and Karen D. Hughes, "Patterns of Deviance in Crime News," *Journal of Communication* 47 (1997).

6. Peter Elikann, *Superpredators: The Demonization of Our Children by the Law.* Plenum Press, 1999. See also Howard Spivak and Deborah Prothrow-Stith, "Stop Demonizing Our Youth," *The Boston Globe,* July 27, 1997.

7. William J. Bennett, John J. DiIulio, and John P. Walters, *Body Count: Moral Poverty and How to Win America's War Against Crime and Drugs.* New York: Simon & Schuster, 1996.

8. James Alan Fox and Jack Levin, "Homicide Against the Elderly: A Research Note," *Criminology* 28 (1991): 317–327.

9. *The Indianapolis Star,* "Turn Up Heat on Meth Makers," August 31, 2002.

10. Bernard Cohen, James Alan Fox, and Marvin E. Wolfgang, *The Memphis and Shelby County Crime Report—1996.* Guardsmark, Inc., 1996.

11. William G. Doerner, "A Regional Analysis of Homicide Rates in the United States," *Criminology* 13 (1975): 90–101.

4

Intimate and Family Murder

The family unit encompasses a wide constellation of relationships, many of which are linked by bloodlines. Understandably yet tragically, the around-the-clock opportunity for conflict and discord within families often causes that same blood to spill. Notwithstanding all the positive and nurturing aspects of family life, it is quite telling that the study of homicide has so many expressions within the family unit—instances when affection turns unhappily to aggression, including "domicide" and "spousicide" (spouse killings), "patricide" and "matricide" (the murder of fathers and mothers, respectively), "fratricide" and "sororicide" (killings of brothers and sisters, respectively), and "infanticide" (murders of young children), among other less common forms of intra-familial homicide. That criminologists have established so many labels to describe killings by and of family members indicates the pervasiveness and diversity of this phenomenon.

As shown in Table 4.1, more than 100,000 Americans were killed by family members or other intimate partners from 1976 to 2002. On average, nearly 4,000 of such homicides occur annually, with about 60 percent of these involving spouses, ex-spouses, or boyfriends/girlfriends.

TABLE 4.1 *Intimate and Family Homicides, 1976–2002 Combined*

Relationship	Cases	Percent
Spouse	37,719	36.3%
Ex-spouse	2,601	2.5%
Parent	8,893	8.5%
Child	15,804	15.2%
Sibling	6,101	5.9%
Other family	11,781	11.3%
Boyfriend/girlfriend	21,148	20.3%
Total	104,047	100.0%

Killing for Profit

Murder in the family and other intimate relationships spans a wide range of motives, from jealousy to revenge, from attention-seeking to mercy. It is one of the most insidious motives, if only for its selfish cold-bloodedness, when the family unit occasionally becomes a vehicle for profit. Murders involving strangers, as we would expect, frequently involve the profit motive. Yet greed knows no limits. Blood may be thicker than water, but not always when cash is involved.

On Halloween 1974, as other Houston residents prepared treats for the neighborhood children, Ronald Clark O'Bryan replaced the white sugary powder inside several Pixy Sticks with cyanide, one of which he placed in his own son's bag of goodies. O'Bryan's dastardly plan was to kill his own eight-year-old son and collect on a $20,000 insurance policy. He had hoped that rampant concern for treat tampering as a form of adolescent Halloween trickery and the discovery of similarly contaminated candy in other children's bags (which fortunately was not eaten) would provide a convenient cover-up to his selfish deed. O'Bryan's plan failed. He was convicted of first-degree murder and himself poisoned to death ten years later in the form of Texas's lethal injection ritual.

On October 23, 1989, the Boston police received an urgent call from a man using his car phone to report that he and his pregnant wife had just been shot by a stranger who had jumped into the backseat of their car. The caller, identified as 29-year-old Charles Stuart, claimed that he and his wife had been attacked by the black intruder dressed in a jogging suit as they drove home from a birthing class in the predominantly black Mission Hill section of the city. Charles Stuart survived the attack, but his wife and unborn child were not so fortunate.

Bostonians quickly rushed to support Charles Stuart with an unparalleled outpouring of sympathy. Everyone in Boston had heard the tape of his heart-wrenching call to 911. Everyone was shaken by his sorrowful eulogy to his wife Carol read at the funeral he was too sick to attend. Even the most die-hard cynic was moved when, despite the severity of his injuries, Stuart begged to be taken across town to cradle his dying infant son in his arms. With the skill of a Shakespearean actor, Stuart played the role of a grieving husband/father.

By January 1990, however, as the police investigation into the homicide continued feverishly, Charles Stuart's story started to crumble. He had indeed shot his wife to death after she refused to abort the pregnancy. Stuart had sensed that fatherhood would put a major chink into his ambitious career plans. Once the hoax was discovered, Stuart jumped off a bridge to his death rather than face public scorn, not to mention state prison.

In the very same year as the Stuart murder, millionaire Joseph Menendez and his wife Mary were shot to death execution-style as they slept in their posh Beverly Hills home. José Menendez, a Cuban refugee, had built his fortune in the video distribution business, and the police suspected, based on the crime scene and the victim's business dealings, that the murder may have been a Mafia hit.

As the police tracked down leads in the case, the Menendez children, 19-year-old Erik and 22-year-old Lyle, split the first portion of their large inheritance and began to pursue the lifestyle of rich bachelors. After seven months, however, as the organized crime theory dissolved, the police scrutinized apparent inconsistencies in the Menendez brothers' alibis.

The two brothers eventually broke down under police interrogation and admitted to the murders. Erik and Lyle Menendez were convicted of murder, after two jury trials in which their claim of having been abused by their father seemed far less plausible than the motive of greed.

Greed can also motivate women to kill their intimates. Toni Cato Riggs was convicted of first-degree murder and conspiracy and sentenced to life without parole after she hired her brother to murder her husband, Anthony. He was a Gulf War veteran who had only been home a few weeks when he was gunned down by Toni's brother so that she could collect his $150,000 life insurance proceeds. At first, there was not enough evidence to charge Toni Riggs with the homicide. Years later, however, she became involved in drug smuggling and confessed to undercover agents posing as drug dealers that she had in fact carefully planned her husband's death.

Obsession and Jealousy

The killer's desired reward in domestic murder cases is often something other than money, but rather securing the love and/or affection of another person. Tufts University professor William Douglas, a middle-age family man, had grown so helplessly obsessed with prostitute Robin Benedict that he wanted her all to himself. Embezzling funds from various federal grants, Douglas placed Benedict on his research payroll to compensate her for sexual exclusivity. As time progressed and Douglas's obsession grew deeper, however, Benedict resisted his jealous possessiveness.

On March 5, 1983, Douglas, unable to accept the thought of his beloved Robin sexually entwined with another man, bludgeoned the 21-year-old call girl to death with a sledgehammer and dumped her body in a trash bin off Route 95, south of Boston. Although her body was never recovered by the police, the prosecution forged ahead with murder charges against the disgraced biochemist. Faced with a murder rap, Douglas pleaded guilty in exchange for a reduced charge of manslaughter.

The figurative "romantic triangle" has three points, and at each nexus we find a person with sufficient motivation for murder. Occasionally, the triangle's apex—the unfaithful two-timer—is murdered for his or her infidelity by a jealous and spiteful mate or lover. Forty-five-year-old Clara Harris, a dentist, tried everything to keep her husband from leaving her for another woman. She scheduled liposuction and breast augmentation surgery, went to a tanning salon, hired a personal trainer, lost 20 pounds, lightened her hair, and wore more provocative clothing. When none of this worked, Harris repeatedly ran over her husband in a hotel parking lot, while his daughter (her stepdaughter) looked on in horror. Although Harris claimed the whole episode was an accident, a videotape of the incident, recorded by the private investigator hired by Harris to follow her philandering husband, showed her running over him multiple (perhaps as many as five) times. Harris was convicted of murder and sentenced to 20 years in prison and given a $10,000 fine. The Texas jury sent a clear message that it is hardly acceptable to kill an unfaithful mate rather than face rejection.

More often, however, it is one of the competing rivals who is killed in order to clear the path for romance. On April 29, 1997, 33-year-old Craig Rabinowitz of Merion, Pennsylvania, an affluent suburb outside of Philadelphia, reported to the police that he had discovered his wife, Stefanie, dead in the bathtub, apparently the victim of an intruder. But in the following weeks, his story dissolved in the face of forensic evidence and the revelation of a web of obsession and financial debt that served as a powerful motive for murder. Rabinowitz had secretly fantasized sharing a life with an exotic dancer nicknamed "Summer" and spent more than $100,000 on trips and private "couch dances" with the object of his desire. Unable to maintain his innocence any longer, Rabinowitz confessed to killing his wife, not only to remove her as an obstacle to romantic bliss but to receive almost $2 million in life insurance to pay off his personal and business indebtedness.

Romantic triangles can also lead to the violent expulsion of an outside threat to an existing relationship. While money and passion combined to drive Rabinowitz to murder his wife, affairs of the heart are often sufficient in themselves to inspire a homicide. When David Graham, popular high school student/athlete from Mansfield, Texas, confessed to his sweetheart, Diane Zamora, about his sexual tryst with sophomore Adrianne Jones, Zamora flew into an uncontrollable rage. As Graham tried to calm her, Zamora jealously insisted that Jones had to be killed. In order to prove his remorse and devotion, Graham conspired with Zamora in the December 1995 beating and shooting death of Jones. The two lovers then went off to become cadets in military academies and vowed to keep the crime as their dark secret. However, Zamora later broke the pact by admitting her involvement to her roommates.

Power, Control, and Abuse

The extraordinary cases of family and intimate homicide described thus far involve a selfish and cold-blooded scheme to commit murder in order to achieve a financial or romantic goal. Most instances of homicide within intimate relationships, however, are more likely to represent an expression of power or a defensive response to it, rather than an instrumental means for satisfying some other personal objective.

More often than not, the use of lethal force by a spouse is not the first violent episode within the relationship. Jacquelyn Campbell of Johns Hopkins University found in her examination of 250 cases of women murdered by their intimate partners that nearly two-thirds had been assaulted by their mate in the past. Murder was not so much a spontaneous, unpredictable act or a behavior out of character for the perpetrator but the culmination of a consistent and growing pattern of abuse within the relationship.[1] While the jury in the criminal trial of ex-football star O. J. Simpson may, for example, have been unconvinced that he had murdered his estranged wife, Nicole Brown, and her friend Ronald Goldman, it was incontrovertible that he had assaulted and terrorized her in the years leading up to her violent death. The jury, like millions of Americans, heard 911 tapes of her desperate pleas for help while O. J. Simpson stormed her apartment. Notwithstanding his guilt or innocence, the potential for lethal violence had clearly been evidenced.

The most troubling and perplexing cases of domestic violence involve relationships held together not so much by intimacy and affection but by intimidation and aggression. In some marriages, the husband's sense of ego and self-worth depends on his ability to control, dominate, and manipulate his wife and children—not just to be in charge of traditional male responsibilities such as the family finances but to have complete and absolute authority over the household. Should his position of authority be questioned by what he perceives (or misperceives) as insolence or disobedience from his subordinate partner, he may use violence or the threat of violence to enforce his rule and reestablish command. The frequency and level of violence within such a relationship typically escalate as the abuser/controller constantly expands and tests the limits of aggression, possessiveness, and control. His wife may threaten to leave for the sake of the children, if not for herself, yet he may try to exploit her needs and feelings of guilt by begging for forgiveness and promising to change. Usually, the only change to occur is for the violence to increase in its brutality as he attempts to tighten his control.

Despite widespread efforts in this country to emancipate victims of domestic violence, we have not successfully resolved all the legal, financial, and emotional ties that can strangle a woman as much as her abusive spouse can. Many women remain in a violent and potentially lethal relationship out of emotional or financial dependency or a perception, even if a false one, that staying together is better for the children.

Domestic violence expert Lenore Walker has characterized the response of some abuse victims as "learned helplessness."[2] Frustrated in her ineffectual struggles to repel early episodes of abuse, a woman may come to develop a sense of resignation that she is helpless in controlling her own fate or that of the children. Seeing no way out while perhaps hoping things will improve, she may stay in the abusive marriage, sometimes until the level of violence becomes deadly.

Similar to the so-called Stockholm syndrome used to describe the compliant behavior of wartime hostages, some domestic abuse victims who feel trapped in a violent relationship can become even more closely bonded to their attacker.[3] Initially, she may strive to please and appease her abuser as a means of sheer survival. As she becomes more isolated from others, she may grow increasingly dependent on her abuser for whatever bits of attention and meager rewards he concedes her. In extreme cases, she can identify so closely with her controlling mate that she focuses exclusively on his real or imagined good points, unable psychologically to see him in a more accurate light.

As an alternative response to sustained abuse, a woman may grow in her determination to survive. Rather than give up hope and give in to their victimizers, many women find the courage and will to fight back—figuratively, if not literally—by seeking help and refuge from friends and family or legal and social services.[4]

Although the survival instinct may be healthier both physically and emotionally, on occasion attempts to escape and survive can instigate retaliatory acts of lethal violence. A move to terminate the relationship occasionally becomes the innocent precipitant to murder, sparked by what Dutton has called "abandonment rage."[5] For example, among a group of nearly 300 women murdered by their intimates, Kathryn Moracco of the University of North Carolina found that 42 percent had either separated or threatened to separate from their assailant.[6] It is the fear of this kind of deadly outcome that ultimately keeps many women in violent relationships.

When a woman does attempt to break away from an abusive partner, he may see her effort to take over control of the relationship as nothing less than a capital offense, punishable by death. In 1991, for example, 39-year-old James Colbert of Concord, New Hampshire, killed his estranged wife and three daughters, before taking his own life by leaping off a bridge into the water below. Learning that his wife had started a new relationship, Colbert reasoned, "If I can't have her and the kids, then no one can." As an ultimate expression of control, Colbert—and definitely not his wife—would be the one to decide when, where, how, and on what terms their marriage would end.

Although the most typical scenario involves lethal violence as the offensive climax to escalating abuse by a husband, in 40 percent of domestic murders it is the wife who deals the fatal blow. In some cases the woman is the aggressor in the marriage, murders in response to her husband's infidelity, kills him to collect life insurance, or kills in order to be with her lover. But, more than men, domestic homicides committed by women are frequently a self-protective response to intimidation, threats, and physical, emotional, or sexual abuse.[7]

In a 1977 murder case made famous in the TV film *The Burning Bed* starring actress Farrah Fawcett, 30-year-old Francine Hughes of Dansville, Michigan, poured gasoline around the bed where her ex-husband Mickey lay sleeping off his latest drinking binge. After lighting a match and setting her former husband ablaze, she boarded her children into the car and drove straight to the police station where she confessed. To the detectives, it had seemed like a simple case of domestic homicide. But after hearing testimony detailing 14 years of battery and death threats, the jury surprised the legal community, if not the nation, by finding Hughes not guilty by temporary insanity.

Ever since the "Burning Bed" case, the courts have struggled with the "battered woman syndrome" as a defense to murder.[8] A chronic abuse victim feels trapped as a consequence of her prolonged history of physical, sexual, or psychological punishment. In the tradition of English common law, in order to invoke self-defense, the risk of aggression has to be immediate and with no reasonable means of escape. Yet increasingly, the courts have excused or at least lessened responsibility when violence was not imminent but a day-to-day, continuing threat. As for the requirement of taking flight, the courts have begun to recognize that legal ties and financial dependencies, if not feelings of sheer terror, often prevent what ordinarily would appear to be opportunities for escape.

Partially due to the efforts by battered women advocacy groups, the incidence of domestic homicide has fallen nationally over the past quarter century. Overall, the number of homicides of husbands and wives has declined steadily from just under 2,200 in 1976 to less than 800 in 2002, a drop of almost two-thirds.

Some critics have suggested that this downturn in spousal homicide is little more than a demographic artifact, the result of changes in domesticity—or living arrangements—than any real progress in reducing violence between marital partners. By this theory, as divorce rates have risen and rates of marriage have declined, fewer men and women are "eligible" to be murdered by their spouses. As some support for this view, the number of unmarried women murdered by boyfriends has increased somewhat over the past quarter century, from 354 in 1976 to 475 in 2002. Although this growth is consistent with the expanded number of unmarried women in the population, it does suggest that non-marriage as well as divorce has put fewer women at risk, at least for spousal homicide.

Over the latter half of the 20th century, divorce laws have indeed been liberalized. By contrast to an earlier era when the marital ties could not be easily broken without proof of cause, such as mental or physical cruelty or adultery, no-fault divorce laws have permitted couples to split before the level of discord reaches extreme and violent proportions. Yet for relationships in which violence is indeed a form of control, the easy availability of divorce can be a cruel illusion. The "if I can't have you, no one can" threat would generally prohibit an amicable no-fault divorce. Fortunately, improvement in the economic status of women has eroded the patriarchical control men have historically had over their spouses.

Another factor behind the decline in intimate homicide is that the social stigma associated with being an abused spouse (as well as a divorcee) has greatly diminished. During a less enlightened era, victims of domestic abuse often internalized blame and guilt for their own victimization. "If only I were a better wife, a better cook, a better lover, he wouldn't get mad and beat me." Today, as the topic of domestic violence has been brought more into the open, victims are less likely to feel responsible for their plight and thus more likely to make a move to exit the relationship.

Besides divorce, more immediate legal and social interventions—such as restraining orders, mandatory police arrest procedures, abuse hotlines, shelters for battered women, and support groups and counseling for victims of domestic violence—have helped provide abused women with a viable escape route. More than ever, a woman has alternatives to picking up a loaded gun and shooting her loaded husband. As shown in Figure 4.1, it is ironically the men who have benefitted the most from intervention strategies designed to protect women. The steepest decline in intimate homicides has been in women killing their partners (husbands, ex-husbands, or boyfriends), down from 1,357 in 1976 to 342 in 2002, a remarkable 75 percent decline. Given the expanding array of legal and social interventions, murder is less often the only or last resort for a woman to protect herself from a current or former intimate who abuses or stalks her.

By contrast, the improvement in the number of women killed by their intimates has been more modest and relatively recent. From 1976 to 1993, the incidents of women killed by intimates fluctuated between 1,400 and 1,600 with no indication of a trend in either direction. Apparently, men were unconcerned about the increasing array of interventions available to victims of domestic violence. In fact, some men were inspired in a decidedly violent way in the face of restraining orders and other initiatives by their wives or girlfriends to escape.

We read frequently of domestic disputes that escalate rapidly to deadly proportions, especially if a gun is available. In fact, 66 percent of homicides by intimate partners involve a gun. The firearm may have been purchased ostensibly to protect and defend the family from an outside intruder, but ultimately it is fired offensively against a loved one in a moment of rage or revenge. In their analysis of cases in Tennessee, Washington, and Ohio, for

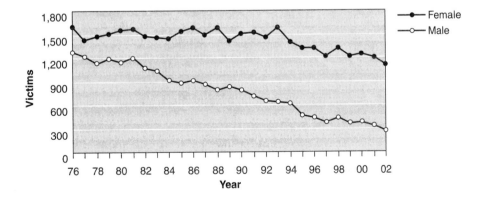

FIGURE 4.1 *Intimate Homicides by Sex of Victim, 1976–2002*

example, Arthur Kellermann and his colleagues found that a gun in the home increased the likelihood of domestic homicide by nearly a factor of three.[9]

It is only in the past few years, since 1993, that the number of men killing wives and girlfriends has declined as well, from 1,581 in 1993 to 1,111 in 2002. This downturn coincides with the implementation of the Brady Law, which mandated background checks (and for the first few years waiting periods as well) prior to purchases of firearms. It is difficult to establish whether this gun legislation made the vital difference, but it is noteworthy that virtually the entire decline (88%) in women murdered by their partners since 1993 has been in gun-related incidents.

The availability of social and legal interventions to abuse victims is, unfortunately, not equally extensive in all parts of the country. Figure 4.2 shows the percentage of homicides that involves an intimate partner by the urbanness of location. It is primarily in the larger cities that we observe a decline in the percentage of homicides that involves an intimate. It is in these same locales where the greatest emphasis has been placed on providing resources such as shelters for battered women. In many suburbs and especially rural areas, a victim of abuse may not have access to these escape routes and may even remain in a dangerous and potentially lethal relationship to avoid the stigma within her small community.

In the final analysis, people often wonder in cases of cold-blooded spousal homicide, "Why didn't he just get a divorce?" For some killers, lethal dissolution of their marriage has far greater benefits—monetary and otherwise—than the legal alternative in divorce court. Clearly, some estranged husbands and wives are motivated to keep all of the marital assets, leaving aside any extra profit from life insurance. Another "asset" they do not want to share is custody of the children. In 2002, for example, 43-year-old Harold Stonier of Concord, Massachusetts, paid a significant sum of money to a "hitman" who turned out to be an undercover agent. Stonier apparently wanted his wife dead, even if it meant paying a sum greater than what he may have forfeited in a divorce settlement. According to his taped statements, he did not want to lose custody of his son, Jamie. The only way to ensure he got custody, Stonier reasoned, was to eliminate his wife. Liberalized divorce laws may therefore have had a greater impact on husbands killing wives than on wives killing their husbands.

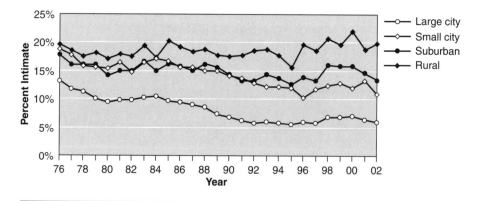

FIGURE 4.2   *Percentage Intimate Homicides by Location Type, 1976–2002*

Family Annihilation

Most family homicides involve a single perpetrator (usually the husband/father) and a single victim (usually his wife). Even when only one person is attacked, others in the household—typically the children—become secondary victims, suffering indirectly by witnessing violence and by having to live with its consequences—that is, having a murdered mother and an incarcerated father.

On occasion, however, the domestic murderer doesn't stop with just one victim but may extend his carnage through the entire family. Although the children may have little or nothing to do with his grudge or grievance, they may still be linked in his mind with the primary victim—after all, they are *her* children. In what has been called "murder by proxy," innocent people are sometimes targeted in order to punish the primary victim even further.[10]

Although his castle was little more than a ramshackle home, Ronald Gene Simmons was the king in his kingdom. He ruled the household, his wife, children, and grandchildren with absolute control, a pattern not so uncommon in rural southern communities like Dover, Arkansas. Simmons dictated where his family members could go, when, and with whom.

By Christmastime 1987, however, he was losing his grip—not on reality but on his family. Simmons's family life seemed to be crumbling around him. Although the kids still obeyed, they now did so without a shred of respect for their father. They had grown rude and insulting toward him. To a former military man like Simmons, this "verbal abuse" was sheer insubordination. But insubordination was nothing compared to desertion. Simmons was aware that his wife was on the verge of leaving him and taking the kids with her.

In a final desperate act of control, Simmons executed his entire family, not only his wife, children, and grandchildren who lived with him but also his older children and their families in succession as they came to the house to visit for Christmas. By the end of a five-day siege, Simmons had killed 14 family members in the largest family massacre in U.S. history. Even then, he wasn't quite finished. After annihilating his family, he launched a 45-minute rampage through the nearby town of Russelville in which he killed 2 and wounded 4 others.

Family massacres are generally committed by the head of household who perceives that he has total say over his clan, in life and in death. He feels entitled by his position to determine his family's destiny. However, a few family annihilations have also been committed by children as a violent reaction to this same type of parental domination and control. In 1976, for example, 18-year-old Harry De La Roche, Jr., methodically executed his mother, father, and two brothers in their beds in order to free himself of his dad's domination. Home from college for Thanksgiving vacation, De La Roche could not bring himself to face his father with his decision to quit school. Murder would be the easier way out.

Annually, above 300 parents are slain by their children or stepchildren, and over half of these parricides involve a child or stepchild under the age of 25. Of these younger perpetrators, as shown in Figure 4.3, most incidents involve fathers killed by their sons or stepsons (53 percent), followed by mothers slain by sons or stepsons (34 percent), fathers by daughters (7 percent) and mothers by daughters (6 percent).

Criminologist Kathleen Heide has proposed a three-category typology for parricides.[11] According to her view, the crime is most frequently committed in response to severe physical or sexual abuse. As with preemptive attacks by battered wives, the act of parricide is often

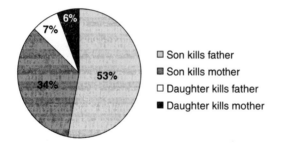

FIGURE 4.3   *Parricides by Type, 1976–2002 Combined*

more defensive than offensive. The defensive strike can also come on behalf of another person, typically protecting a mother from her abusive husband or boyfriend. In January 2000, for example, an 8-year-old Tennessee boy confessed to stabbing his mother's boyfriend to death, after witnessing a pattern of physical violence directed against her.

Heide's other two classifications involve psychological rather than situational disorders. Some children who murder their parents do so under the influence of a severe mental illness, such as schizophrenia. Still others simply have bad character, classifiable as an antisocial personality disorder (or, for especially young offenders, a conduct disorder). In Allentown, Pennsylvania, for example, two chronically delinquent brothers—ages 15 and 17—who fashioned themselves as white supremacist skinheads, killed their father when he refused to let them drive the family car. They also murdered their mother and their 11-year-old brother.

Infanticide

Very young children virtually never commit murder, of course, but they are clearly at risk for being murdered. As shown in Figure 4.4, 600–700 children under the age of five are killed each year, with boys having a slightly greater level of victimization than girls. Although the number of such cases appears to have risen over the past two decades, the increase is actually no greater than corresponding changes in the population of young children.

Infanticide is a remarkably different event from most any other form of homicide. Because of the small stature and physical vulnerability of young children, firearms are rarely used—or needed—to kill them. Most commonly, victims of this tender age are killed with hands or fists through strangulation, suffocation, beating, or shaking. Infanticide typically occurs during a fit of anger by an adult against a defenseless baby or following a chronic pattern of child abuse that turns fatal.

As shown in Figure 4.5, the majority of the perpetrators of infanticide are parents, not stranger abductors or intruders. Other than parents, the next largest category of perpetrators consists of male friends or acquaintances, very often the mother's boyfriend. Overall, fewer than 5 percent of infanticides are committed by babysitters or nannies.

The internationally publicized murder trial of 19-year-old English au pair Louise Woodward in the 1997 "shaken baby" death of 8-month-old Matthew Eappen of Newton,

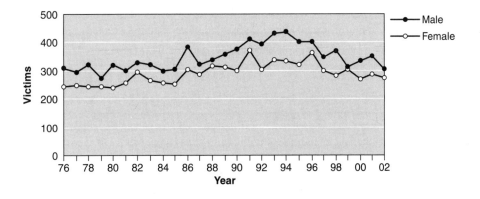

FIGURE 4.4 *Infanticides by Sex of Victim, 1976–2002*

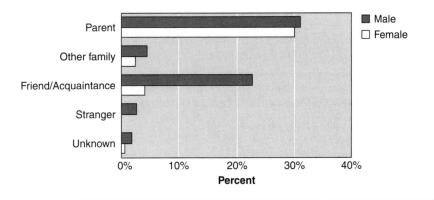

FIGURE 4.5 *Infanticides by Offender Type, 1976–2002 Combined*

Massachusetts, gave many parents pause to think about the caretakers to whom they entrusted their young ones. Babysitters have been known to murder children for reasons of ill-temper and poor training, but these are few and very far between. Although parents are, of course, wise to investigate fully those in whom they place so much trust, murder is generally the least of their concerns (especially compared with the much higher likelihood of accidental death).

Because of the overwhelming statistical tendencies in cases of infanticide implicating parents, the focus of the investigation into the death of 6-year-old JonBenet Ramsey of Boulder, Colorado, during Christmas 1996 centered, rightly or wrongly, on the girl's parents, John and Patsy. When they refused to cooperate with the police, suspicion grew. And when Patsy could not be ruled out as the author of a ransom note found at the scene of the crime, many people became convinced that JonBenet's mother had murdered her young daughter. Although child abductions by strangers do sometimes occur, in general parents have a much greater range of motivations for committing infanticide than do acquaintances or strangers.

Because of our steadfast belief that parents should be protectors rather than executioners, we tend to accept alternative explanations for child homicide, despite the strong statistical pattern favoring parents as suspects. This was what 23-year-old Susan Smith of Union, South Carolina, counted on when she and her estranged husband went before a national television audience in October 1994 and begged tearfully for the lives and safety of her two sons, 3-year-old Michael and Alex, age 14 months.

According to the distraught mother, a black stranger had jumped into her Mazda Protege while she was stopped at a traffic light. The carjacker had reportedly ordered her out of the vehicle and then sped off with Smith's two boys still trapped in the backseat. The police were cautiously skeptical, however, because of some discrepancies in her description of the incident. Within days, after failing a polygraph test, Susan Smith confessed that she had rolled the car into a nearby lake with her children strapped helplessly inside.

In some instances of infanticide, a young parent responds violently when unable to handle the stress of a difficult crying baby. Some instances may be aided by hormonal changes after childbirth, ranging from the "baby blues" to clinical postpartum depression. In recent years, some movement has even been seen in raising a postpartum defense to murder charges.

In March 2002, Andrea Yates of Houston, Texas drowned her five children, ages 7, 5, 3, 2 and 6 months. Yates was spared the death penalty, but was sentenced to life in prison with eligibility for parole after 40 years. Although she admitted planning the murders in advance, Yates plead not guilty by reason of insanity due to an obviously severe case of postpartum psychosis (PPP). She had a history of institutionalization, suicide attempts and previous postpartum depression. Yet jurors believed that Yates knew what she was doing was wrong and therefore failed to qualify for insanity under Texas law.

Yet occasionally, as in Susan Smith's case, the use of lethal force against a young innocent is far more selfish and reprehensible than just the inability to cope with parenthood. Smith had learned that her new boyfriend would not stay with or marry her because she had children. She apparently chose to sacrifice her children in the pursuit of romance.

Sadly, children are sometimes exploited for a number of self-serving reasons—for profit, for love, even for attention. In what is known as Munchausen syndrome, adults and children have been known to feign illness or even self-inflict sickness or injury for the sake of attention.[12] For some people who may otherwise feel insecure and unloved, the attention received from family, friends, even the medical professionals when sick can become psychologically addictive, so much so that the sympathy is worth the suffering. In a derivative condition, Munchausen syndrome by proxy, parents and other caretakers have been known to cause injury or illness to a child, an elderly parent, or other dependent in order to claim center stage and inject themselves into an exiting or emergency situation.

For Marybeth Tinning of Schenectady, New York, the sympathy afforded a grieving mother grew irresistible. Craving attention, she learned that the support given to a new mother only lasts so long. She also learned, when her third child, baby Jennifer, died shortly after birth following a week-long struggle with hemorrhagic meningitis, that the attention surrounding a death could be as sustaining as that surrounding a birth. For the span of some dozen years, Marybeth gave birth to a series of children, all of whom eventually died, usually of what had been diagnosed as SIDS (sudden infant death syndrome) or "crib death."

Marybeth responded routinely following each loss of another child. She called all her friends and relatives to announce the latest reduction in the Tinning family, expecting the customary round of pity and attention. Her death announcements had become as emotionally arousing for her as the birth announcements; both would make her the center of attention.

Marybeth began theorizing—almost bragging—about a genetic defect that she was passing on to each of her babies. But as children numbers six, seven, and eight died, sympathy for Marybeth started turning into suspicion.

For five years after the death of their eighth child, Marybeth and her husband, Joseph, remained childless. After years with an "empty nest," the Tinnings were ecstatic over the birth of their ninth child, Tami Lynne, in August of 1985. The baby girl was beautiful, healthy, and full of life, yet those closest to the Tinnings quietly predicted that there would soon be another funeral to attend.

According to Marybeth, early in the morning of December 20, she went to check on her baby and found her lying on her stomach, motionless and breathless. Despite efforts to restore her breathing, Tami Lynne was pronounced dead. Unable to ignore what had become painfully clear, Marybeth's sister-in-law this time went to the police with her suspicions. Tami Lynne was autopsied carefully and thoroughly, with new and improved methods for distinguishing SIDS from induced asphyxiation. According to the coroner's report, the baby had not died of natural causes but instead had been suffocated. Despite the fact that implicating evidence from earlier deaths had long since been buried, there was enough direct and circumstantial evidence to charge and convict Marybeth with murder.

In Munchausen syndrome by proxy, the victims are exploited as pawns to fulfill the perpetrator's emotional needs. Infanticides, as we have seen in other cases, can also result from a desire for more practical rewards, such as profit, companionship, or even vengeance.

On Father's Day 1999, Amy Shanabarger of Franklin, Indiana, returned home from her job as a grocery store cashier only to find her 7-month-old son Tyler dead, lying face down in his crib. After an autopsy, the coroner determined that the cause of death was SIDS. Just hours after the funeral, however, the boy's father confessed to the police that he had suffocated the infant, while his wife was at work, by wrapping his head in plastic. Ronald Shanabarger, age 29, admitted his motive was revenge against his wife, planning the homicide even before the child was conceived. He was angry and resentful that in 1996 Amy, before they were married, had refused to cut her vacation cruise short to comfort him following the death of his father. According to the confession, Shanabarger fathered the child, waited until his wife bonded with the infant, and then murdered him so that his wife could experience the same kind of pain she had insensitively ignored years earlier.

Killing for Love?

One of the lesser common, yet especially insidious forms of family homicide involves the victimization of elders who, because of advanced age, infirmity, or dependency, are vulnerable to family members. Sons, daughters, and other relations have been known to abuse elders for emotional reasons or even murder them greedily to hasten an expected inheritance.

Within families, murder can also be an expression of love and compassion. Despite the laws prohibiting euthanasia, occasionally children kill elderly and dying parents, and parents kill sickly children to spare them the misery of living. Sometimes it is a case of assisted suicide in which the victim is too weak to execute the fatal procedure. Other times, a loving family member may make a decision for the victim in a merciful and loving act of homicide.

Family annihilations of perfectly healthy loved ones can also reflect the same notion of love, albeit twisted and depression-inspired. To the murderer, life on earth may be so miserable that he feels his loved ones will be better off dead. In what psychiatrist Shervert Frazier termed "suicide by proxy," the killer sees his loved ones as an extension of himself.[13] He feels personal responsibility for the well-being of his wife and children and sees no other way out of his predicament.

Lawrence DeLisle, age 29, of Lincoln Park, Michigan, had become so overwhelmed with despair that he deliberately drove his station wagon straight into the Detroit River in an effort to murder his entire family—his wife, three kids, and himself. After hitting the water, his survival instinct overtook his self-pity and he successfully swam to safety, as did his wife. The children were not so lucky, however. Unable to extricate themselves from their seat belts, they drowned within minutes. Despite his suicidal intentions, DeLisle was convicted of three counts of murder.

While it is easy to be suspicious of DeLisle's motives, other family murderers have been better able to follow through on their suicide mission. By May 1990, 37-year-old Hermino Elizalde, described by friends and neighbors in Chicago as a devoted father, had become hopelessly despondent over his recent firing. He was even more concerned about his ex-wife's attempt to exploit his lapse in employment to win custody of their four daughters and one son, after she accused him of mistreating them. Rather than losing his beloved children, he decided to keep them together at all cost . . . at least spiritually. Elizalde doused his sleeping children with gasoline, lit a match, and set them afire one at a time. When he was sure they were dead, he set himself on fire. By killing them all, Elizalde felt assured that they would be reunited in a better life after death.

One of the less common yet particularly insidious types of family homicide is murder-suicide, typically involving current or ex-spouses or significant others. Although the media seems to cover more of the cases that occur in younger couples, recent research by Donna Cohen found the rate of murder-suicide to be twice as high among the over 55 age group than among younger couples.[14] Extrapolating from Florida cases, Cohen estimated that there are approximately 1,000–1,500 episodes of murder-suicide each year in the U.S. (involving about 2,000–3,000 deaths). Her research also suggested that this phenomenon may be on the rise. In older couples, it is most common for the husband to be the perpetrator and the wife to be the unwilling victim, typically shot while asleep. Many episodes may stem from the husband's inability to cope with a care-giving role. He may rationalize his crime as an act of love or compassion, but it may actually have a more selfish motive.

To any casual observer of current events, the occurrence of family murder seems endless. Yet despite the tragedies in so many households across the country, the number of family murders has actually declined, from over 3,600 victims annually in the late 1970s to just under 2,000 in 2002. The percentage of all homicides traced to familial relationships has dropped as well. Though the trend may be in the right direction, the thousands of instances each year when men, women, and children are murdered by people they love, be it for power, passion, or profit, offend our sense of the sanctity and safety of marriage and family. The words "until death do us part" should be a loving promise, never a loathsome threat.

Endnotes

1. J. McFarlane, J. Campbell, S. Wilt, C. Sachs, Y. Ulrich, and X. Xu, "Stalking and Intimate Partner Femicide," *Homicide Studies* 3 (1999): 300–316.

2. Lenore E. Walker, "Battered Women and Learned Helplessness," *Victimology: An International Journal* 2 (1977): 525–534.

3. Dee L. R. Graham, Edna Rawlings, and Nelly Rimini, "Survivors of Terror: Battered Women, Hostages, and the Stockholm Syndrome," in Kersti Yllo and Michele L. Bograd, eds., *Feminist Perspectives on Wife Abuse.* Newbury Park, CA: Sage Publications, 1998.

4. Edward W. Gondolf and Ellen R. Fisher, *Battered Women as Survivors: An Alternative to Treating Learned Helplessness.* New York: Lexington Books, 1988.

5. Donald G. Dutton, *The Domestic Assault of Women: Psychological and Criminal Justice Perspectives.* Vancouver: University of British Columbia Press, 1995.

6. Kathryn E. Moracco, Carol W. Runyan, and John D. Butts, "Femicide in North Carolina: A Statewide Study of Patterns and Precursors," *Homicide Studies* 2 (1998): 422–446.

7. See Ann Goetting, "Homicidal Wives: A Profile," *Journal of Family Issues* 8 (1987): 332–341.

8. See R. K. Thyfault, "Self-Defense: Battered Women Syndrome on Trial," *California Western Law Review* 20 (1984): 485–510.

9. A. L. Kellermann, F. P. Rivara, N. B. Rusforth, J. G. Banton, B. T. Reay, J. T. Francisco, A. B. Locchi, B. A. Prosdzinski, B. B. Hackman, and G. Somes, "Gun Ownership as a Risk Factor for Homicide in the Home," *New England Journal of Medicine* 267 (1993): 1084–1090.

10. Shervert H. Frazier, "Violence and Social Impact," in J. C. Schoolar and C. M. Gaitz, eds., *Research and the Psychiatric Patient.* New York: Brunner/Mazel, 1975.

11. Kathleen M. Heide, *Why Kids Kill Parents: Child Abuse and Adolescent Homicide.* Columbus, OH: Ohio State University Press, 1992.

12. Charles V. Ford, "Munchausen Syndrome," in Claude T. H. Friedmann and Robert A. Faguet, eds., *Extraordinary Disorders of Human Behavior.* New York: Plenum Press, 1982. Also see Richard Firstman and Jamie Talan, *The Death of Innocents.* New York: Bantam Books, 1998.

13. Shervert H. Frazier, op. cit.

14. Donna Cohen, "Homicide-Suicide in Older People," *Psychiatric Times* 17 (2000): 49–52.

5

The Coming and Going
of the Young Superpredators

The decade of the 1990s may long be remembered for its technological advances—the expanding power of personal computers, the ubiquitousness of the Internet, as well as the proliferation of wireless communications. Yet to those who closely monitor crime trends, the 1990s will be remembered as the decade when the murder rate fell.

By the end of the 1990s, the rate of killing in America had sunk to levels not seen for 30 years. As citizens across the country celebrated New Year's 2000 with incredible fanfare and relief that the Y2K computer bug was little more than a scare, police departments rejoiced in their own sense of victory.

Criminologists had warned of an impending juvenile crime wave[1] created by a new breed of "superpredators."[2] Despite the dire forecast, as the 1990s drew to a close, city after city reported spectacularly low homicide rates. Boston closed out 1999 with as few as 31 murders, compared with 152 in 1990. Philadelphia's homicide toll reached below the 300 level for the first time in well over a decade. New York City, despite a slight increase in 1999, tallied 667 murders, substantially below its 1990 peak of 2,245. Chicago recorded 641 killings, its lowest level in many years.

While these reductions as well as declines in many other cities were worthy of celebration, the murder rate was not at a 30-year low point for all segments of the population. Only when we look much more closely into the trends do we begin fully to understand the great crime drop of the 1990s.

An Epidemic of Youth Homicide

Figure 5.1 displays the overall rate of offending—offenders per 100,000 population—for all age groups combined. Similar to the pattern shown earlier (in Figure 3.1) for the rate of homicide victims, the rate of offending peaked in the 1980s at nearly 12 per 100,000, declined by about 25 percent to the mid-1980s, rose sharply through 1991 to another peak of 11 per 100,000, and declined thereafter to a low of just over 6 offenders per 100,000 population.

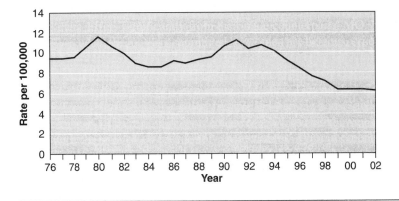

FIGURE 5.1 *Homicide Offending Rate, 1976–2002*

Probing deeper into these trends by comparing different age groups uncovers a very different picture. As shown in Figure 5.2, the rate of murder at the hands of adults, ages 25 and older, declined slowly yet steadily through the 1980s and 1990s, without any rise during the violence-filled years of the late 1980s. All of the changes in homicide were among younger offenders. From 1985 to 1993, the rate of killing among young adults, ages 18 to 24, rose 93 percent, before dropping by nearly a third by 2002. Young adults have traditionally had the highest rates of offending, and this gap grew even wider in recent years.

The most remarkable change, however, occurred among teenagers. Prior to 1985, teens committed homicide at the same low rate as their parents' generation. However, since the mid-1980s, the pattern of offending for adolescents much more resembled that of their older siblings. From 1985 to 1993, the rate of murder committed by teenagers tripled, from 9.8 to 30.2 per 100,000, before its recent sharp decline.

What happened in the mid-1980s that drove the youth homicide figures into record territory? Although there are many factors that would underlie such a sharp trend as this, the most compelling and important was the emergence of crack cocaine as a popular street market drug in cities across America. Although the pharmacological effects of crack co-

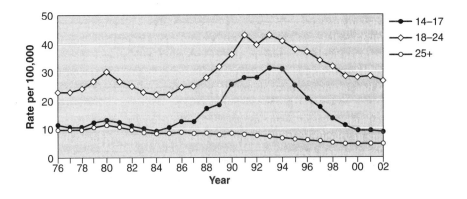

FIGURE 5.2 *Homicide Offending Rates by Age, 1976–2002*

caine were worrisome, involving a lessening of impulse control as well as unpredictable effects on the body, the real damage to our society and the crime problem surrounded the dynamics of the crack drug market.[3]

When the crack market developed, the usual economic forces of supply and demand created fierce and violent competition for business. The demand for crack, which unlike other drugs was sold in small single-hit quantities, was so great that dealers had to recruit large numbers of street merchants to distribute the contraband. In light of this intense demand, teenagers were aggressively recruited and enlisted as street sellers. Not only were they willing to take on the risks for some quick cash (and free drugs), but they did so at a lower level of compensation. It was also perceived that, if caught, they would be treated more leniently by the courts.

Because of the violence associated with the trade, guns were an essential tool for survival. Youngsters trafficking in crack cocaine armed themselves for added muscle as well as for protection.[4] As soon as some teenagers were armed, their peers—even those uninvolved in crack as sellers or users—began to acquire guns as well.[5]

A virtual teen arms race spiraled out of control, instigated by, but not limited to, crack activity. Some kids carried guns for offensive purposes, others for self-defense, and still others for status among their friends and rivals. The arming of America's youth created a volatile mix of impulsivity and firepower, as trigger-happy youth used their weaponry for reasons large and small—from the elimination of a rival gang member to the execution of someone who insulted them.

As shown in Figure 5.3, the entire increase in teen homicide was gun related. From 1985 to 1993, the number of teenagers who killed with a gun quadrupled, before tailing off in recent years. There was no appreciable increase in juvenile homicides by other means.

It has long been true that many teenagers are impatient, imprudent, and impulsive, willing to act spontaneously without fully thinking through the consequences of their actions. The availability of a gun in the hands of quick-triggered kids clearly had an impact on the murder rate.

The increase was also related to gang activity. As shown in Figure 5.4, the number of homicides associated with gangs soared in the late 1980s and early 1990s. In detailed analyses of homicide reports in Chicago and Los Angeles, moreover, Cheryl Maxson has shown

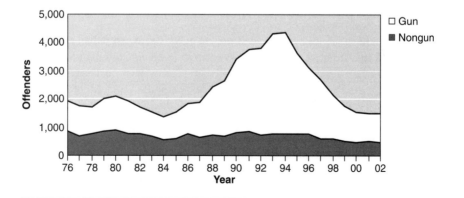

FIGURE 5.3   *Teen Homicide Offenders by Weapon, 1976–2002*

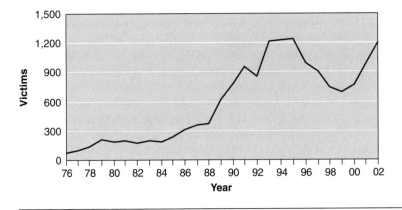

FIGURE 5.4   *Gang Homicides, 1976–2002*

that gang killings represented an increasing number and percentage of all murders from the mid-1980s to the mid-1990s.[6] During the 1980s, several national gangs (e.g., the Bloods and the Crips) expanded their membership as more and more kids were attracted to what gangs had to offer. Many observers have characterized the growth of gangs as a process of intimidation—as a gang member you were protected from attacks.

The definition of "gang," not to mention "gang-related homicide," can be problematic. At what point does a group of kids involved in delinquent activities become a gang? Would we include a homicide involving a gang member as an offender, a victim, or both? Would we include one gang member killing another in a love triangle? Or, would we include a gang member killing his parents? Are these all gang-related homicides?

Even with a fairly broad definition of what constitutes a gang (most police departments use their own discretion as to whether or not a homicide is gang-related), gang homicides are still relatively uncommon—approximately 5–7% of the total homicides committed each year. Of course, the representation of gang homicides would increase somewhat if the same standards applied to inner-city youths were applied to middle-class suburban teenagers who commit crimes in a group. Most people would probably not consider the so-called Trenchcoat Mafia at Columbine High School a gang, yet two of its members (Dylan Klebold and Eric Harris) shot to death 13 people.

But there are many other functions to gang membership than just protection.[7] Gangs provided an alternative socializing mechanism, as the institution of the family weakened in this capacity. By joining a gang, a child could feel special, feel as if he belonged to something important, and be a member of a group that praised him. Moreover, it was a source of excitement and even economic resources. Where illicit drugs were sold, impoverished inner-city gang members gained not only a quick way to make large amounts of money but also a way to serve an apprenticeship in a growing business—the drug industry.[8]

One of the features that tends to distinguish juvenile murder from killings perpetrated by older offenders is the involvement of group dynamics. As shown in Figure 5.5, not only are teen murderers significantly more likely to commit homicide with the help of accomplices, but the percentage of juvenile murders involving two or more perpetrators has grown.

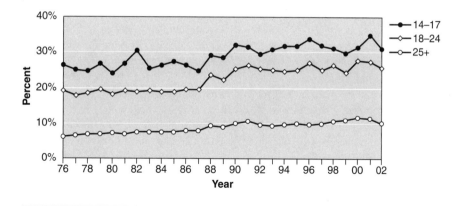

FIGURE 5.5 *Multiple Offender Homicides by Age, 1976–2002*

Individuals—and especially children—often act differently in a group setting than they do on their own. Sometimes peer pressure can encourage someone to conform to a pro-social norm, but frequently it can provide strong encouragement to do the wrong thing. In group settings, the activity may be secondary to inter-personal dynamics. A group leader may feel good that others are willing to follow his lead even into areas of behavior that are cruel and vicious. At the same time, the followers can feel good about the praise they receive from the leader (and other group members) in joining along. In group settings, so-called mob psychology can sweep participants into committing even horrible crimes that no one in the group really wants to do. In situations of a "shared misunderstanding," each group member wrongfully believes that everyone else but him actually desires to commit an offense.[9] Concerned about their reputation among friends, they all participate.

The group effect can operate within large mobs of people—such as in the widely pub-licized episodes of wilding or even in lynchings—and in collections as small as a pair of accomplices. Following the arrest of two Vermont teenagers, 17-year-old Robert Tulloch and 16-year-old James Parker, for the January 2001 brutal murder of Dartmouth College professors, Half and Susanne Zantop, numerous theories were proposed for a possible con-nection between the victims and the perpetrators. Some observers suggested that it may have been a hate crime related to the victims' German roots. Others speculated that they all had been members of the same hiking club. These and other proposed linkages proved wrong. The victims were selected just because they had something the assailants wanted—cash, to help fund their dream of traveling to Australia.

Rather than a connection between victims and offenders, it is instead the close bond between the two assailants that holds the key to understanding this tragic episode. Tulloch exalted in his leadership position, feeding off the admiration of his younger partner, while Parker sought the praise and approval of his older mentor. Had Tulloch and Parker been apart, arguably this crime would never have occurred. In tandem, they brought out the worst in each other.

The subculture of violence notion described earlier, if updated and modernized, is quite helpful in understanding the violence readiness of many young urban dwellers. For inner-city youth, the "American Dream," appearing absolutely unattainable, can be little more than a cruel nightmare. Alienated from mainstream society, minority youngsters instead often obey the "code of the streets" in which respect is the fundamental and most vital commodity of daily life. In order to earn respect and then guard against losing it, according to sociologist Elijah Anderson, a youngster must comport himself at all times in a manner showing that he's ready and willing to be violent. According to Anderson, being disrespected is a fate worse than being murdered.[10]

Another feature that strikingly distinguishes juvenile murders from those committed by older individuals is the particularly senseless character of the youthful impulses and motivations. By contrast to the inspirations of profit, jealousy, and control that characterize most adult homicide, children often, if not typically, kill for trivial reasons—a leather jacket, a romantic brush-off, a challenging glance, or no reason in particular. In a Los Angeles suburb, for example, two teenage girls murdered their best friend because they were jealous of her slender figure, waist-length auburn hair, good looks, and popularity with boys. In Miami, a 12-year-old boy killed a homeless man over a dispute involving a piece of pizza. And in Independence, Missouri, a teenager murdered a Good Humor man because the vender refused to give him a free frozen treat.

Criminologists who have focused heavily on the problem of rising teen homicide rates have been criticized for unfairly painting an entire generation with the same broad brush.[11] Despite a growing number of juvenile murderers, it absolutely remains the case that the vast majority of youngsters do not even come close to committing homicide. Even among the highest rate group—young black males—for every youngster who commits homicide, literally hundreds never will.

Those who do commit homicide tend to differ from those who do not in several important respects besides demographics. Kenneth Busch and his colleagues, for example, studied the case histories of 71 juvenile murderers and compared them with similar data for a sample of 71 non-violent delinquents, matched for age, race, sex, and social class. Overall, the young murderers were significantly more likely to have come from a violent family, to have abused alcohol, to have had severe educational deficiencies, and to have participated in gang activities.[12] More generally, the large body of research on violent youth has suggested a wide range of risk factors including: poor medical care and nutrition during early age as well as prenatally; drug and alcohol dependency; inadequate supervision and ineffective parenting; emotional, physical, and sexual abuse; poverty; learning disabilities and academic problems; isolation from peers or contact with delinquent peers; and exposure to violent media and entertainment, among many others.[13] Yet none of these conditions, even in combination, is sufficient to produce homicidal behavior. Risk factors represent predispositions, not predestination.

Explaining the 1990s Decline

Just as the increase in the U.S. homicide rate in the late 1980s and early 1990s can be linked to the crack epidemic, the subsequent decline can also be associated, at least in part, with a contraction or maturation of the crack market.[14] Typical of most fads in the marketplace—from Furbies in the toy world to skirt length in the fashion industry—the crack market passed through a natural evolutionary process. Although there had been street warfare over market shares in the early years of the drug, by the 1990s, the turf lines were being settled through survival of the fittest and the fiercest. Certain drug sellers were able to muscle or shoot out the competition—many of the losers had been incarcerated, had been killed, or had moved away from their neighborhood in a big city—and the crack frenzy began to dissipate. Also by virtue of some widely publicized horror stories about the dangers of crack (e.g., the death of basketball star Len Bias), the demand for crack dwindled.

The crack market had largely devastated a particular cohort—those born from 1968 to 1974, especially blacks. When the crack market first hit the streets in the mid-1980s, they were old enough to be up to taking the risk, but not old enough to know better. Known as the "big brother effect," those born after the early 1970s were scared away from crack by the devastation they saw in their older siblings and others in their communities. As a result, the rate of homicide by young black males in particular plummeted in the mid-1990s. As shown in Figures 5.6a and 5.6b, while similar trends existed for white and black males, the rise and subsequent fall in homicide were especially steep among young black males.

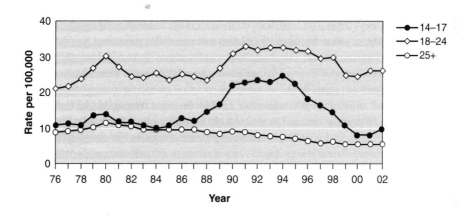

FIGURE 5.6A *Homicide Offending Rates by Age, White Males, 1976–2002*

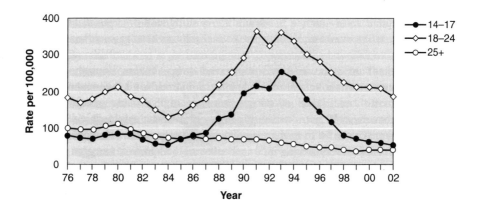

FIGURE 5.6B *Homicide Offending Rates by Age, Black Males, 1976–2002*

On a statistical basis, murder by juveniles actually has fallen since 1993, but it fell from a level that was an all-time record when the crack epidemic wreaked havoc on America's youngsters, especially minority youth in urban centers such as New York, Chicago, and Baltimore. It would be a serious mistake to frame the decline in crack-related violence as solely a market driven trend that law enforcement passively watched from the sidelines, waiting for this fad to play itself out. Rather, police agencies, in implementing community-oriented strategies, had much to do with arresting the violence associated with crack, as well as guns and gangs. In Boston, for example, the police negotiated a cease-fire with warring gangs after having gotten everyone's attention by sending away to prison a major gang leader on federal weapons charges. The New York City police confiscated guns from the hands of teenagers through aggressive (aka "zero-tolerance") stop-and-frisk strategies.

It would also be a mistake to leave the impression that the decline in youth murder was solely a result of the decline in the drug wars or police intervention. The level of youth violence subsided not only for murder but over a range of episodes from simple assault to rioting, first in large cities but eventually in smaller cities as well. Perhaps precipitated by the incredible growth of violence associated with big-city drugs, many Americans around the country became desperate for solutions. Afraid to walk the streets in their own neighborhoods or to do shopping downtown, they became sick and tired of feeling like victims. In urban centers across the country, residents sought to re-establish a sense of community as they began to recognize that they could make a difference in the lives of local youth. At the grassroots level, parents, teachers, psychologists, religious and business leaders, social workers, college students, and the police worked together to repair the moral, social, and economic damage done to young people over a period of 20 years and to take the glamour out of destructive behavior. Through a myriad number of new programs, adults gave back to teenagers, especially what they had lacked for more than two decades—more supervision, structure, guidance, and hope for the future.[15]

Local schools were at the center of effective community efforts to reverse the scourge of teenage violence, often taking on responsibilities previously performed by the family. High school principals adopted a strict policy regarding students who carried firearms to school, making classrooms safer from the threat of gun violence. During the 1996–97 school year, there were an incredible 6,093 expulsions for gun possession in schools around the country. In addition, by means of effective conflict resolution programs built into the curriculum, many local schools began teaching their students what parents used to teach: to have empathy for victims, to control their anger, and to manage their impulsive behavior. Finally, schools provided what was lacking after the school day ended—adult supervision, guidance, and control. No wonder, then, that for most of our children and teenagers, the school hours were by far the safest hours of the day.

Schools were not the only local institutions that stepped forward to fill guiding roles. Churches ran athletic and gun-buy-back programs. Community policing placed more officers in strategic positions in high-crime areas. Probation officers rode in patrol cars to keep an eye on youthful probationers. Increasing numbers of local college students served as mentors, tutors, and peer-mediators in neighborhood schools. Parents and teachers volunteered more to supervise after-school programs in athletics, drama, and art. Local businesses generated more summer jobs, at least some of which led to careers with the companies. More community centers opened their doors to local teenagers. Municipalities beefed up funds for community policing, with residents forming more partnerships with police.

In Boston, which has been seen as a model in dealing with teenage crime,[16] the murder count plummeted from 34 teen offenders in 1990 to only 3 in 1998. Over the same period, the city saw a proliferation of programs geared toward at-risk teenagers. The "wake-up call" for Boston's community leaders came during a funeral service in 1992 at the Morning Star Baptist Church. As a crowd of mourners looked on in horror, a gang of local youngsters chased another teenager into the church, where they repeatedly stabbed him into submission. Shocked by this crime, a group of local Boston ministers decided that enough was enough, and that it was time to act. Rather than wait for troubled youngsters to come to their churches, they decided to take their congregations to the streets and the gangs, working with the police to identify the most recalcitrant young offenders and to provide alternative programs for those teenagers whose lives could be turned around.

Boston's attack on juvenile violence has been multi-faceted, emphasizing prevention, tough and effective law enforcement, as well as the formation of partnerships with local residents. The community policing effort has increased communication between police and neighborhood youngsters. Perhaps taking their cue from Boston's churches, moreover, other local institutions—businesses, government, universities, schools, police, and parents—were suddenly more willing to get involved in the lives of local youth. The juvenile crime rate in Boston finally began to reverse direction, and sharply so.

The Boston model continues to influence public policy nationwide. Although generating much political controversy concerning the separation of church and state, President George W. Bush's emphasis on allowing federal funding for faith-based organizations is an attempt to bring the church into the loop of providing services to at-risk youth as well as ex-offenders, the homeless, the hungry, substance abusers, those with HIV and AIDS, and welfare-to-work families.

Because of all these efforts in Boston and elsewhere, the rate of youth homicide is back where it was before the deadly crack wars in the late 1980s and early 1990s. Moreover, the nation's murder rate in general seems to have stabilized—virtually unchanged from 1999 through 2002. This is not the time, however, to rest on our laurels or to conclude that youth violence is no longer a problem. To the contrary, there are indications that gang-related murder is once again on the rise. As shown in Figure 5.4, the number of gang-related killings has nearly doubled since 1999, back to the level witnessed during the early 1990s. This sharp increase can be traced primarily to the Los Angeles area and to a lesser extent to Chicago. But, as we learned painfully during the last wave of gang violence, what starts on the West Coast can eventually spread across the nation.

There are several reasons why gang violence has re-emerged. First, many of the gang leaders who were sent away to prison in the '80s and early '90s are returning back to their old neighborhoods and their old gang affiliations. At the same time, young recruits who did not witness the bloodshed in those earlier years are attracted to the excitement, thrill, and status of gang membership. Finally, many cities have slashed their budgets for anti-gang initiatives, believing that the problem had been resolved. Hopefully, cities will respond quickly, before gang violence gets anymore out of hand.

Selling Evil

Despite the magnificently successful effort in Boston as well as elsewhere to reduce the level of teenage violence, especially that related to street gangs and guns, the problem is hardly resolved. Although crack- and gang-related violence may have taken a nosedive, the nation must still contend with long-term issues, from supervision and television (too little of one and too much of the other) to adolescent angst and alienation.

It is easy enough to implicate the mass media—especially motion pictures, television, and video games—for the occurrence of hideous violence on a national level. Certainly, there is a good deal of evidence collected over several decades that a steady diet of media-depicted violence can help to desensitize our young people, distorting their perceptions of social reality, and even inspiring hideous, brutal crimes. And the average child now grows up observing tens of thousands of murders on TV, more than 100,000 acts of violence. Cumulatively, this has an effect, although the exact size and nature of the effect have been debated for almost as long as television has existed.

Communication research conducted for decades suggests that people who watch many hours of television every day tend to overestimate the percentage of the world population that is white and male, underestimate the amount of poverty in our country, and exaggerate the amount of violence they are likely to encounter. Heavy viewers also overestimate the proportion of jury trials in our courts and the number of miracle cures performed by doctors. They are socialized to accept a false view of social reality because this is precisely what they see on TV every evening beginning at 8 p.m.

According to George Gerbner, those children who view excessively tend to develop what he has labeled a "mean world view."[17] Wherever they look—in their neighborhood after dark, on the streets on the way to school, on the playground with their peers—they see violence and the threat of violence. They grow up feeling intimidated, threatened, and paranoid. In line with the television version of life, they exaggerate their likelihood of becoming a victim of violent crime.

Everywhere you turn on the TV dial, you find violence. Because violence sells, it keeps the ratings high, it keeps programs on the air; it is entertaining.[18] The list of violent programs seems *endless—Inside Edition, Dateline NBC, America's Most Wanted, 20/20, 60 Minutes, 48 Hours, Walker Texas Ranger, Martial Law, NYPD Blue, Law and Order,* not to mention all local and network newscasts. Actually, our entire popular culture has increasingly become a culture of murder and violence. Rap lyrics proudly extol the virtues of shooting women and attacking whites, gays, and the police. Heavy metal musically expresses themes in which blacks, immigrants, gays, and women are brutalized. White power rock calls for a racial holy war, which white Christians would ultimately win.

Even more troubling, perhaps, are the new forms of hero worship that have always been an integral part of the process whereby young people—adults in training—are socialized to internalize society's most cherished norms and values. Over the decades, we have celebrated those members of society who have reached the pinnacle of success in their fields by honoring them in movies, documentaries, magazine profiles, and even on trading cards. More recently, we have extended our celebration to what some consider our new anti-heroes, those who have distinguished themselves in the worst possible ways by reaching the pinnacle of "success" as murderers. We celebrate evil.

Professional wrestling could be a metaphor for the way that we now honor wrongdoing. Prior to the 1990s, wrestling matches represented morality plays, featuring good against evil. During the 1980s, for example, Hulk Hogan was widely regarded as a paragon of virtue—until he was caught pumping himself up with steroids. By the mid-1990s, professional wrestling was looking more and more like an episode of the Jerry Springer Show—Hulk had become Hollywood Hogan, and he was joined by a lengthy list of filthy fighters with names like "The Undertaker" and "Chainsaw Charlie." Most of the good guys were gone from the ring and were replaced by a host of evil wrestlers battling evil wrestlers.

In 1985, the *National Lampoon* spoofed America's glorification of murderers by publishing a series of Mass Murderer Trading Cards, complete with photos, autographs, and statistics on "all your favorite slayers." As a parody, the *Lampoon* had placed despicable multiple killers in a context generally reserved for superstars.

What was meant as social satire in 1985 has since become a social reality. In 1991, a California trading card company published its first series of mass and serial killer cards, spotlighting such infamous criminals as Jeffrey Dahmer, Theodore Bundy, and Charles Manson. Selling for ten dollars per pack (without bubble gum), it was no joke. Several other card makers soon followed suit, hoping to cash in on the celebrity of multiple murderers.

Even comic books have been used as a vehicle for celebrating the exploits of vicious killers like Jeffrey Dahmer, rather than traditional superheroes. By giving him a starring role once held by the likes of Batman and Superman, the killer is unnecessarily glorified, as in Marshall McCluhan's famous adage, "the medium is the message." The victims' memory is trivialized by placing them in a comic book format.

In a more respectable context, the coveted cover of *People* magazine has become a spotlight for infamous criminals. It was bad enough that Milwaukee's confessed cannibal Jeffrey Dahmer was on the cover of *People* three times, an honor usually reserved for Hollywood stars and Washington politicians. But this magazine also chose Dahmer as one of its "25 Most Intriguing People of 1991" and later placed him on its list of the "100 Most Intriguing People of the Century."

Consider how *People* magazine has changed since the 1970s when celebrities selected for the cover included First Lady Pat Nixon, Barbara Walters, Richard Burton, Joe Namath, Ralph Nader, and Mary Tyler Moore—individuals who were honored for their achievements in politics, industry, sports, and entertainment. By the late 1980s, many of the cover stories had turned negative—JFK and the mob, Robin Williams's love affair with his son's nanny, Jimmy Swaggart's sex scandal, Drew Barrymore's alcoholism, Kristy McNichol's drug addiction, the troubled life of Christina Onassis, why everyone hates Robin Givens, the scandal behind the Tawana Brawly rape case, and on and on. And finally, *People*'s covers began to feature rapists, murderers, and other criminals: Robert Chambers (the preppie murder case), schoolyard sniper Laurie Dann, Leona Helmsley, Mike Tyson, Joel Steinberg, Jim and Tammy Bakker, Charles Stuart, the Menendez brothers, Amy Fisher, David Koresh, Heidi Fleiss, the Bobbitts, O. J. Simpson, Luke Woodham, Louise Woodward, and, of course, Jeffrey Dahmer.

Television has also helped to turn our criminals into celebrities. Docudramas—the "Sunday Night True Crime Movie of the Week"—are often biographies of vicious criminals—many of whom are played by leading actors and actresses, like Mark Harmon as Theodore Bundy, Brian Dennehy as John Wayne Gacy, and Jean Smart as Aileen Wuornos. Having glamorous actors cast in the role of vicious killers unfortunately infuses these killers with glamour and romance. In addition, a variety of news magazine programs regularly feature the biographies of multiple murderers, delving into every minute detail of their past. Highlighting the way in which they suffered as children places them unjustifiably in the role of helpless victims.

The glorification of mass killers has created a big-money market for almost anything that they say or do: the artwork of John Wayne Gacy who got the death penalty for killing 33 young men and boys in Des Plaines, Illinois; the paintings of mass murderer Richard Speck, who slaughtered 8 nurses in Chicago; the refrigerator in which Jeffrey Dahmer had stored his victims' body parts; songs written by Charles Manson; the poetry of Danny Rolling, who brutally tortured, killed, and mutilated five college students in Gainesville, Florida; the writings of Theodore Kaczynski, the Unabomber; T-shirts bearing the image of serial killer Ted Bundy; and calendars featuring the Hillside Strangler, Kenneth Bianchi.

Celebrating evil and murder in popular culture may be having a particularly profound impact on teenagers who want to feel important but are routinely ignored by parents, peers, and teachers. The lesson for youngsters may be: Behave yourself and adults won't notice; go on a rampage at school, and you become a big-shot superstar.

Almost 60 percent of our children and teenagers lack adequate parental supervision, living with a single working parent or in a household where both parents hold full-time jobs.[19] Although many may enjoy substitute forms of supervision provided by extended family, neighbors, or day care, as many as 5 million youngsters have no regular monitoring by adults. As a result, many children come home from school to an empty house, grab milk and cookies from the refrigerator, and watch anything they want on their own TV. If their sets lack cable channels showing their choice of a grotesque movie, they can always run down to the video rental center a block away and rent a nasty R or unrated movie. Or, they can play a violent video game in which they rehearse—in a virtually realistic manner—stabbing, shooting, bombing, or running down other people. Or, they can surf the Internet, visiting an array of pornographic, violent, and hate-filled Websites.

In some respects, violence in television and film, which has been the focus of most of the debate, is relatively tame. It represents a passive form of entertainment, as compared to the more active participation provided by video games. Rather than just lie on the living-room couch and witness a massacre on television, children can cybernetically kill on demand—and learn to enjoy it—through one of many violent action games available to them in computer game stores or on the Internet. Although these games are fantasy, with multimedia sound and advanced graphics, the line between virtual reality and stark reality can become rather thin.

Concern for the effects of violent entertainment of all forms on impressionable children is hardly new. As early as the 1960s, parents and child advocates were alarmed about exposing young viewers to unrealistic images of "cleaned-up violence." That is, because television programs and motion pictures of the day failed to depict the destructive aspects of punching, stabbing, and shooting, youngsters were growing up believing that violence didn't have consequences. In order to placate anxious parents, moreover, a voluntary code of the motion picture industry—movie ratings—was established to give them an opportunity to censor their children's viewing choices.

Beginning in the 1970s, the problem of sanitized film violence was replaced by a much more troubling phenomenon. In order to lure young people to the box office, producers frequently gave them exactly what they wanted—more graphic sex and violence. The movie rating system soon became a media version of "forbidden fruit"—more a guide for children in determining what they really "must see" than a guide for parents on what their children must not see. Experimental studies of factors influencing viewer selection have found that teenaged boys, in particular, prefer programs and films with an R rating or a parental warning, regardless of their content.[20] From the perspective of a young viewer, if you're not part of the "mature audience," then you must be part of the "immature audience," and what self-respecting, red-blooded American adolescent wants to be labeled that?

Experiments have also shown that a steady diet of R-rated films in which violence and sex are fused together actually desensitizes youngsters to the plight of rape victims and tends to make them more aggressive. For teenagers who are having trouble making the transition into adulthood, such films may also confuse them into believing that they cannot have sex without violence, that the one is inseparable from the other.[21]

The impact of media violence can be aggravated or mitigated, depending on the circumstances in which children grow up. It isn't that the mass media are so powerful; it is that our other institutions—our families, our schools, our churches and synagogues, our neighborhoods, our businesses, our political system—have become so weak with respect to raising children.

In Japan, by contrast, television programs are much more violent than their American counterparts. Yet the level of street violence in Japan remains comparatively low. Part of the reason involves the continuing power of Japanese traditional values on its youth. But another important difference is that Japanese parents hardly use television as a babysitter the way that it is more typically used in the United States. In Japan, children watch television with an adult—a parent, a grandparent, a family friend—who monitors, guides, interprets, and explains. This is the crucial difference.[22] Thus, the fundamental issue is not just what children are watching, but who is watching the children.

In the United States, rather than provide creative alternatives to parental supervision, politicians and entertainment industry leaders have sought to develop a method for allowing parents to continue working full-time while still having remote control over their children's access to violent television. As of January 2000, all new TV sets (with at least 13-inch screens) must come equipped with a V-chip (V for violence), with which parents theoretically can filter out the most offensive programs from their children's after-school viewing options.

It may be naive to assume that unsupervised teenagers—left alone in front of their V-chip controlled TV sets—will instead tune into *National Geographic,* read Shakespeare, or take up chess. More likely, they will bypass their parents' attempts at absentee censorship by renting a grotesque film on videotape, play a violent video game, or listen to the hate-filled lyrics of rap and heavy metal on the family CD player. Or, they might just go over to a friend's house whose parents don't use a V-chip.

Looking Ahead

Citizen concern over the impact of television, motion pictures, video games, and the Internet on children continues to be strong. Of course, the possibility of an angry public response to media violence may be expected to fade, as more and more Americans realize that the crime rate is on its way down. Indeed, in the face of rosy crime statistics, citizens may come to believe falsely that we have won the war against youth violence.

Complacency would be a terrible mistake. We dare not relax our efforts in the area of youth crime because we have a new crop of teens every five years—today's teen will be tomorrow's young adult, and today's child will be tomorrow's adolescent—with each new cohort of teens looking to express its passion for rebellion and thirst for excitement. In addition, demographic change could make matters worse. The next few years will bring an expansion of the teenage population as the so-called baby-boomerang generation (children of the baby boomers) matures into adolescence.

There are about 40 million children in America under the age of 10, more than at any time since the original baby boomers were in grade school. This newest group of youngsters will be teenagers before too long. Over the next few years, the number of teens, ages 14 to 17, will swell, which may indeed bring increased problems of teen suicide, venereal disease, drug abuse, joblessness, and, of course, violence. The growth in the youth population will be particularly great among blacks and Latinos.

Given the difficult conditions in which many of these youngsters grow up—with inferior schools, disrupted homes, and violence-torn neighborhoods—many more of them will be at risk in the years ahead. The hopeful news is that there is still time to stem the tide—to prevent the next wave of youth crime. But we must act now while this baby-boomerang generation is still young and impressionable and will be impressed with what a teacher, a preacher, or some other authority figure has to say. If we wait until these children reach their teenage years and another wave of youth killings is upon us, it may be too late to do much about it. It is far easier and considerably less expensive to build the child than to rebuild the teenager. It is more effective to "prehabilitate" early than to rehabilitate later. At the same time, we should never be willing to give up on an entire generation of youngsters, even if they have reached their teenage years lacking what might have helped place them in the mainstream. Indeed, most teenagers with a juvenile record do not grow into adult offenders.

Even if youth homicide were to increase in the years ahead, the overall murder rate should continue to decline. This is because the fastest-growing segment of the population consists of senior citizens. The 65 million baby boomers, hardly babies anymore, are fast becoming card-carrying members of AARP, doing their part to bring down the crime rate just by aging. It is important, however, that we not be fooled by the graying of America, and be blind to the problems of youth. The future of American society may depend on our collective ability to reach unsupervised youngsters, to make them feel that someone besides a drug dealer cares about them.

Endnotes

1. James Alan Fox, "The Coming Juvenile Crime Storm," *Population Today,* September 1996.

2. John J. DiIulio, "The Coming of the Super-Predators." *The Weekly Standard* (November 27, 1995): 23–28.

3. Alfred Blumstein, "Youth Violence, Guns, and the Illicit Drug Industry," *Journal of Criminal Law and Criminology* 86 (1995): 10–36.

4. See Joseph F. Sheley and James D. Wright, *In the Line of Fire: Youth, Guns and Violence in Urban America.* New York: Aldine, 1995.

5. David Hemenway, Deborah Prothrow-Stith, Jack Bergstein, Roseanna Ander, and Bruce Kennedy, "Gun Carrying Among Adolescents," *Law and Contemporary Problems* 59 (1996): 39–53.

6. Cheryl Maxson, "Gang Homicide: A Review and Extension of the Literature," in M. Dwayne Smith and Margaret A. Zahn, eds., *Homicide: A Sourcebook of Social Research.* Thousand Oaks, CA: Sage Publications, 1999.

7. See Jeffrey Fagan and Deanna L. Wilkinson, "The Functions of Adolescent Violence," in Delbert S. Elliott, Beatrix A. Hamburg, and Kirk R. Williams, eds., *Violence in American Schools: A New Perspective.* New York: Cambridge University Press, 1998.

8. Felix M. Padilla, *The Gang as an American Enterprise.* New Brunswick, NJ: Rutgers University Press, 1992.

9. See David Matza, *Delinquency and Drift.* New York: Wiley, 1964.

10. Elijah Anderson, *Code of the Street: Decency, Violence, and the Moral Life of the Inner City.* New York: W. W. Norton, 1999.

11. Franklin E. Zimring, *American Youth Violence.* New York: Oxford University Press, 1998.

12. Kenneth G. Busch, Robert Zagar, John R. Hughes, Jack Arbit, and Robert E. Bussell, "Adolescents Who Kill," *Journal of Clinical Psychology* 46 (1990): 472–485.

13. Rolf Loeber and David P. Farrington, eds., *Serious and Violent Juvenile Offenders.* Thousand Oaks, CA: Sage Publications, 1998. David P. Farrington, "Predictors, Causes and Correlates of Male Youth Violence," in Michael and Mark H. Moore, eds., *Youth Violence.* Chicago: University of Chicago Press, 1998.

14. Andrew Lang Golub and Bruce D. Johnson, *Crack's Decline: Some Surprises Among U.S. Cities.* Washington, DC: National Institute of Justice, 1997. Alfred Blumstein, "Disaggregating the Violence Trends," in Al Blumstein and Joel Wallman, eds., *The Crime Drop in America.* New York: Cambridge University Press [forthcoming].

15. Jack Levin, "An Effective Response to Teenage Crime Is Possible—and Cities are Showing the Way," *Chronicle of Higher Education* 35 (May 7, 1999): 14.

16. Janet Reno, *Youth Violence, A Community-Based Response—One City's Success Story.* Washington, DC: U.S. Department of Justice, 1996.

17. George Gerbner, *Television and Its Viewers: What Social Science Sees.* Santa Monica, CA: Rand Corporation, 1976.

18. James T. Hamilton, *Channeling Violence: The Economic Market for Violent Television Programming.* Princeton, NJ: Princeton University Press, 1998.

19. James Alan Fox, *Trends in Juvenile Violence: A Report to the United States Attorney General on Current and Future Rates of Juvenile Offending.* Boston: Northeastern University, March 1996.

20. Joanne Cantor and K. S. Harrison, "Ratings and Advisories for Television Programming." In *National Television Violence Study,* Vol. 1 (pp. 361–410). Thousand Oaks, CA: Sage Publications, 1996.

21. Neil M. Malamuth and Edward Donnerstein, *Pornography and Sexual Aggression.* New York: Academic Press, 1984. Edward, Daniel Linz, and Steven Penrod, *The Question of Pornography: Research Findings and Policy Implications.* New York: Free Press, 1987.

22. Jack Levin and William C. Levin, *The Human Puzzle: An Introduction to Social Psychology.* Belmont, CA: Wadsworth, 1988.

6

Well-Schooled in Murder

Just as Americans were beginning to enjoy plunging rates of youth violence and murder, a new phenomenon emerged on the radar screen of crime problems to worry about. On October 1, 1997, 16-year-old Luke Woodham walked into a Pearl, Mississippi, high school just hours after having killed his mother. Pulling a gun out from under his trench coat, the chubby, bespectacled youngster immediately murdered two schoolmates and then sprayed bullets into a crowd of students, injuring seven more. His motive? To take over the school, kill all the students, and escape to Cuba.

In the aftermath of the Pearl, Mississippi, shooting spree, parents, teachers, and students around the country became extremely anxious about school safety. Their fears were more than confirmed by subsequent events. Exactly two months later, on December 1, 1997, 14-year-old Michael Carneal, a freshman at Heath High School in West Paducah, Kentucky, opened fire on an informal prayer circle held in the school's lobby, killing three girls and wounding five other students. Then on March 24, 1998, two boys, 11-year-old Andrew Golden and 13-year-old Mitchell Johnson, pulled the fire alarm at their Jonesboro, Arkansas, middle school and then began shooting at students and teachers as they filed out of the building. When the gun smoke cleared, four students and a teacher were dead, and many more injured.

Months later, it happened twice more in the same week. On Tuesday, May 19th, a Fayetteville, Tennessee, high school senior shot and killed a classmate over a romantic rivalry. Then on Thursday, May 21st, Kipland Kinkel, a 15-year-old freshman from Springfield, Oregon, armed with a .22 caliber semi-automatic rifle, turned his high school cafeteria into a battlefield, after having been suspended a day earlier for bringing a gun to school. At Thurston High, Kinkel killed 2 students and wounded 22 more. At home, he had killed his parents.

Blaming Parents

Elevated juvenile crime rates and well-publicized episodes of school violence have prompted many Americans to question the role of family and parenting. Under the assumption that bad kids are products of bad homes—parents who are neglectful and psychologically or physically abusive—many communities have enacted parental responsibility laws in an attempt to threaten parents with fines or jail time into taking their job more seriously.

Although the important role of parenting cannot be denied, much of the time teenagers become violent despite the best efforts of parents. The struggles of dedicated parents can nowadays be overpowered by the negative influences of peers and media or by a child's emotional and developmental challenges. Until a child is 8 or 9 years of age, it is still realistic to expect the family to exercise a large measure of control over his or her behavior. By the time a youngster has reached the age of 10 or 11, however, adolescence has already set in, making a child incredibly susceptible to peer group influences and everything that goes along with it—video games, violent movies and television, and dangerous Websites on the Internet.

It would, of course, not be possible to hold Bill and Faith Kinkel legally responsible for their son Kip's violent outburst at his high school in Springfield, Oregon, just a short drive up Route 5 from Silverton where the first parental responsibility law was passed. They were executed by their boy in stage one of his deadly assault, yet this has not prevented them from being charged in the court of public opinion. In the aftermath, public sentiment was accusatory: How could they have given their son permission to buy a gun—not one but several, including a semi-automatic rifle? Why didn't they instead get him some help?

The truth is that the Kinkels did try to get their son the help that he needed. For years, they tried to provide him with whatever was required to overcome his learning and social deficiencies. Throughout his childhood, Kip Kinkel never fulfilled his parents' hopes and expectations. Dyslexic and physically awkward, Kip struggled academically and socially. He surely wasn't as talented as his older sister, Kristin, and could never measure up in the eyes of his parents, both of whom were highly regarded schoolteachers. With each failed attempt to find activities and pursuits in which he could excel, Kip Kinkel's frustration only grew more intense.

Regrettably, Kip did seem to have a passion for bomb-making and guns, much of which he learned over the Internet. His cyber-contacts not only provided him with the inspiration but also reinforced his darkening character and mood. As the demands of high school and the perceived disappointment of his parents increased, Kinkel turned his attention to the school shootings in Pearl and Jonesboro. He yearned to feel important, to satisfy his parents' standards, and to be accepted by his classmates.

Copycat Shootings

The recent rash of school shootings has raised questions about what's different about kids today that would explain this kind of behavior. Actually, in many respects, kids today are no different than youngsters from earlier generations. There has been teenage alienation so long as there have been teenagers. There has been school bullying so long as there have been schools. What is different is today's culture and the weapons to which youngsters have access.

Thirty years ago, an angry high school student would not even have considered the idea of bringing a gun into the classroom. Instead, he might have thoughts about breaking a few windows or spray-painting graffiti in order to vent his anger. The notion of turning the school into a battleground would never come to mind. Sadly, because of widely publicized school shootings around the country, youngsters have been given new deadly examples to follow. And getting a gun—even a semiautomatic—is no problem.

In the aftermath of the highly publicized school shootings, most children identified with the pain of the victims. They grieved for the slain students whom they only knew through television reports, discussed their fears with parents and classmates, and prayed that history would not repeat itself in their own school.

Yet more than a few students—those like Kip Kinkel who felt alienated and frustrated—apparently identified instead with the power of the perpetrators—the foundation for the copycat phenomenon. Some may have fantasized, or worse, about following in their "hero's" footsteps. Not only was the new breed of youthful mass killers featured on the covers of most national publications, but there were even Websites published on the Internet that served as a tribute to their bold heroism and martyrdom.

It is no coincidence that nearly all recent episodes of school multiple murders have involved white teenaged boys from small towns. Although this may reflect lesser preparedness in rural areas, the copycat effect is strongest when there is close similarity between hero and follower. A youngster from Oklahoma might identify with the plight of a kindred spirit from Arkansas or Kentucky, whose shooting spree is covered in the news. By contrast, for a black youngster living in a Chicago project, the same episode would not be something with which he could identify.

At the very least, the copycat phenomenon can determine the timing and form of a murderous attack. If the publicized killers strike a school, then they provide the idea to murder in the classroom rather than at a shopping mall or a law firm. If the killers use a firearm, then those who imitate are also likely to use a gun rather than a knife, explosives, or a hammer. Finally, the copycat effect is short-lived, causing a number of similar attacks to be committed over a limited period.

Thus, many vicious murders cluster together in time. For example, in the 1997–1998 school year, when Kip Kinkel went on his shooting spree, there were eight multiple-victim homicides at American Schools—as compared to two during the previous academic year. For a few disturbed individuals, the media hype and publicity given to killers can provide a source of role models for their own behavior, even inspiring them to realize their dreams of stardom and grandeur. There are fads among killers just as there are fads among dress designers.

In September 1988, for example, 19-year-old James Wilson of Greenwood, South Carolina, went on a shooting spree at a local elementary school, killing two innocent children. When the police searched his home, they discovered that Wilson had pinned to his wall a photo of his hero taken from the cover of *People* magazine. His hero was 36-year-old Laurie Dann, a woman who a few months earlier had committed a similar crime at a school in Winnetka, Illinois.[1]

In general, the copycat phenomenon tends to occur when a murder receives much media attention. For example, within days of the widely publicized shooting spree by gunman Colin Ferguson on a Long Island commuter train in December 1993, two men were arrested for making threats of violence against Long Island railroad employees and passengers. Similarly, mass killer George Hennard, Jr., who, in October 1991, shot to death 23 people as they were having their lunch at a Luby's cafeteria in Killeen, Texas, had just watched a videotaped documentary about James Huberty's 1984 rampage at a McDonald's restaurant in San Ysidro, California.

Even motion pictures about fictional killers such as in *Exorcist 3, Warriors,* and *Natural Born Killers* have inspired copycat murders around the country. Just prior to his killing spree in Gainesville Florida, for example, Danny Rolling had seen the film, *Exorcist 3*. Based on characters and scenes in the movie, he called himself "Gemini" and decapitated one of his victims.

Twenty years ago, a child might have been inspired by his or her friends down the block. Now, thanks to the pervasiveness of television, he or she is just as likely to follow the lead of teenagers in Pearl or Springfield. Like their adult counterparts, teenaged killers can be inspired by other killers, but they may also be inspired by fictional portrayals in films and video games. Kip Kinkel had been fascinated with the popular movie version of Shakespeare's *Romeo and Juliet*. In the small town of Moses Lake, Washington, 14-year-old Barry Loukaitis shot to death two students and a teacher after reading Stephen King's short story about a school massacre and watching the film, *Natural Born Killers*.

In June 1998, after a seemingly relentless string of school shooting episodes, summer vacation mercifully arrived. Over a two-month summer vacation, would the contagion effect dissipate? When school opened in the fall, parents were scared. In fact, a 1998 poll conducted by the Shell Oil Company found that three-quarters of parents surveyed were very anxious about school shootings and violence, topping the list of school-related concerns, well ahead of worries about peer pressure, declining academic standards, poor quality of teaching, and limited availability of educational equipment and supplies. For parents, the adage applied: safety first.

Explaining School Massacres

Despite parental concerns arising from the previous year's bloodshed, the 1998–99 school year was relatively uneventful, that is until April 20, 1999, when a school shooting of such immense proportions occurred that it radically, if not permanently, altered public thinking and debate about student safety and security. After months of planning and preparation, 18-year-old Eric Harris and 17-year-old Dylan Klebold armed themselves with guns and explosives and headed off to Columbine High School in Littleton, Colorado, to celebrate Adolph Hitler's birthday in a manner fitting their hero. By the time their assault ended with self-inflicted fatal gunshots, a dozen students and one teacher lay dead.

In understanding the horrific actions of schoolyard snipers, it is as important to examine friendships as it is to delve into family background. At Columbine, Harris and Klebold were generally seen as geeks or nerds, from the point of view of any of the large student cliques—the jocks, the punks, etc. Though excluded from mainstream student culture, they banded together and bonded together with several of their fellow outcasts in what they came to call the "Trench Coat Mafia." The image they attempted to create was clearly one of power and dominance—the gothic incivility, the forces of darkness, the preoccupation with Hitler, the celebration of evil and villainy. Harris and Klebold desperately wanted to feel important; and in the preparations they made to murder their classmates, the two shooters got their wish. For more than a year, they plotted and planned, colluded and conspired to put one over on their schoolmates, teachers, and parents. They amassed an arsenal of weapons, strategized about logistics, and made final preparations—yet, until it was too late, not a single adult got wind of what Harris and Klebold intended to do.

Birds of a feather may kill together. Harris, the leader, would likely have enjoyed the respect and admiration from Klebold, who in turn would have felt uplifted by the praise he received from his revered buddy. In their relationship, the two boys got from one another what was otherwise missing from their lives—they felt special, they gained a sense of belonging, they were united against the world. As Harris remarked, as he and his friend made last-minute preparations to commit mass murder: "This is just a two-man war against everything else."

When the scourge of school shootings emerged, some criminologists speculated that it was just the next phase of the youth violence epidemic. What had started in the inner city, according to this view, had spread to middle America. With the public, the issue of lethal violence inside of schools struck a nerve. Unlike crack and gang violence that had infested primarily minority neighborhoods in the urban core, school shootings occurred in suburbs and rural communities that had been largely immune from the urban bloodshed. Indeed, this may help explain why such extraordinary murders occurred where they did. The residents of towns like West Paducah, Springfield, Littleton, and Pearl felt impervious to crime, violence, and poverty—what they regarded as big-city problems. As a result, they never prepared for the possibility that teenagers in their town might become so alienated and marginalized as to go on a shooting spree at school in order to get even with teachers and classmates. Whereas urban schools initiated programs and policies in the area of conflict resolution, peer mediation, and counseling, small-town and suburban schools tended to rest on their laurels.

Political observers capitalized on this uneven public response to youth homicide in cities versus elsewhere as a clear indication of racism. Most Americans seemed apathetic when, to an increasing extent, black kids were shooting each other, but once murder spread to the hinterlands, the demand for action was heard loud and clear. Although this allegation is likely valid, there was another major change in the pattern of school violence that cried out for media and public attention—the emergence of mass murder.

As shown in Table 6.1, school homicides are actually down, roughly parallel to the decline in youth killings generally. Though homicides arising from a conflict between one victim and one perpetrator are newsworthy at the local level, these episodes rarely make national news, whether or not the participants are black, white, or Latino. Yet the events of the 1997–98 school year got everyone's attention, all the way to the White House, which established a

TABLE 6.1 *Homicides at School*

School Year	Incidents	Victims
1992–1993	43	45
1993–1994	42	45
1994–1995	17	17
1995–1996	25	30
1996–1997	22	24
1997–1998	26	35
1998–1999	12	25
1999–2000	19	21
2000–2001	15	16
2001–2002	2	2
2002–2003	4	4

Adapted from "School Associated Violent Deaths," The National School Safety Center, Westlake Village, CA.

Presidential Advisory Committee in the wake of an episode in Clinton's home state of Arkansas. As the body counts grew larger, murder grabbed the attention of the nation.

Mass murder at school by disgruntled pupils was a scary new wrinkle. A decade earlier, schoolyards were the targets of imbalanced adults looking to hurt society where it hurt the most. School snipers were likely not to be teenagers but middle-aged adults like Laurie Dann, the 36-year-old resident of Glencoe, Illinois, who, in May 1988, went on a rampage with a 22-caliber handgun in a Winnetka elementary school. Actually, there were 12 different school shootings in 1988 through early 1989, the last of which was Patrick Purdy's January assault on the Cleveland Elementary School in Stockton, California. He murdered five Southeast Asian children as they played at recess.

It is not an incidental fact that the recent shootings occurred at schools, rather than at some other location. Notwithstanding research findings suggesting that most schools do not experience serious forms of violence, the school day itself can present certain issues and risks. Not only do children congregate in large numbers while at school, thereby creating occasions for conflict, but the school setting can sometimes breed feelings of inadequacy, anxiety, fear, hostility, rejection, and boredom. For some vengeful or alienated children, school can represent an ideal place, both logistically and symbolically, for getting even or settling a score.

Responses to School Shootings

After Columbine, schools around the nation went on red alert. Many heightened security— installing metal detectors, surveillance cameras, entry control devices, and even armed guards—to try to protect the school setting from the latest threat. Although these responses to the school violence panic are quite understandable, they have cost our school districts hundreds of millions of dollars since 1999, and yet, most of this technology can do little to deter the truly motivated and determined student from seeking revenge. Metal detectors and other security measures are hardly foolproof; there are many ways in which a student can smuggle weapons past these devices. Besides, a vengeful student can still kill his victims in the schoolyard (as in Jonesboro, Arkansas) or even on the bus. Security might even be regarded as a challenge to be overcome by a rebellious student who would like to show up the administration. Overreliance on a law enforcement approach may also give us a false sense of security, causing school officials to think that the problem has been resolved.

Administrators also responded with tough "zero tolerance" policies against weapons or even menacing words, putting students on notice that guns, knives, or threats of violence would not be tolerated. Applied rigidly, this has resulted in the suspension of elementary school children in Georgia for making a list of people they wanted to hurt (including the Spice Girls and Barney, the purple dinosaur), a girl in Colorado who brought the wrong lunch bag to school that contained an apple and a paring knife, and a second-grader in Maryland who made a gun out of construction paper. On other occasions, this no-nonsense stance may have inspired additional feelings of alienation. Six months after the Columbine massacre, another student at the now infamous high school in Littleton was overheard threatening to finish the job.

In the aftermath of the Columbine tragedy, much of the focus (and finger-pointing) was about warning signs that were reportedly missed or ignored. For example, Harris and Klebold had made a movie about blowing up the school. Mitchell Johnson gave his Jonesboro, Arkansas, classmates advance warning that "something big" was going to happen the next day at school. Yet all of the warning signs were disregarded.

Barry Loukaitis, who killed a teacher and two students during a February 2, 1996, shooting spree in his algebra class at Frontier Junior High in Moses Lake, Washington, was fascinated with books and movies about rampaging youth (see Table 6.2). But Loukaitis did more than just consume stories of violence; he also wrote them. Before going on his deadly rampage, Loukaitis had submitted to his English teacher a poem about killing:

> *Murder*
> It's my first murder
> I'm at my point of no return
> I can't let him live now
> He'd go to the cops for sure
> So I finish.
> I look at his body on the floor
> Killing a bastard that deserves to die
> Ain't nothing like it in the world
> But he sure did bleed a lot

Many of the warning signs were even more direct. Mitchell Johnson, Andrew Golden, and Luke Woodham all told friends in advance and in no uncertain terms that they planned to shoot classmates. Whether or not the "confidants" took the shooters' words of warning seriously, the powerful code of silence obeyed by many teenagers may still have discouraged them from "snitching" even if it meant preventing a murder.

Ignored warning signs and threats, on the one hand, and falsely accused students, on the other, have placed school administrators in a quandary. How aggressively should they respond to rumors of a threat, and how can they distinguish misguided but harmless attention-seekers from the truly dangerous outcasts?

The Bureau of Alcohol, Tobacco, and Firearms hopes it has the answer by teaming up with a California software company to test out a computerized threat assessment program for violent students. High-tech right down to its name, the "Mosaic 2000" system evaluates students on a scale from one to ten, to identify the "few bad apples" before they wreak havoc on their classmates.[2] This approach is actually just the latest in a growing list of checklists and guidebooks, available from such diverse groups as the American Psychological Association and the U.S. Department of Education, which attempt to aid school personnel in picking up on the supposedly telltale warning signs of impending violence.[3] Even the FBI is getting into the act, working with educators to develop a list of 60 red flags to help school personnel profile potentially violent students.[4]

Predicting violent behavior, especially in rare and extreme forms, is enormously difficult. In terms of the "few bad apples" theory, there are lots of apples that are not quite perfect in color, size, or shape but are fine just beneath the skin. There are lots of kids who look, act, or dress like our image of the schoolyard shooter—they might wear black trench coats, scary tattoos, or gang headgear. Yet very few of them will translate their deviant adolescent attitudes into dangerous acts of violence. The few accurate predictions will be far outnumbered by the many "false positives."

TABLE 6.2   *Characteristics of Selected School Massacres*

Shooter(s)	Where/When	Victims	Weapon/ Source	School/Size/ Security
Barry Loukaitis, 14	Moses Lake, Wash. 2 p.m., Feb. 2, 1996	1 teacher and 2 students killed, 1 student wounded	30-.30 cal. rifle; home	Frontier Junior High, 600 students, no security guard
Luke Woodham, 16	Pearl, Miss. 8:10 a.m., Oct. 1, 1997	2 students killed, 7 wounded, mother fatally stabbed	30-.30 cal. rifle; home	Pearl High School, 1,000 students, no security guard
Michael Carneal, 14	West Paducah, Ky. 7:30 a.m., Dec. 1, 1997	3 students killed, 5 wounded	.22-cal Ruger pistol; stolen from neighbor's father	Heath High School, 600 students, no security guard
Andrew Golden, 11 & Mitchell Johnson, 13	Jonesboro, Ark. 12:35 p.m., Mar. 24, 1998	1 teacher and 4 students killed, 10 wounded	3 rifles, 7 handguns; stolen from relatives	Westside Middle School, 250 students, no security guard
Kipland Kinkel, 15	Springfield, Ore. 8 a.m., May 21, 1998	2 students killed and more than 20 wounded, killed parents	22-cal. semi-automatic rifle, 2 pistols; presents from father	Thurston High School, 1,400 students, no security guard
Eric Harris, 18 & Dylan Klebold, 17	Littleton, Colo. 11:25 a.m., Apr. 20, 1999	1 teacher and 12 students killed, 23 wounded	Handgun, rifle, and 2 shotguns; some bought by friends	Columbine High School, 1,900 students, armed sheriff's deputy

Adapted and reprinted with permission from *Time Magazine,* May 31, 1999.

In addition, any attempt to single out the potential troublemakers could actually do more harm than good, by stigmatizing, marginalizing, and traumatizing already troubled youth. "Don't play with Johnnie—he's a bad apple." Already ostracized and picked on by his peers, Johnnie will now sense that even the teachers and the administration are against him. The "bad apple" label could even become a self-fulfilling prophesy, encouraging doubly alienated children to act out in a violent manner.

Following the April 1999 attack at Columbine High in Littleton, Colorado, two government agencies—the U.S. Department of Education and the U.S. Secret Service—collaborated to study 37 student-perpetrated school shootings that occurred in the United States from 1974 through 2000.[5] The results were revealing. Many of the attackers had felt bullied or persecuted by other students; many had considered suicide. Most did not threaten their victims prior to their attack, but they had access to weapons and knew how to use them. Yet, the researchers indicated the futility of profiling potential perpetrators. Too many non-violent students had the same characteristics.

Stressing how to identify characteristics of the individual troublemaker also lets schools off the hook. By turning the problem of schoolyard homicide into a lesson in abnormal psychology, the blame can be located outside of the school setting. From this per-

Family Situation	Mental Health	Cultural Influences	Precipitant
Suicidal mother was planning to divorce father	Severe depression; inferiority complex	Movie: Natural Born Killers; book: Stephen King's Rage	Was teased by jock (one of the victims)
Father left family when Luke was 11	Erratic coping skills; lack of empathy; sensitive to insults	Music: Marilyn Manson; heroes: Hitler and Nietzsche	Girlfriend broke up with him, called pudgy and gay
Both parents at home, smart older sister	Depressed; erratic fears; pleaded guilty and mentally ill	Movie: Basketball Diaries; video games: Doom, Quake	Called gay in school paper, had a crush on a female victim
Johnson's parents divorced; Golden's parents both at home	Johnson—a bully and aggressive; Golden—tough and mean-spirited	Johnson—music: Tupac Shakur; video game: Mortal Kombat	Both rejected by girlfriends, Johnson teased for being fat
Both parents at home; smart, popular older sister	Depressed, took Ritalin, then Prozac; loner	Music: Marilyn Manson, Nirvana; Internet junkie	Expelled from school, about to be sent to troubled-youth program
Both from two-parent families; Harris' brother good athlete	Harris took antidepressant Luvox; Klebold shy and sad	Music: Marilyn Manson; hero: Hitler; video games: Doom and Quake	Teased by jocks, labeled "Trench Coat Mafia," called "faggots"

spective, students have to change, not the schools. A recent study of city schools suggests that elementary-level administrators who have failed to institute anti-violence policies and programs are especially likely to take the "abnormal psychology" approach.[6] They tend to regard their students as victims of inadequate upbringing, family conflict, excessive exposure to media violence, and parental abuse and neglect (that is, bad apples not falling far from the tree). Under such circumstances, anti-violence programs in the schools would be mistakenly considered a waste of scarce economic resources.

Focusing on the individual child also ignores the fact that students often act in group settings far differently than when they are alone. To understand the course of events in Jonesboro, Littleton, and Pearl, we must examine the relationships and interactions among the perpetrators as closely as we scrutinize their personal backgrounds and individual pathologies. To children, the expectations and approval of close friends can be all-important, especially when parents and other adults are not around. The issue may not be one of a few bad apples, but of a poorly tended orchard.

The best approach to reducing the potential for violence through prediction involves reducing the caseload of teachers and guidance counselors.[7] Smaller classes and increased staffing would allow school personnel to observe even subtle issues, which cannot be easily determined from a simplistic checklist, an anonymous phone call, or an elaborate computer algorithm. More important, our focus should not be on the potentially violent kid, but on the unhappy kid (although at times these may be one in the same). We should use warning signs, but to reach troubled youngsters, long before they become troublesome. If we wait until a student has murderous intentions, we have waited much too long.

Healthy and Safe Schools

It is likely that eventually we will find that the recent spate of school massacres is an aberration rather than a permanent feature of American public education. Fads come and go, especially those involving youthful perpetrators, and in many respects, crime contagion spreads and expires very much like fads in fashion, dance, and games. At this juncture, the thousands of angry, alienated children in America who are ostracized and bullied have several violent role models to copy. Once the contagion passes, the same children may return to less malicious yet equally vengeful actions like breaking windows, stuffing school toilets, and putting stink bombs in lockers.

Despite the school violence hype and panic, schools actually are the safest place for our kids to be.[8] With structure and regular supervision, the rate of violence in schools (literally one homicide per 1 million schoolchildren) is lower than it is on the street corner, in shopping malls, even at home. Youngsters are more likely to be killed riding their bike to school than they are to be murdered by an armed classmate.

Yet concern with school violence is not completely misplaced and may even motivate much positive change. As noted in the recent school violence research of Crystal Garcia, officials charged with developing school safety plans have begun to recognize that costly weapon detection systems and cumbersome entry control devices are not the school violence panaceas that many had hoped they would be.[9] In fact, administrators now acknowledge that these technologies are fairly ineffective at preventing serious school violence and in some instances may violate students' rights. Principals have looked to invest in other strategies—mainly school resource officers, security guards, mental health personnel, and prevention programs. For example, many high school and middle school principals have recognized violence prevention as a priority and adopted effective conflict resolution and peer mediation programs, have encouraged after-school programs, have instituted anti-hate curricula, and have worked to bring community resources into the school in the form of tutors and mentors.

There are also efforts underway to bring about structural changes that would give more attention to children who desperately need it. Such measures include reducing the size of the schools and the size of the classes, extending the school day, providing meaningful alternative school programming for suspended and expelled students, reinstating extracurricular activities that have fallen victim to budget cuts, hiring more school psychologists and guidance counselors, expanding school resource officer programs, recruiting parents to help patrol crime prone areas such as parking lots and athletic fields, and bringing other volunteers from the community to meet with needy students.

One of the most promising strategies adopted by administrators around the country in the aftermath of the school slaughters was to respond directly and aggressively to bullying. Rather than ignoring incidents of harassment and intimidation or recommending that victims stand up and fight back, educators are intervening in two ways to prevent bullying: by implementing programs designed to increase sensitivity and empathy among students and teachers to the plight of victims, and by training staff to recognize even subtle forms of intimidation.

Without destroying the civil liberties of young people and harming many innocent students with false accusations, we may never be able to identify each and every would-be shooter before he opens fire in a crowded classroom. Even if reliable predictions were possible, we may not be able to intervene effectively in all cases. By contrast, focusing on changing schools rather than schoolchildren has much broader potential. In the process of improving school climate, we can enhance the health and well-being of all children and, at the same time, hopefully avert senseless murder.

Endnotes

1. James Alan Fox and Jack Levin, *Overkill: Mass Murder and Serial Killing Exposed.* New York: Plenum Press, 1994.

2. Lisa Richardson, "Schools Testing Threat Analysis," *The Los Angeles Times,* December 18, 1999, p. B3.

3. American Psychological Association, *Warning Signs.* Washington, DC, 1999. U.S. Department of Education, *Early Warning, Timely Response: A Guide to Safe Schools.* Washington, DC, 1998.

4. Janet Bingham, "FBI Puts 'Risk List' Out for Schools: 60 Factors to Help ID Violent Students," *The Denver Post,* November 9, 1999, p. A1.

5. United States Secret Service and United States Department of Education, "The Final Report and Findings of the Safe School Initiative: Implications for the Prevention of School Attacks in the United States," Washington, DC, May 2002.

6. Jack Levin and Heather Beth Johnson, "Youth Violence and the Urban Public School Response," *Journal of Research in Education* 7 (1997): 3–7.

7. See Denise C. Gottfredson, *School Size and School Disorder.* Baltimore, MD: Center for Social Organization of Schools, Johns Hopkins University, 1985.

8. Elizabeth Donohue, Vincent Shiraldi, and Jason Ziedenberg, *School House Hype: School Shootings and the Real Risks Kids Face in America.* Justice Policy Institute, September 15, 1998.

9. Crystal A. Garcia and Sheila S. Kennedy, "Back to School: Technology, School Safety and the Disappearing Fourth Amendment," *Kansas Journal of Law and Policy* (2003): 273–288.

7

Serial Killers

Thanks in part to a fascination with anything that is "serial," whether it be murder, rape, arson, or robbery, there has been a tendency to focus a good deal of attention on the timing of repeated murders. Thus, the FBI distinguishes between spree killers who take the lives of several victims over a short period of time without a "cooling off" period versus serial killers who murder a number of people over weeks, months, or years, but in between their attacks live relatively normal lives.[1] In 1990, for example, Danny Rolling brutally murdered five college students in Gainesville, Florida, at three different crime scenes over a 72-hour period, and therefore technically qualifies as a spree killer. Similarly, Andrew Cunanan, in 1997, murdered four victims—two in Minneapolis, one in Chicago, and another in New Jersey—over the period of a few days. He too would appear to fit the definition of a spree killer.

The problem is that the distinction between spree and serial can easily break down. Staying on the loose after killing his four victims, Cunanan turned up in Miami two months later when he shot to death fashion designer Gianni Versace. Cunanan's revised body count—five victims—was accumulated over a period of months, not days. Is he still a spree killer or is he a serial murderer? Or, does it really matter that much?

It turns out that Danny Rolling had slaughtered three people in Shreveport, Louisiana fully eight months before his Gainesville attacks. Should Rolling be labeled a serial killer? Or, should he instead be regarded as a mass killer for murdering the three Louisiana victims in a single assault? Again, does it really matter?

The point is that rigidly focusing on the timing of attacks, while interesting, is far less important to our understanding of multiple homicide than attempting to assess the killer's motivation. It might also be valuable to distinguish full-time from part-time repeat killers, whether or not they choose to murder their victims over a short or long period of time. Over a three week time span in October 2002, the DC Snipers took the lives of 10 people. During this entire period, aside from eating and sleeping, their time was apparently consumed by planning, executing, escaping, and hiding from the police. For most serial killers, murder is a part-time hobby. They typically return to their normal activities—holding a job, attending classes, playing with their children—after every murder they commit.

It should also be noted that we tend to overlook certain types of serial killers, even when their body counts are high. Most media attention is focused on sexual sadists. Little attention is given to mothers who kill their children, nurses who poison their patients, or armed robbers who repeatedly take the lives of their victims.

Because of the massive publicity devoted to such crimes as the grisly slayings of at least 17 males by cannibalistic necrophile Jeffrey Dahmer, the term "serial murder" has become part of everyday vocabulary. Serial killers like David Berkowitz ("Son of Sam"), Kenneth Bianchi ("The Hillside Strangler"), and Theodore (better known as Ted) Bundy are featured in prime-time TV docudramas and mass market paperbacks, no longer just in obscure detective magazines. Stretching the limits of decency, moreover, serial killers have, as described in Chapter 5, clearly become a fixture in our popular culture, featured in both trading cards and comic books as well as on T-shirts. Further glamourizing and romanticizing their crimes, journalists and true-crime writers often assign colorful nicknames to their murderous activities (see Table 7.1).

It is difficult to gauge the full extent of serial homicide. Because of complexities in linking murders committed by the same perpetrator but at different times and even differ-

TABLE 7.1   *Selected Serial Killer Monikers*

Killer(s)	*Moniker*	*Killer(s)*	*Moniker*
Richard Angelo	Angel of Death	Carlton Gary	The Stocking Strangler
David Berkowitz	Son of Sam	Ed Gein	The Ghoul of Wisconsin
Kenneth Bianchi & Angelo Buono	The Hillside Stranglers	Vaughn Greenwood	The Skid Row Slasher
William Bonin & Vernon Butts	The Freeway Killers	Donald Harvey	Angel of Death
Ian Brady & Myra Hindley	The Moors Murderers	William Heirens	The Lipstick Killer
Jerry Brudos	The Shoe-Fetish Slayer	Theodore Kaczynski	Unabomber
Ted Bundy	Ted	Patrick Kearney	The Trash Bag Murderer
David Carpenter	The Trailside Killer	Edmund Kemper III	The Co-Ed Killer
Richard Chase	The Vampire of Sacramento	Paul Knowles	The Casanova Killer
Douglas Clark	The Sunset Strip Killer	George Metesky	The Mad Bomber
John Norman Collins	Co-Ed Murderer	John Allen Muhammad & Lee Boyd Malvo	The DC Snipers
Adolfo De Jesus Constanzo	Godfather of Matamoros	Richard Ramirez	The Night Stalker
Dean Corll	The Candy Man	Melvin David Rees	The Sex Beast
Juan Corona	The Machete Murderer	Gary Leon Ridgway	The Green River Killer
Jeffrey Dahmer	The Milwaukee Monster	Timothy William Spencer	The Southside Slayer
Albert DeSalvo	The Boston Strangler	Carol Eugene Watts	The Sunday Morning Slasher
Nannie Doss	The Giggling Granny	Wayne Williams	The Atlanta Child Murderer
Larry Eyler	The Interstate Killer		
Albert Fish	The Cannibal	Randall Woodfield	The I-5 Killer
John Wayne Gacy	Killer Clown		

ent places, no precise estimate of the prevalence of serial killers is even possible. Still, in sharp contrast to the rampant interest and enormous fascination with serial murderers, we can be confident that the rate of serial homicide is far from epidemic. Although a large percentage of all killers featured in TV dramas, news magazine programs, and true-crime books commit serial murder, the death toll linked to serial killers in reality represents only about 1 percent of all murders in the United States, a couple hundred victims per year at most. At the same time, it is sobering to recognize that just a handful of murderers, about one to two dozen annually, can account for as many as 100–200 victims.

A Profile of Serial Killers

There is a multitude of different motives that provoke serial killers and help them to justify their actions. Some, such as Marybeth Tinning discussed earlier in Chapter 4, have slain a series of children to satisfy a pathological need for attention and sympathy. As described later in Chapter 10, a few serial killings have occurred in the context of cult activity. A charismatic cult leader like Charles Manson or Adolfo De Jesus Constanzo inspires his followers to commit homicides, often ritualistic or excessively brutal in nature, both to achieve some political or spiritual goal as well as to nourish the leader's excessive need to be in charge. A few serial killers are driven not by a charismatic cult figure but by the commandments of delusional forces that place them on a relentless mission of murder. Still other serial killings are expeditious cover-ups. "Railway killer" Angel Maturino Resendez, for example, was charged in 1999 with killing nine people in Texas, Kentucky, and Illinois, all near railroad tracks, in the process of robbery and burglary primarily to eliminate the potential victim-witnesses. By far, however, the most common form of serial murder surrounds the killer's quest to satisfy his own sadistic urges or excessive need for control. He exploits his victims as a means of satisfying personal, and often sexual, desires.[2]

There are several myths that have long existed about serial killers, and other legends that are rather recent in origin.[3] One of the oldest misconceptions is that of the serial murderer as a human monster, surely derived from or reinforced by Hollywood creations such as Jason of *Friday the 13th* in which these killing machines are portrayed as glassy-eyed lunatics, whose entire existence is centered on satisfying their compulsion for human destruction.

Actually, it would be somewhat comforting if the Hollywood image were at all accurate. If serial killers indeed looked like crazed maniacs and acted in a patently bizarre fashion, they would be easily avoided on sight. Unfortunately, in very many respects, most serial killers are extraordinarily ordinary, and, as such, extremely deadly.

Quite opposite to the Hollywood stereotype, a more modern image describes these killers as unusually handsome and charming, perhaps generalizing from one of the most celebrated cases of modern years, that of Theodore Bundy who murdered dozens of women from Washington State to Florida and was indeed a "lady killer," in more ways than one. Richard Rameriz, the so-called Night Stalker of Los Angeles, also was sought after by numerous adoring women, even in prison, and actually married one.

Aspiring to marry a convicted and imprisoned serial killer may say much more about the mental health of the brides-to-be than the charm of the killers themselves. Marrying someone in prison is one way an insecure woman can be assured that her man is not cheating on her (at least with other women). He may be behind bars, but not in the bars looking for a good time. She always knows where he is.

It is tempting to focus only on defects in the killer groupies—their lack of self-esteem and bad judgment—to explain their attraction to serial killers. Some of them find a mission in their relationship. They must tell the world that their man is innocent, that he is only a victim of injustice, not a hardened criminal. Others may be reticent about making a commitment, but can claim a relationship on a superficial level. Still others may feel special because their man shared his most personal and intimate thoughts. Only she sees his gentler side.

Aside from the needs of killer groupies, what deserves to be acknowledged as well is society's complicity in making these murderers into attractive and appealing celebrities. In some cases, serial killers have received more national publicity than rock stars or rap artists. Moreover, most serial killers are extremely manipulative. They know exactly how to lure vulnerable women into a relationship, just as they understood how to lure their poor victims into a position of total vulnerability in order to take their lives.

It would be wrong, however, to characterize all, or even most, serial killers as debonaire, charming, and handsome. Some are decidedly undesirable by conventional standards, and still others suffer from intense shyness. In fact, for some serial killers, murder can be their only strategy for seeking sexual gratification and even enjoying the company of others.

Leonard Lake, a middle-age recluse who lived in the woods just east of San Francisco, was painfully aware of his limitations when he outlined on videotape, with chilling calmness and clarity, his motives for abducting women. Balding and paunchy, Lake fully recognized his dilemma. The kind of women to which he was attracted—young women and teenage girls perhaps as young as 12—would not give him the time of day. On the other hand, he had no desire at all for more mature females who might show a sexual interest in him. He decided that he would have to take what he wanted.

As an introverted, quiet type, Lake also disliked most of the non-sexual aspects surrounding the mating ritual. He only really wanted women for sex and housework but had no interest in conversation or companionship. With the help of his buddy Charles Ng, Lake constructed a holding cell inside a bunker next to his home in which he kept a steady supply of slaves. He used them for so long as they were appealing and satisfying and then violently discarded them as human trash.

Although Leonard Lake was as intelligent as he was self-absorbed, it is also part of the modern mythology that serial killers are typically brilliant—like Hannibal Lector from Thomas Harris's novel, *The Silence of the Lambs.* Although some serial killers such as California's Lawrence Sigmund Bittaker have genius-level IQs, others clearly have sub-par intelligence.

Grover Godwin collected data about 107 serial killers and their 728 victims from a variety of sources including local police departments, the FBI, and newspaper reports, but predominantly from the Homicide Investigation and Tracking System (HITS) database in Washington State.[4] All of the cases he examined had been solved. Godwin determined that only 16 percent of the serial murderers he studied had attended college and only 4 percent graduated with a bachelor's degree. The majority were employed in blue-collar jobs working for other people. Regardless of social class, IQ, or level of educational attainment, however, most serial killers—at least those who successfully remain at large for long time periods—typically do possess a certain degree of cunning, criminal *savoir faire* needed to accumulate a significant body count. Many of them are exceptionally skillful in their presentation of self, so much so that they are beyond suspicion and thus are difficult to apprehend.

The most prolific serial killers also tend to be the most organized psychologically. They methodically stalk their victims for the best opportunity to strike so as not to be seen, and they smartly dump the bodies far away so as not to leave any clues. The discovery of a body in a dump site does not provide the crime scene where most of the forensic evidence—hairs, blood, fibers, semen—is located. In a sense, becoming a serial killer is a process of self-selection. A confused assailant who kills in a frenzied way cannot successfully plan, execute, and cover up the crime. The most dangerous, cunning murderers are a great challenge for law enforcement authorities. Notwithstanding advances in forensics, computerized offender tracking, and even behavioral profiling, when these crimes are solved, luck generally plays a significant role.

It may not exactly be fair to law enforcement to characterize these apprehensions as lucky because they still involve the police doing their job. While killers like Theodore Bundy and Gary Heidnik may have been caught in routine traffic stops and Berkowitz was linked to the Son of Sam killings due to a parking ticket, these are obviously important police activities—even if not requiring tremendous technical skill—and highlight the significance of a police presence in our society.

There is also some evidence that the most organized killers can begin to deteriorate over time. Bundy began his killing career with a duffle bag filled with weapons, disguises, and tools and had several ruses he used to lure women (e.g., his arm was in a sling and he needed help loading something into his car). By the time he committed the Chi Omega sorority house murders at Florida State University, however, Bundy used a log he found at the crime scene as his murder weapon and left bite marks on his victim's body. Apparently, Bundy's transformation was from a highly organized to a quite disorganized killer.

The notion that serial killers subconsciously wish to be caught and for this purpose carelessly leave telltale clues at crime scenes or act impetuously and recklessly may hold in detective novels but has little validity when applied to most real cases. When serial killer Andrew Cunanan traveled from the midwest to the east coast in a series of stolen cars, many law enforcement experts speculated that his incautious actions, such as using his victims' cell phones, indicated a latent desire to be apprehended. Despite this wishful thinking on the part of investigators, Cunanan remained at large for months, claiming five victims—two in Minnesota, one each in Illinois and New Jersey, and finally celebrity designer Gianni Versace in Miami. Even as the police cornered him on a Miami houseboat, Cunanan still controlled when, where, and how the killing spree would end. On July 23, 1997, as police and media helicopters circled above, the 27-year-old killer took his own life rather than be taken alive. Perhaps it was a death wish, but clearly not an arrest wish.

Another widely held belief—but one that is true—is that serial killers are typically white males in their late 20s or 30s. Criminologist Eric Hickey has assembled a long-term historical database of nearly 400 serial killers in which 84 percent were male, 20 percent were black, and the average age at which they first committed murder was 27.5.[5] Godwin's results were similar to those obtained by Hickey—in his sample of serial killers, 95 percent were males, 16 percent were black, and their average age was 30.

Despite these commonalities, there are of course exceptions to the white-male rule of thumb. There are more female serial killers than perhaps many casual observers of the topic would believe, although as we shall discuss later how the MO or modus operandi of female serial killers differs significantly from their male counterparts' MO.

Even when the murders committed by women are heinous, cruel, and sexually predatory, the tendency is still to portray the offenders as victims. Karla Homolka fully and willingly participated in the brutal rapes and murders of three girls, one of whom was her own younger sister, to satisfy her own sexual fantasies. Gwendolyn Graham and Catherine Wood, convicted of killing five elderly people in a nursing home (and suspected of as many as 10 deaths in total) used their murders as foreplay, sneaking away afterwards into vacant rooms to have sex and discuss fondly their victims' dying moments. Aileen Wuornos, a Florida prostitute who murdered seven men, told the jurors during her trial that she hoped their daughters would be raped.

Dozens of women have murdered children, stepchildren, husbands, mothers, and fathers for the benefit of collecting on their life insurance. Given the reluctance to label the most brutal female killers as serial predators, profiles of the female serial killers may be off the mark. Much more weight appears to be given to a female killer's past history of child and domestic abuse, portraying her as a victim, as mentally ill, and as not responsible for her actions.[6] Criminologists are only now beginning to recognize the existence of a female sexual predator. Women, like men, can develop deviant psychosexual needs. Women can only begin to achieve equality with men if their predatory, violent, and murderous behavior is acknowledged as a product of their free will to kill, and punished accordingly.

The percentage of black serial killers is not much greater than their population share but appreciably lower than the substantial percentage of blacks among murderers of all kinds. The involvement of blacks in serial murder, however, may be somewhat understated. Serial murder, like murder generally, tends to be intra-racial; serial killings of black victims, especially those who are impoverished and marginalized politically, are less likely to be connected, prioritized for investigation, and subsequently solved. Because of victim characteristics, therefore, black serial killers may be more likely to remain unidentified.

One of the most striking dissimilarities between serial murder and criminal homicide generally is the nature of the victim-offender relationship. Unlike single-victim murder, which commonly arises from some dispute between partners, family members, or friends, serial murder is typically a stranger-perpetrated crime. According to Godwin, some 90 percent of serial killers' victims were total strangers to their assailants; only 3 percent were friends and 1 percent were family members. To some extent, the abundance of stranger victims reflects the predatory patterns of these killers as well as the greater ease with which stranger attackers can escape apprehension and therefore be free to amass a large tally of kills.

In addition to their lack of a prior relationship with their assailants, serial murder victims also tend to share one important trait—their vulnerability. Although virtually anyone can be targeted, serial killers tend to prefer children, prostitutes, and the elderly as victims. To some extent, this may reflect their sexual desires. But this victim preference also reflects the relative ease with which the offenders can abduct and slay certain targets. Pedophile Wesley Allen Dodd of Washington State encountered little difficulty in snatching children from parks and other public spaces. Arthur Shawcross made a habit of trolling Rochester's red-light district, not needing even an ounce of force to find streetwalkers willing to enter his web of control.

Like serial murderers, their victims tend to be white—in Godwin's study, 81 percent. The age range is quite broad, reflecting the disparate classes of favored victims. The gender characteristics of serial killer victims are quite different from those of killers generally. Given the strong sexual element in the motivations of male serial murderers, their victims tend to be female—fully 67 percent. Despite the greater number of females slain, moreover, some serial killers are gay or bisexual and purposely target male victims for rape and murder. In Godwin's study, 20 percent of the victims were males who were raped by their attackers.

One of the most striking and intriguing aspects of serial murderers is the nature of their motivation. Although it has been loosely described as "motiveless," there is indeed one—to satisfy an intense appetite for power and sadism. The serial murderer tends to kill not for love, money, or revenge but just for the fun of it—because it makes him feel good.

The typical serial killer is someone like Hillside Strangler Kenneth Bianchi who, along with his cousin Angelo Buono, raped, tortured, and murdered ten young women in the Los Angeles area in the late 1970s. The "Hillside Strangler" moniker is quite telling. Unlike most other types of murderers, the serial killer hardly ever uses a firearm. Too easy, too clean, and much too distant, a gun would only rob him of his greatest pleasure: exalting in his victim's suffering. Some observers have suggested that to a sexual sadist a gun is phallic, and shooting bullets like an ejaculation[7]; yet very few, if any, serial killers have ever used a gun to sodomize a victim—fists, vegetables, and other objects, but no gun barrels. The sadistic serial killer enjoys the whole experience of murder—squeezing a throat rather than a trigger—squeezing from his victim's body her last breath of life, killing her slowly and with great suffering on her part.

Like Bianchi and his favorite cousin and killing partner Angelo Buono, many serial killers operate in teams—as many as 20 percent. They encourage each other to do the wrong thing and are more likely than their counterparts who operate alone to torture their victims. For Lawrence Bittaker and Roy Norris, killing was a team sport. They called it the "birthday game," seeking to kill teenage girls of different ages (13, 14, 15, etc.), like trophies. Bittaker and Norris preferred blondes and tortured them in their specially equipped van, which they called "Murder Mac." The pair tape-recorded the torture sessions so they could relive them later in their spare time.

Some teams include mixed couples. Doug Clark, the so-called Los Angeles Sunset Strip Killer, did the murdering and decapitating, while his girlfriend, Carol Bundy (no relation to Theodore), assisted. She even prepared the severed heads of victims for him to use as sex objects in the shower. She would do anything for her guy and for the sake of their love. Similarly, Janice Hooker helped her husband, Cameron, abduct young women for his sex torture sessions. So long as her husband had sex slaves around the house, he would leave her alone.

The Murdering Mind

Many laypeople assume that anyone who kills for fun, pleasure, or sport must be psychotic and out of touch with reality. Some serial killers have been driven by severe mental illness, such as Herbert Mullen of Santa Cruz, California, who killed 13 people in a span of four months in order to avert an earthquake—or at least that's what the voices told him.[8]

By contrast, Godwin found little evidence of serial killers suffering from profound mental disorders. Only 28 percent of all the murderers in his study had a history of receiving any kind of treatment for mental illness; even fewer (20 percent) had a history of being treated for alcoholism or drug abuse. Most serial murderers are not insane in a legal sense or psychotic in a medical sense. Though they know right from wrong, know exactly what they are doing, and can control their desire to kill, they typically choose not to do so. Even the serial killers who remember childhood abuse, experience hallucinations, and "discover" multiple personalities at trial time may be suffering from mental disorders manufactured by defense attorneys who employ the insanity plea as a last resort.

Psychologically, most serial killers are sociopaths (or antisocial personality types). They possess a disorder of character rather than of the mind, involving a lack of conscience and feelings of remorse, an inability to feel empathy for others, pathological lying, a manipulative style, impulsivity, and a total concern for maximizing their own pleasures in life.[9] Other people are seen merely as tools for fulfilling their own needs and desires, no matter how perverse or reprehensible. The serial killer is more bad than mad—simply put, he is evil.

Some killers are not only remorseless but are even proud of their conquests and boast to the press, to the relatives of their victims, even to each other with considerable pleasure. Almost half of all serial killers collect souvenirs of their crimes.[10] Joel Rifkin, for example, who in 1993 confessed to murdering 17 prostitutes in New York, kept his victims' underwear, shoes, sweaters, cosmetics, and jewelry in his bedroom. Jeffrey Dahmer proudly displayed pictures of his victims on the walls of his apartment and kept body parts in his refrigerator.

Missouri's Robert Berdella, a 40-year-old man who held captive six male sex slaves, had a particularly rich collection of souvenirs, including two human skulls and over 200 photographs of his victims in a variety of degrading poses before and after death, and with various vegetables inserted into their body cavities. He also chronicled his "human experiments" in a detailed diary of his tortures.

Berdella's collection of souvenirs served several important purposes. First, for a man who had otherwise led an unremarkable life, his treasures made him feel accomplished. They represented the one and only way in which he had ever distinguished himself "as a real pro." More important, the souvenirs became tangible reminders of the "good times" Berdella had spent with his "playmates." With the aid of his photographs, he could still get pleasure, even between captives, from reminiscing, daydreaming, fantasizing, and even masturbating. In fact, serial killers have lasting memories as well as incredibly rich, vivid, detailed, elaborate fantasies. Through murder and mayhem, they literally chase their dreams.[11]

Many serial killers have various paraphilias—sexual attractions to unusual or bizarre objects. Rather than just a fetish (a sexual attraction to a non-human object such as feces or shoes), some have multiple paraphilias including cannibalism, pedophilia and necrophilia. At what point does their paraphilia become a mental disorder that they cannot control? Almost never in a court of law as illustrated by the rejection of Jeffrey Dahmer's plea of insanity based on his necrophiliac and cannibalistic desires.

Even though serial killers tend to be sociopaths, totally lacking in concern for their victims, some actually do have a conscience and the capacity for remorse but are able to neutralize or negate their feelings of guilt. There is a powerful psychological process—known as dehumanization—which allows many serial killers to slaughter scores of innocent people by viewing them as worthless and, therefore, expendable. By targeting marginalized groups—prostitutes, the homeless, runaways—they can rationalize (if they need to for their own sense of emotional comfort) that they are doing something good for society . . . or at least nothing that bad.

Jeffrey Dahmer actually viewed his crimes as a sign of love and affection. He told Tracy Edwards, his final victim who managed to escape and led the police to Dahmer's apartment of horrors, that if he played his cards right, he too could give his heart to Jeff. He meant it literally of course, but, according to Edwards, he said it in an affectionate, not a threatening, manner.

Many serial killers skillfully compartmentalize the world into two groups—those whom they care about and everyone else. Kenneth Bianchi, for example, could be kind and loving to his wife and child as well as his mother and friends, yet be vicious and cruel to those he considered expendable. He and his cousin started with prostitutes (and first a black prostitute for whom they had very little concern), then later, when comfortable with killing, branched out to middle-class, more respectable targets.

According to Stephen Giannangelo, serial killers are also eased into their murderous avocation by the clumsiness and impulsivity of their first kill.[12] He likens the first murder to the sexually inexperienced teenager who fumbles in the backseat of a car as he attempts to have sex with his date. For a serial killer, what might begin as a rape or an assault is transformed in the excitement of the moment into homicide. Almost inadvertently, the killer crosses the threshold separating fantasy from fact. Whatever shame he may feel for having committed a serious offense is completely overshadowed by the "rush" that he acquires from finally discovering what he needs.

It has been estimated that 1 in 20 males in our society could be considered sociopathic. Of course, most sociopaths are not violent: they may lie, cheat, steal, harass, or womanize, but rape and murder are not particularly appealing to them. The other critical ingredient to the profile of the serial killer is a strong tendency toward sexual sadism. More generally, these men have a craving for power and control. They tie up their victims in order to watch them squirm, torture their victims to hear them scream. They rape, sodomize, degrade, bludgeon, and mutilate their victims in order to feel powerful, dominant, and superior.

One of Lawrence Bittaker's victims pleaded, "Please, if you're going to kill me, tell me so that I can pray first." Bittaker was exhilarated by his victim's begging. He assured her that she would not die and then slammed an icepick in her ear. He just loved the control.

The sexual sadist derives intense pleasure through the pain, suffering, and humiliation of another person. In a pure sense, sexual sadists enjoy the act of inflicting pain upon another, non-consenting victim. Yet the pleasure may also flow from the result—the screams and degradation of the recipient, rather than from just the act itself. Sexual sadists can also relish vicariously when another person (an accomplice or even an actor in a film) causes a victim to suffer. Thus, a pair or team of serial killers can enjoy not only personal satisfaction from raping and torturing a victim, but the feeling of superiority can be enhanced by the power of the partnership.

Power and control may be critical themes in the character of serial murderers, yet these traits are also common in many successful people in the worlds of business, politics, and even academics. The willingness to win at all cost, no matter who is hurt in the process, may insulate many winning individuals from looking back at those they exploit along the road to success. A vital difference between serial killers and those who backstab only figuratively may be access to legitimate opportunity.

At the same time, the sadistic sexual fantasies of the serial killer may also pattern the form of his search for power. It appears that many serial murderers, from an early age, become absorbed deeply in a rich fantasy life involving images of sex and violence. As they mature into adolescence, their fantasies become more and more consuming, increasing in their power as internal drive mechanisms that motivate them to cross the line into murderous behavior.

Not all children who fantasize about sadistic forms of violence grow up to be serial killers. The fact that most serial murderers do not initiate their murder sprees until well into their adult years indicates the important role of adult experiences—successes in relationships and at work—in the making of a serial killer. Many individuals who have suffered profoundly as children grow into healthy and non-violent adults. They benefit later from positive experiences with peers, romantic partners, and co-workers who give them the support and encouragement that they lacked when they were young.

This was unfortunately not true of Danny Rolling, who turned to murder at the age of 36, killing three in his hometown of Shreveport, Louisiana, and five more in Gainesville, Florida. Not only had Rolling been the victim of an abusive parent, but his adjustment and personal problems continued through adolescence into early adulthood. A brief marriage ended in divorce, his adult relationship with his parents continued to be severely strained, and he couldn't manage to hold a job. Instead, he drifted first from job to job, next from state to state, then from prison to prison, and finally from murder to murder.[13]

Amazingly, given the abuse and horror of their childhoods, serial killers rarely kill themselves. Their own suffering is not internalized but rather externalized—they blame others. Occasionally, a serial killer will attempt suicide. Gary Heidnik attempted to take his own life 13 times. How can someone who is so skilled at killing others be so inadequate at killing himself? Clearly the answer is that he did not want to die. Herbert Baumeister, an exception to the rule, committed suicide in 1996 but only after the discovery of thousands of bone and teeth fragments on his family's estate in Carmel, Indiana.

Although only four of Baumeister's victims were positively identified, the fragments were of at least 11 bodies. A father, husband and businessman, he may have also been the I-70 killer during the late 1980s as his businesses often took him from Indiana to Ohio over this highway. Baumeister's victims were gay men whom he had picked up in gay bars in Indianapolis. This case is also an example of how serial killers can remain undetected and uninvestigated for so long when their victim pool is a marginalized group. It is unlikely that Baumeister's murderous career would have gone on so long if he had elected to slay college students or professors.

Childhood Origins

Whenever the case of an infamous serial killer is uncovered, be it a cannibalistic sadist or a not-so-merciful mercy killer, journalists and behavioral scientists alike tend to search for clues deep within the killer's biography that might explain his or her seemingly senseless or excessively brutal murders. Many writers, for example, have emphasized Theodore Bundy's concerns over having been born illegitimate, and biographers of "Hillside Strangler" Kenneth Bianchi capitalized on his having been an adopted child.

Researchers are not of one mind, however, in explaining what produces the psyche of the serial murderer. Some stress genetic or biological factors in accounting for such defects as sociopathy. Moffit and Henry suggest, for example, that damage to the right hemisphere of the brain may be responsible for losses of "social sensibilities," including lack of empathy and difficulties with bonding.[14] Other investigators point instead to early childhood experiences and repeated psychological trauma during development, such as insufficient bonding of the child to his parents or even physical and psychological abuse. Interestingly, shyness has been identified as a factor that may protect against delinquency, perhaps as a trait that limits the number of peer contacts.[15] However, shyness—and particularly shyness with women—is a characteristic that appears in many case histories of male serial killers.

There is a long tradition of research on the childhood correlates of homicidal proneness. For example, John Macdonald long ago hypothesized a triad of symptoms—enuresis, firesetting, and cruelty to animals—which he viewed as reactions to parental rejection, neglect, or brutality.[16] Although the so-called Macdonald's Triad was later refuted in controlled studies, the connection between parental physical/sexual abuse or abandonment and subsequent violent behavior remains a continuing focus of research. On an anecdotal level, moreover, it appears that many serial killers have as children reportedly expressed sadistic behavior toward animals.

Indeed, a number of more recent studies have purported to support the hypothesis that violent individuals are also abusive toward animals.[17] For example, Kellert and Felthous found significantly more childhood animal cruelty among aggressive criminals than among either nonaggressive criminals or non-criminals.[18] Moreover, tracking the criminal records of 153 animal abusers compared with 153 non-abusers, sociologist Arnold Arluke and colleagues determined that the animal abusers were five times more likely to commit acts of human violence including murder, rape, and assault.[19]

Yet as described in the case studies of Steve Egger's *The Killers Among Us,* serial murderers don't just abuse animals but torture and dissect them. Egger's description of serial killer Jerry Marcus notes how the killer set pregnant cats on fire and poured hot water on hungry dogs—and after these sadistic acts he felt pride and joy. Jeffrey Dahmer started his killing spree on neighborhood pets when he was a child. He had a pet cemetery, and a long history of animal decapitation and vivisection. It appears that much more attention should be given to those who abuse animals as there is ample evidence that in many cases, the animals just get bigger. People of any age who achieve joy via the suffering of any living creature may come to have a long future of child abuse, partner violence, rape, or murder.

It is often suggested that because of deep-rooted problems stemming from childhood, serial killers suffer from a profound sense of powerlessness, which they compensate for through extreme forms of aggression to exert control over others. The biographies of most serial killers reveal significant physical and psychological trauma at an early age. Based on in-depth interviews with 36 incarcerated murderers, Ressler and his colleagues found evidence of psychological abuse (e.g., public humiliation) in 23 cases and physical trauma in 13 cases.[20] Eric Hickey reported that among a group of 62 male serial killers, 48 percent had been rejected as children by a parent or some other important person in their lives.[21] Of course, these same types of experiences can be found in the biographies of many "normal" people as well. More specifically, although useful for characterizing the backgrounds of serial killers, the findings presented by Ressler and Hickey lack a comparison group drawn from non-offending populations for which the same definitions of trauma have been applied.

Therefore, it is impossible to conclude that serial killers have suffered as children to any greater extent than others have.

The emphasis on child abuse as a "cause" of murderous rage has become the latest excuse of serial killers who attempt to deflect blame for their actions. Unfortunately, murderers who might exploit the "child abuse syndrome" to their own advantage frequently receive a sympathetic ear. As a sociopath, the serial killer is a particularly convincing and accomplished liar. As a professional trained to be supportive and empathic, his psychiatrist may be easily conned. The case histories of such malingerers as Kenneth Bianchi and Arthur Shawcross, both serial killers who fooled mental health professionals with fabricated tales of child abuse, remind us to be skeptical about the self-serving testimony of accused killers eager to escape legal responsibility for their crimes.

As a related matter, more than a few serial killers—from David Berkowitz to Joel Rifkin—were raised by adoptive parents. In the "adopted child syndrome," an individual displaces his anger for birth parents onto adoptive parents as well as other authority figures. According to Kirschner, the syndrome is often expressed, early in life, in "provocative antisocial behavior" including firesetting, truancy, promiscuity, pathological lying, and stealing.[22] The deeply troubled adopted child may, in fantasy, create an imaginary playmate who represents his antisocial impulses. Later, he may experience a dissociative disorder or even the development of an alter personality in which his murderous tendencies become situated.

The apparent overrepresentation of adoption in the biographies of serial killers has been exploited by those who are looking for simple explanations for heinous and senseless crimes. In reality, the way in which this link operates has not been completely explained. That is, possible triggering mechanisms might include the effects of rejection by birth parents, maternal deprivation during the critical first few months of life, poor prenatal care by the birth mother, or genetic deficiencies passed on from both biological parents.

Some neurologists and psychiatrists have suggested that many killers—especially killers who commit senseless acts of brutality—have incurred severe injury to the limbic region of the brain as a result of profound or repeated head trauma, generally during childhood. Dorothy Otnow Lewis and Jonathan Pincus, for example, examined 15 murderers on Florida's death row and found that all showed signs of neurological irregularities.[23] In addition, Joel Norris reported that excessive spinal fluid was found in the brain scan of serial killer Henry Lee Lucas; Norris argued that this abnormality was caused by an earlier series of blows to Lucas's head.[24]

There is compelling reason to believe that severe head trauma and resulting injuries to the brain can potentially have dire effects on behavior, including violent outbursts, learning disabilities, and epilepsy. Henry Lee Lucas was reportedly beaten by his mother with lumber and broom handles. He later claimed to have experienced frequent dizzy spells and blackouts. Bobby Joe Long, who was convicted by the state of Florida in 1986 and 1994 of a total of nine counts of murder, also appears to have received several severe head injuries. In three different episodes, at the age of five or six, Long fell off a swing, from a horse, and off his bicycle, suffering repeated brain concussions in the process.

There are important possible causal order problems with theories about brain damage and violent behavior. If the individual is a thrill-seeker, then the same set of personality factors may lead to head injuries (e.g., horseback riding, motorcycles, bicycles, and playground equipment). In the presence of other negative social contexts (e.g., physical and sexual abuse, substance use and abuse), the same thrill-seeking need may also act as a predisposing factor to violence. Thus, head injuries may be a result of aggressive and violent behavior rather than their cause.

It is often said that "hindsight is 20/20." This is definitely true in terms of explaining serial murder. Following the apprehension of a serial killer, we generally hear mixed reports that "he seemed like a nice guy, but there was something about him that wasn't quite right." Of course, there is something about most people that isn't "quite right." However, when such a person is exposed to be a serial murderer, we tend to focus on the red flags in his character and biography that were ignored. Even the stench emanating from Jeffrey Dahmer's apartment, which he explained to the neighbors as the odor of spoiled meat from his broken freezer, was unexceptional until after the fact.

The methodological problems in predicting violence in advance are well known. For a category of violence as rare as serial murder, the low base rate and consequent false-positive dilemma are overwhelming. Simply put, there are thousands of white males in their late 20s or 30s who are sadistic, thirst for power, and lack strong internal controls and tortured animals as children and may have been adopted or abused—but the vast majority of them will never kill anyone.

Victim Selection

Although some serial killers have targeted co-eds, they are much more likely to target particularly vulnerable individuals—runaways, prostitutes, homeless people, or patients in nursing homes and hospitals. Serial killers rarely choose professional athletes, bodybuilders, or NRA conventioneers as their victims. Unlike homicides in general, most victims of serial killers are women, especially prostitutes. Some research in serial murder has suggested that the victim actually has a symbolic value for the killer; for example, Ted Bundy selected women who physically resembled a girlfriend who had dumped him.[25] The problem with this line of reasoning is that so many of the women in high schools and colleges in the 1970s looked the same. It was popular to wear long, straight hair, parted down the middle. Rather than a Norman Bates-like complex regarding their mothers or their girlfriends, serial killers more likely choose women in general because of their heterosexuality and the inability of most women to defend themselves.

Moreover, the marginality of prostitutes, drug addicts, and runaways gives the killer a special advantage. It generally takes considerable time for a missing person's report to be filed, even longer to recognize that a woman has become a victim of homicide. By the time the police locate a body, they are typically left with skeletal remains—no DNA, fingerprints, fiber, or hair. Indeed, they are lucky to be able to identify the victim, let alone the killer. In November 2003, Gary Leon Ridgway, the Green River Killer, in a plea bargain to avoid the death penalty, admitted to killing more than 48 prostitutes in the Seattle area over a 16-year period. In his statement, Ridgway said he targeted prostitutes "because I thought I could kill as many as I wanted without getting caught." According to the serial killer, "they were easy to pick up without being noticed" and "they would not be reported missing right away, and might never be reported missing." Additionally, the psychological process of victim dehumanization, described earlier, enabled Ridgway to kill prostitutes without remorse. He recalled this thought while strangling one of his victims: "You made me do it, you bitch, you whore, you worthless piece of garbage."

Finally, there is so little pressure on the police to solve a string of prostitute killings or those of certain other marginalized groups like homeless drug addicts. Most middle-class individuals don't feel personally threatened. After all, its only criminals killing criminals!

Endnotes

1. Robert K. Ressler, John E. Douglas, Ann W. Burgess, and Allen G. Burgess, *Crime Classification Manual.* Lexington, MA: Lexington Books, 1992.

2. Janet Warren, Roy R. Hazelwood, and Park E. Dietz, "The Sexually Sadistic Serial Killer," in Thomas O'Reilly-Fleming, ed., *Serial and Mass Murder: Theory, Research and Policy.* Toronto: Canadian Scholars' Press, 1996.

3. James Alan Fox and Jack Levin, "Serial Murder: Myth and Reality," in Dwayne Smith and Margaret Zahn, eds., *Homicide Studies: A Sourcebook of Social Research.* Thousand Oaks, CA: Sage Publications, 1998.

4. Grover Maurice Godwin, *Hunting Serial Predators: A Multivariate Classification Approach to Profiling Violent Behavior.* Boca Raton, FL: CRC Press, 1999.

5. Eric W. Hickey, *Serial Murderers and Their Victims.* Belmont, CA: Wadsworth, 1997.

6. Patricia Pearson, *When She Was Bad.* New York: Penguin Books, 1998.

7. David Abrahamsen. *The Murdering Mind.* New York: Harper & Row, 1973.

8. Donald T. Lunde, *Murder and Madness.* San Francisco, CA: San Francisco Book Company, 1976.

9. Robert D. Hare, *Psychopathy: Theory and Research.* New York: Wiley, 1970.

10. Godwin, op. cit.

11. R. A. Prentky, A. W. Burgess, F. Rokous, A. Lee, C. Hartman, R. Ressler, and J. Douglas, "The Presumptive Role of Fantasy in Serial Sexual Homicide," *The American Journal of Psychiatry* 146 (1989): 887–891.

12. Stephen J. Giannangelo, *The Psychopathology of Serial Murder: A Theory of Violence.* Westport, CT: Greenwood Publishing Group, 1996.

13. James Alan Fox and Jack Levin, *Killer on Campus.* New York: Avon Books, 1996.

14. T. F. Moffit and B. Henry, "Neuropsychological Studies of Juvenile Delinquency and Juvenile Violence," in J. S. Miller, ed., *Neuropsychology of Aggression.* Boston: Kluwer, 1991.

15. Donald J. West and David P. Farrington, *The Delinquent Way of Life.* London: Heinemann, 1977.

16. John M. Macdonald, "The Threat to Kill," *American Journal of Psychiatry* 120 (1963): 125–130; Daniel S. Hellman and Nathan Blackman, "Enuresis, Firesetting, and Cruelty to Animals," *American Journal of Psychiatry* 122 (1966): 1431–1435.

17. Alan R. Felthous, "Childhood Cruelty to Cats, Dogs and Other Animals," *Bulletin of the American Academy of Psychiatry and the Law* 9 (1981): 48–53.

18. S. Kellert and Alan R. Felthous, "Childhood Cruelty Toward Animals Among Criminals and Non-Criminals," *Human Relations* 18 (1985): 1113–1139.

19. Arnold Arluke, Jack Levin, Carter Luke, and Frank Ascione, "The Relationship of Animal Abuse to Violence and Other Forms of Antisocial Behavior," *Journal of Interpersonal Violence* 14 (1999): 963–975.

20. Robert K. Ressler, Ann W. Burgess, and John E. Douglas, *Sexual Homicide: Patterns and Motives,* Lexington, MA: Lexington Books, 1988.

21. Eric W. Hickey, *Serial Murderers and Their Victims.* Belmont, CA: Wadsworth, 1997.

22. David Kirschner, "Understanding Adoptees Who Kill: Dissociation, Patricide, and the Psychodynamics of Adoption," *International Journal of Offender Therapy and Comparative Criminology* 36 (1992): 323–333.

23. Dorothy Otnow Lewis, Jonathan H. Pincus, M. Feldman, L. Jackson, and B. Bard, "Psychiatric, Neurological and Psycho-Educational Characteristics of 15 Death Row Inmates in the United States," *American Journal of Psychiatry* 143 (1986): 838–845.

24. Joel Norris, *Serial Killers: The Growing Menace.* New York: Doubleday, 1988.

25. Hickey, op. cit.

8

Medical Murder

It is a sad fact of life that hospitals, clinics, and nursing homes are places where some people go to die. More tragically, they are places where a few go to be murdered. Several different forms of murder, serial in nature, can be grouped together because they occur in health care settings. It has become increasingly common to find medical professionals charged with homicides committed in the line of duty.

For our purposes, medical murder includes nurses, doctors, nurse's aides, emergency medical technicians, nursing home aides, and other medical professionals who intentionally kill their patients. Excluded from this classification, however, are domestic and other homicides committed by people who just happen to be doctors or nurses. There are many cases of doctors and nurses killing a family member for profit or murdering their spouse during a nasty separation or divorce. Perhaps none is as well-known as that of Dr. Claus Von Bülow who was convicted in 1982 of overdosing his diabetic wife with insulin to stake claim to her fortune. In addition, this class of homicide does not include thousands of patients who may die each year because of medical incompetence, malpractice, and error. By "medical murder," we mean murders that are intentionally committed by medical staff against patients.

These killers have often been called "Angels of Mercy" and "Angels of Death," but there is nothing angelic or merciful about their crimes. While euthanasia and physician- or other-assisted suicides (e.g., Kevorkian style "medicides") are legally a form of homicide in almost all areas of the United States, assisted-suicide implies participation by the patient—a wish to die. But the victims of medical murders are patients who not only had no wish to die, but in most cases, had expected the medical staff to help them get well.

Medical murder is certainly not a new phenomenon—from 1907 to 1912, Amy Archer-Gilligan ran a home for the aged in Connecticut where she poisoned as many as 40 people. Jane Toppan, a nurse's aide in turn-of-the-century New England, confessed to killing at least 30, but is suspected of poisoning as many as 100 people.

The Medical Murderer by Rupert Furneaux (1957) and *One Hundred Years of Medical Murder* by John Camp (1982) provide details on several cases of nurses and doctors who murdered patients during the 19th and early 20th centuries.[1] Moreover, the first serial killer to be hanged in the United States was Dr. H. H. Holmes (a.k.a. Herman Webster Mudgett) who may have slain as many as 200 women in Chicago from 1892 to 1896. In many of these early medical murder cases, the motive was profit. So although medical professionals and nursing home staff have a long history of murdering patients in their care, we have only fairly recently (in the last 30 years or so) discovered medical murderers with motives other than financial gain. Like the definition for serial murder in general, our notion of medical murder does not include medical professionals who have killed "only" one patient and, thanks to diligent staff, were stopped before they could repeat the crime.

Also not included in our scope of medical murder are mass killings in medical settings. For example, in April 2003, a female doctor went berserk in a hospital in Madrid, Spain, killing two and wounding six people with a knife. Her attack was aimed at colleagues and patients, and, according to co-workers, she was clearly suffering from mental illness in the time frame before the attack—but no one removed her from her position.

Almost everyone is familiar with the names of serial killers Theodore Bundy, John Wayne Gacy, and David Berkowitz. But few can name notorious medical killers who were responsible for even higher death counts over longer periods of time. For example, few recognize the name Efren Salvidar, a respiratory therapist in California who may have murdered as many as 200 patients between 1989 and 1998, or Donald Harvey, a nurse's aide in Kentucky and Ohio who may have killed as many as 80 people between 1970 and 1987.

Counting Medical Murders

Unlike school shootings, family massacres, and workplace shootings, it is often years before a medical murderer's crimes are discovered. Since these deaths occur in a setting where death is a part of the job and often assumed to be a result of the initial reason for admission to the hospital or nursing home, the death itself may not be suspicious. Thus, an accurate assessment of the number of medical murders is rather difficult. Since media interest in medical murders has grown during the last 30 years, many assume that this type of murder has increased. We have no way of knowing, however, whether there has been a real increase in the occurrence of medical murder or if there is simply improved reporting and detection.

In the United States, two cases of medical murder were reported during the 1970s, nine in the 1980s, nine in the 1990s, and several thus far since 2000.[2] An inspection of known cases suggests that most of the detected murders are in the United States, but this may be related to the higher surveillance levels in our medical care settings compared to other countries. There seem to have been more instances in England than would be expected by chance, but this too may be due to better surveillance systems.

Examination of the known cases over the last 30 years indicates that many of these killers may have taken a life once or twice a month during their active phases (e.g., Harold Shipman and Orville Lynn Majors). We can assume that there are far more medical murders that go undetected, particularly when the killers work in several medical settings over the course of their careers.

As illustrated by the long active periods of many of the perpetrators, medical murders are not revealed as homicides until long after the fact. As a result, official crime reporting sources, such as the FBI's *Uniform Crime Reports,* do not count these deaths in statistical tallies. Also, a number of hospitals have conducted investigations into suspicious deaths although no suspect was ever charged with murder. For example, there were at least five deaths and several other suspected attempts that occurred in a Michigan Veteran's Hospital in 1975, but no member of the staff was ever arrested or charged. An investigation of Springfield Community Hospital in Dayton, Ohio, that began in 1985 (but was halted and then launched again in 1993) discovered that as many as 30 patients may have been killed. Empty bottles of Pavulon were found in various places around the hospital. Although there was a primary suspect, again no one was arrested.

An attempt to estimate the frequency of medical murder can use cases over the past couple decades as a starting point. During the 1980s, as many as six to eight cases were detected during any given year. If these offenders followed the pattern of one or two murders per month (as appears to be the average for Orville Lynn Majors, Harold Shipman, and others), then 16 deaths a month would result in nearly 200 deaths per year—and these only include the six to eight offenders who were identified. If only a small proportion of these murders are uncovered, or if the monthly average death toll per offender was say four (as in the Springfield, Ohio, case) rather than one to two, then the number of medical murders each year could easily be as high as 500 to 1,000. This is a significant number given that the total number of U.S. homicides is now approximately 16,000 per year. As our surveillance systems improve, time will tell how many of these murderers have been on decades-long killing sprees in our hospitals, nursing homes, and hospice centers—not to mention the home health care industry where detection of foul play is even more challenging.

Although medical murderers to date have been more likely to be nurses and nurse's aides than other types of medical workers, this may be somewhat artifactual. It seems likely that because nurses have formal ties to patients, their connections are more easily discovered and investigated. Any number of aides or other medical staff members may be in and out of patient rooms at various and unrecorded times of day. Combined with less traceable methods of killings often used in these settings (e.g., suffocation with a pillow or pinching off an oxygen flow), the number of cases of medical murder committed by ancillary medical staff may be particularly undercounted.

Motives and Types of Medical Murderers

Medical murderers are similar to other serial killers in that they choose vulnerable populations as their victims—the sick, the elderly, and children. There are, however, some unique gender ratios for medical murderers. Other researchers have discovered relatively few females among serial killers generally. Eric Hickey's research found only 16 percent committed by females, while Godwin found only 5 percent. Thus, the finding that 60 percent of medical murders are committed by women makes this type of murder quite different than most others.[3] Although fewer than 10 percent of nurses and nurse's aides are male, almost 40 percent of known medical murders are committed by males.[4] So, although females make up a greater proportion of medical murderers than other types of killers, men are still overrepresented among them.

We know that medical murders are more likely than most other types of homicides to be committed by females (in part because they are overrepresented in these professions). We also know that the typical medical murder method, poison, is most likely to be the method chosen by female serial killers (suffocation is the second most common method chosen by female medical murderers).[5] Thus, access to poisons and vulnerable populations creates more of the situational components needed to carry out these crimes.

Most female serial killers choose victims with whom they have a relationship—husbands, children, and the like. In medical murder, however, this is generally not the case. More typically, the victim was only a patient for a few hours but is totally dependent on the caretaker. Contrary to the motives of other female serial killers, the motive for the vast majority of medical murderers is not money, but rather some form of power, control, or attention. Also, these cases provide much evidence to refute the widely-held notion serial killers are hardly ever women.

Although personal motives predominate in medical murders, some recent cases appear to have been inspired by profit. Harold Shipman, a British physician, was convicted of killing 15 patients over a period of decades, but he may have poisoned to death as many as 400. He was detected after forging the will of one of his patients, so there was a clear financial component to some of his killings. However, his motives may have been more complex. He had been overheard complaining about the space that the elderly were taking up in hospitals, and even though he killed both male and female patients, an overwhelming number of his victims were elderly women. As is the case with many murderers, there may be more than one motive. And rather than an instrumental motive such as financial gain, medical murderers, like other serial killers, may be motivated by more expressive, intrinsic concerns of power, control, and glory.

An analysis of the methods used in medical murders as well as the context within which they are committed illustrates at least two primary types of medical murderers. One type, the *power killer,* murders in silence, often works the night shift, and seems to be able to continue killing over a longer period of time. The ability to determine who lives and who dies provides the power and control that this offender craves. Although some medical murderers brag about their crimes, the power type kills in relative silence. These nurses and nurse's aides bask in the power of having taken a life and seem to take pleasure in baffling physicians. They may use a substance such as morphine rather than the more "code blue" inducing Pavulon (which paralyzes the respiratory system while the patient remains conscious) or "heart-stopping" substances such as Digoxin. Since their activities take place under quieter circumstances, it may take years before anyone detects the extraordinarily high number of deaths occurring during their shifts. As is noted in Table 8.1, several of the more recent medical murderers have been power killers. Their offenses may also have a sexual component, but interviews with these killers have shed relatively little light on this dimension.

Donald Harvey, a nurse's aide and autopsy assistant, appears to fit the profile of a power killer. He poisoned or smothered patients, neighbors, family, and friends over a 17-year time period. He also had a history of suicide attempts, burglary and other thefts, as well as institutionalization for mental problems that included repeated electroshock therapies. Like many other criminals, these killers have multiple levels of problems and dysfunctional histories.

The other major type of medical murderer is the nurse who craves attention. The *hero killer* attempts to create a life or death emergency with the goal of either watching others scramble to save the life of the victim or, more typically, of thrusting themselves into the center of the crisis. Several of these murderers became known as nurses who functioned very well in "code blue" situations. It is unclear how many of the victims were intended to die. By definition, the nurse takes the victim to the edge of death and, in some cases, may have intended to save the patient's life dramatically rather than to take it.

Even when the patient dies, the murderer has still experienced the excitement of the emergency situation and of baffling other medical professionals as to why the patient died. They may even be praised by family and co-workers for their vigilant attempts to save the life of the victim. Genene Jones, convicted of one murder (and suspected in as many as 47 deaths) in Texas during the late 1970s and early 1980s, worked primarily with sick children. She reveled in the attention and glory of bringing dying young patients back to life in front of their terrified parents. One family was so thankful for her seemingly heroic efforts to save their baby daughter (whose twin had already been murdered by Jones) that they made her the baby's godmother after she rescued the child.

Another medical murderer, Joseph Dewey Akin, was directly linked to 17 suspicious deaths but suspected of as many as 100. His killing marathon likely began in Georgia in 1983 and ended in North Fulton Regional Hospital in Alabama in 1990. Akin had falsely claimed to have earned a four-year nursing degree when he actually had only two years of training. He was also cited for his difficulty in getting along with others on the job. Exaggerated credentials, braggadocio, and difficulty with interpersonal relationships are characteristic of many of the "hero" medical murderers. Nurse Akin chose drugs that induced cardiac arrest, setting the stage for his grand performance as the heroic lifesaving "super nurse."

Medical murderers who create emergency situations in the hope of becoming heroes or at least having the chance to be part of the emergency response, appear to be similar to the isolated cases of firefighters who intentionally set blazes. John Orr, an arson investigator in Glendale, California, who may have set as many as 2,000 fires (in which at least four people died), is serving a life sentence. Orr's motives included being at the scene of an exhilarating event (one that held some sexual excitement for him) and to be held up by his peers as an expert who had special insights into identifying arson fires.[6]

Orr is but one of a number of arsonist firefighters who have come to the attention of authorities. These firefighters appear to be innervated by the same motive that drives nurse murderers to create life or death emergencies for their patients—a desperate need for attention. Certain types of people may seek out professions that offer them excitement and a chance to save lives, but only a relatively few actually create the crisis that will make them a hero.

Interviews with medical murderers suggest that in addition to the primary motives of power/control or attention, these killers may also be motivated in a secondary way by dependent or demanding patients, heavy patient loads, and cover-ups for other crimes. They may be stealing drugs, money, or belongings from patients. Or they may be inspired by hatred, as was Orville Lynn Majors of Indiana who poisoned to death at least six patients. Majors stated that he simply "hated old people" and thought "they should all be gassed."[7]

These killers typically suffer from a variety of personality disorders such as narcissism which includes a grandiose sense of self and a belief that the world needs to recognize their greatness. Despite an arrogant veneer, they may have an overwhelming feeling of worthlessness and lack of control. As with serial murderers in general, medical killers usually suffer childhoods filled with trauma, abuse, and/or neglect. Interestingly, many of them seem to have been more neglected than abused and it is perhaps their accumulated feelings of being neglected that causes them to take such drastic measures to be noticed.

TABLE 8.1   *Thirty Years of Medical Murder (Selected Cases)*

Medical Murderer (name, age, occupation)	Location	Years of Activity	Suspected Victims	Convicted Number
Joseph Dewey Akin 32 Nurse	North Fulton Reg. Hospital, Alabama & Georgia	1983–87 1987–90	Over 100	1
Richard Angelo 26 Nurse	New York	1987–89	At least 10	4
Roberto Diaz 46 Nurse	California	1971–81	12–60 Elderly	12
Jeffrey Feltner 26 Nurse's Aide	Florida	1990	7 Elderly	1
Kristen Gilbert 33 Nurse	Veteran Affairs Medical Center, Northampton, MA	1996	4	4
Gwendolyn Graham 23 & Catherine May Wood 24 Nurse's Aides	Michigan	1987	10	5
Donald Harvey 35 Nurse's Aide	London, KY & Cincinnati, OH	1970–86	32–80	24
Vicki Dawn Jackson 36 Nurse	Texas	2000–01	20–24	Indictment on 4 elderly deaths
Genene Jones 33 Nurse	Bexar County Medical Hospital, Kerrville, TX	1978–82	47 Children	1 homicide & 1 for injuring child
Orville Lynn Majors 38 Nurse	Vermillion County Hospital, IN	1993–95	60–130 Elderly	6
Randy Powers 31 Nurse's Aide	California	1984	12	Convicted of assault on a baby
Brian Rosenfeld 32 Nurse	Largo, FL	1990	23–25	3
Efren Salvidar 28 Respiratory Therapist	Glendale Adventist Medical Center, Glendale, CA	1989–98	100–200	6 Elderly
Bobbie Sue Terrell 29 Nurse	Florida	1984	18	4 Elderly
Michael Swango 44 Doctor	U.S.A. & Zimabawe	1983–97	35–60	4

Being different, feeling like an outsider, and suffering humiliation can lead to feelings of powerlessness and rage. Hale, focusing on the internal motives of serial killers, suggests that serial killers have experienced some form of torment and humiliation early in life.[8] This humiliation turns to rage, and the rage becomes targeted at others—in many cases

Sentence	Method	Motive	Other Factors
15 years plea agreement manslaughter	Lidocaine or epinephrine	Hero	Fired for false credentials; difficulty getting along with others
61 years to life in prison	Pavulon or anectine	Hero	Former fireman and EMT
Death	Lidocaine	Power	Would predict patient's deaths
Life in prison; plead guilty	Smothered	Hero	Police received anonymous tips about unnatural deaths
4 life sentences without parole	Epinephrine	Hero	Trying to impress boyfriend who was security guard at hospital
6 life sentences without parole	Smothered	Power/Sex	Wood never killed, confessed when Graham began threatening babies
4 life sentences	Smothered or hooked patients to empty oxygen tanks; cyanide	Power	Suicide attempts, mental hospital commitments, 21 electroshock treatments 1983–1986; also burglary
Accused	Muscle relaxant, mivacurium chloride	Power	1 victim traced to estranged husband
159 years, parole eligible after 20 years	Succinycholine, Heprin	Hero	Unattractive, needy, liar, sexually promiscuous
300 years	Epinephrine and potassium chloride	Power	Hated the elderly
5 years, released December 1987	Lidocane	Hero	After release, enrolled in EMT program with false name; rejected when real identity discovered
Life in Prison Plead guilty	Mellaril	Power	Targeted victims in geriatrics ward
Life in Prison Plead guilty	Pavulon, Succin	Power	Claimed that other nurses were doing the same thing
Life in prison Plead guilty	Insulin, asphyxiation, or strangulation	Hero	Schizophrenic, overweight and shy
Life in prison Plead guilty	Potassium, cyanide, epinephrine & succinylcholine	Power	Suspected of poisoning co-workers' food

others who may remind the killer of someone who embarrassed them earlier in life. As described in Chapter 2, Erich Fromm viewed destructive aggression as a response to feelings of powerlessness. For the medical murderer, killing makes them the center of attention and through this, makes them feel dominant.

In the medical setting, staff members may be humiliated or embarrassed by others—demanding doctors may snap at overworked nurses or an incompetent nurse may be marginalized by co-workers. Some medical staff may even find the work itself to be humiliating (e.g., bathing the elderly in a nursing home or changing too many bed pans), and so they purposely target their workplace and its captive pool of potential victims in order to seek revenge for perceived mistreatment. Obviously, not everyone who has suffered humiliation and embarrassment turns their feelings into murderous rage, so we must also focus on the other contextual factors that exist in order to explain killings by medical staff.

Administrative Facilitators

While factors that may promote murderous impulses for those operating in medical facilities are similar to those for other serial killers—childhood neglect, abuse, and/or trauma, some special situational circumstances serve as facilitators for medical homicides. Most obvious is the easy access to drugs that are capable of killing patients. Nurses routinely administer medications and narcotics, so they have access not only to the weapon but also to the patients as potential victims. Medical murders committed by nurse's aides who do not have access to drugs more often use other means such as suffocation or poisoning, but not necessarily with controlled substances. Interestingly, the vast majority of the drugs used as murder weapons by medical murderers are not controlled narcotics, and thus are relatively easy to secure and poorly monitored. However, they can be just as deadly as controlled substances like morphine.

In addition to providing access to the murder weapon and the mode of delivery, hospitals and nursing homes may also more directly facilitate murders due to lack of surveillance, or even more directly through actual cover-ups. Only fairly recently have hospitals begun any sort of "mortality analysis" that might indicate an excessive number of deaths in a particular unit and/or shift. In some cases, there may have been a code of silence similar to the code of silence common in policing, in part because what the murderer did was done occasionally by other nurses on the ward.

Co-workers had joked and gossiped about the deaths of patients under the care of Efren Salvidar, but most did not complain to administrators. According to Salvidar, many other people were doing what he did. Interestingly, not only was Salvidar fired, but four other respiratory therapists were also fired and two management personnel resigned. Particularly troubling is that John Bardgett and Efren Salvidar both referred to themselves as "Angels of Death" before they were apprehended by police. Others talked about the patients they had killed, and some even kept souvenirs that they showed to fellow staff members.

Even when suspicions arise that there may be a serial killer working in a hospital, staff may be reticent to contact the police. Investigations may be conducted "in-house" before the police are contacted. When mysterious deaths occur in a hospital or nursing home, there may be some period of time when administrators are attempting to determine if the deaths are due to incompetence or impairment or if they are intentional. There are obvious litigation issues for medical institutions in the event that a caregiver is killing patients. Given the documented cases of hospitals refusing to acknowledge nurse and physician impairment (e.g., drug and alcohol addiction) and many cases of hospitals enforcing little or no disciplinary action against incompetent doctors and nurses, it is easy to imagine similar sorts of cover-ups for intentional medical killings.

Another contributing factor may also be the reluctance of medical professionals to admit that they do not know why a patient died. Rather, they may feel pressured to state a cause of death, however inaccurate or incomplete.

A recent study by the Institute of Medicine found that as many as 98,000 hospital deaths a year may result from error.[9] What proportion of these deaths were intentional errors?

Although medical killers can be very successful in taking the lives of others, they seem to fail in taking their own lives—many of them attempt suicide unsuccessfully multiple times during their very successful murder sprees. Likely their suicide attempts are not intended to be successful (as they clearly know how to kill people), but are rather yet another cry for attention.

There are still other institutional facilitators that make lengthy medical killing sprees possible. Dr. Michael Swango was glaringly incompetent in medical school, but he managed to graduate, albeit behind his classmates. He killed an untold number of patients over a period of almost 20 years as he worked in seven different hospitals. Early on, he also worked as an EMT, when he poisoned a number of his co-workers. At a minimum, Swango's killings began during his Ohio State University Hospital internship from which he was dismissed amidst a frenzy of speculation about the deaths of a number of patients. When Swango applied for jobs, almost no one called to check his references or background. Investigations took place in nearly every hospital where he worked; but in most cases, no charges were ever filed. Finally, several different investigators and school administrators spread the word about Swango, but not before he had killed at least 35 people, and probably many more. As illustrated by the Swango case, the disciplinary records of nurses and other medical professionals are confidential. Thus, it can be very difficult to track incompetent medical staff or even worse, predators who switch hospitals or nursing homes and move from state to state.

Munchausen Syndrome by Proxy

In addition to medical staffers who kill patients during the course of their occupational duties, there are other criminal activities that occur in medical settings. While *Munchausen Syndrome* involves making oneself sick or faking various illnesses usually in order to attract attention or sympathy, *Munchausen Syndrome by Proxy* (MSBP) involves inducing or faking illness in someone else, typically a child. So a MSBP case could involve a mother poisoning or suffocating her child or rushing the child to the hospital after claiming she saw the child having a seizure.

Feldman, Ford, and Reinhold in *Patient or Pretender: Inside the World of Factitious Disorders* comment that many deaths initially diagnosed as Sudden Infant Death Syndrome (SIDS) may have actually been cases of MSBP. At times, a parent's attempt to use illness for the sake of attention can inadvertently result in death of the victim.[10] Although most Munchausen by proxy cases involve mother's who hurt (or kill) their children, a recent study also found that some people gain similar attention (and engage in similar deception/duping routines) by poisoning or otherwise deliberately hurting their pets.[11] These scenarios seem very similar to the nurse or other medical professional who creates a life or death emergency for attention, acts which may subsequently (albeit sometimes not necessarily intentionally) result in the death of the victim.

The common theme among medical murderers and Munchausen moms is an overwhelming need for attention or sympathy. People who crave attention may harm themselves to gain attention from colleagues, doctors, or nurses or they may harm others so that they can be seen as supreme caregivers, devoted parents, or exemplary medical professionals. Karen Sterchi poisoned her son Christopher until she was stopped in 1987 by hospital staff in St. Louis Missouri. Her son, age 6 at the time she was caught poisoning him, had a lifetime of unexplained medical problems. Mrs. Sterchi also had an older son who had health problems that had disappeared after the new baby was born. She had been exposing her son to many types of bacteria (including feces, mold, and stagnant water) and was convicted of assault but served no time in jail. During the medical crises of her son, she basked in the glory of being the ultimate mom, she partook of benefits and fundraisers held for the family and not only financially and emotionally devastated her family but left a child with long term physical problems.

Like medical murder, the frequency of MSBP is impossible to estimate. It is usually only the most extreme cases that come to the attention of hospital staff. Schreier and Libow, in *Hurting for Love: Munchausen Syndrome by Proxy,* discovered several cases in one year in one hospital, and while their research also found that approximately 10 percent of the victims of MSBP die, there are no reliable estimates of the frequency of the syndrome.

MSBP offenders, again typically mothers, may behave like serial killers with cooling-off periods during which they are not making their child sick but still basking in the martyrdom of caring for a sick child.[12] These same types of offenders, both mothers who make their child sick and nurses who poison patients and cause code-blue situations, may be similar to people who falsely report crimes in order to gain the attention of others.

Yorker notes that in most cases, nurses who kill do not have previous criminal histories, but some do have previous histories of Munchausen or MSBP—an earlier sign of their desperate need for attention and power.[13] As noted by Rosenberg, however, most people who have MSBP do not also have Munchausen Syndrome, and many researchers agree that rather than just versions of the same disorder, they are in fact different syndromes.[14]

More detailed research has been conducted into the backgrounds of Munchausen moms, and a common theme that often emerges is their profound feelings of being ignored as children.[15] More specifically, many report a physically or emotionally distant father. Some research has suggested that the doctor may actually represent a father figure to the Munchausen offender. Thus, although these offenders may not have suffered horrendous and overt child abuse, the experience of child neglect can have dire consequences as well.

The nurse or other caregiver who makes victims sick (and sometimes kills them) may manifest motives similar to people with MSBP—they do it to attract attention from parents, coworkers, doctors, friends, and family members. Unfortunately, these killers continue to get attention after they are apprehended, as some of them have been featured on news programs such as *Dateline NBC, 48 Hours,* and *60 Minutes II.*

Prevention and Intervention

Monitoring all of the activities in hospitals and nursing homes, much less in the home health care industry, would seem an impossible task. At a minimum, hospitals should initiate surveillance and mortality analysis systems. These can include data systems that document drug use, patient deaths, etc., by shift, staff, and unit. Obviously, by the time these systems could alert the hospital to an unusual number of deaths, a serial killer would already have enjoyed a significant period of activity at the deadly expense of several patients. Video surveillance may also be an asset for the prevention of both medical murder and MSBP, as many mothers continue to poison or suffocate their children even while they are in the hospital when left alone in an examination room.

In addition, to the extent that nursing shortages and burdensome working conditions contribute to caregivers' desires to end a patient's life; hospitals should be required to maintain suitable staff-patient ratios. More reasonable staffing levels would also allow supervisors to monitor staff activities. In the event that hospitals and nursing homes mandate limits on staff hirings, patients may need to be prepared to be turned away when there are staffing shortages. Obviously, greater attention should be paid to investigating the credentials and previous work histories of applicants for positions in medical facilities; unfortunately, state regulations related to hiring practices and background checks vary considerably across the country. Prevention and intervention strategies should include closer monitoring of drugs (including those that are not controlled substances but nonetheless lethal) and significant legal penalties to hospital administrators for internal (as opposed to police-involved) investigations along with severe penalties for cover-ups.

To track cases of MSBP, hospital registries for both patients and staff members (much like criminal history data bases) may have merit in response to the mobility of perpetrators. Some MSBP parents take their children to different doctors or different hospitals when suspicions arise. Similarly, nurses and other health workers sometimes change jobs when rumors start to spread, only to resume their deadly treatments at a new location.

As is often the case when female perpetrators are at work, the law underplays the seriousness of MSBP. In almost all states, mothers caught poisoning and otherwise intentionally harming their child in a Munchausen scenario are typically charged with low level misdemeanors. Until endangering the life and health of a child is handled more harshly, these offenders will continue to play out their selfish schemes with relative impunity.

Since the deaths of patients in hospitals and nursing homes is to some extent "expected," closer inspection of these deaths by medical examiners and/or coroners is warranted. Many states have created "death review teams" for the investigation of any child's death, and similar types of oversight may be needed in nursing homes.

Now that hospitals and nursing homes have become sensitized to these types of killers in their midst (and have been sued on a few occasions), we may see both an increase and a decrease in these crimes. At least initially, as enhanced surveillance and tracking systems are put in place, a significant number of killers who have been active in the past may come to light. In the long term, these surveillance systems should prevent any one individual from claiming large victim counts. However, since crime is in part a function of opportunity, it is clearly possible that as our population ages and more and more people reside in nursing homes and are treated in some type of medical setting (including in-home care and hospice), these and other related crimes may increase.

This chapter has discussed nurses and doctors who intentionally kill patients. But what about the caregiver who intentionally neglects a patient's bedsores that results in death? At what point is neglect of a patient's needs for food, water, medication, or basic personal hygiene actually a form of slow murder?

A significant number of medical murderers have not been charged with homicide at all. For a number of reasons including difficulty proving intent and a lack of proper medical documentation, forensic deficiencies and a lack of hospital cooperation, many of these killers are convicted of some level of assault or neglect or even something as trivial as distribution of a controlled substance.

In August 2003, the charges against Richard Williams were dismissed. Williams had been charged with 10 counts of first-degree murder of patients in a Missouri Veteran's hospital. The prosecutor was forced to dismiss the charges due to lack of hospital cooperation and incompetent procedures at the private crime laboratory that had handled the forensic evidence from the case. Williams, who was originally suspected in over 40 deaths, is now appealing a civil judgment that found him responsible for the 10 deaths selected for investigation.

Just as the population of prostitutes, the homeless, and runaway kids has provided hunting grounds for the sexual serial killer, hospitals and nursing homes are the hunting grounds of the medical murderer. Looking ahead, the next hunting ground may be our nation's jails and prisons. It has been recently publicized that physicians who have been convicted of crimes and/or lost their medical licenses because of various forms of misconduct are being hired by some states faced with increasing jail/prison populations and growing heath care demands.[16] Physicians who drugged and sexually assaulted former patients are now serving the inmate population. Who will believe the incarcerated felon over the word of a doctor when some form of medical misconduct occurs. Will anyone care about or investigate the unexpected death of a violent prison inmate?

Endnotes

1. John Camp, *One Hundred Years of Medical Murder.* London: The Bodley Head LTD, 1982. Rupert Furneaux, *The Medical Murderer.* New York: Abeelard-Schuman Limited, 1957.

2. Beatrice Crofts Yorker, *Serial Murder in Hospitals.* Presented at the Forensic Nursing Clinical Update, Phoenix, AZ, 2001.

3. Eric W. Hickey, *Serial Murders and Their Victims.* Belmont, CA: Wadsworth, 2002.

4. Yorker, op. cit.

5. Hickey, op. cit.

6. Joseph Wambaugh, *Fire Lover: A True Story.* New York: Harper Collins, 2002.

7. Indiana v. Orville Lynn Majors Jr., Probable Cause Affidavit, December 29, 1997.

8. Robert Hale, The Role of Humiliation and Embarrassment in Serial Murder. *Psychology, A Journal of Human Behavior* Vol. 31, No. 2, 1994.

9. Institute of Medicine, *To Err Is Human: Building a Safer Health System,* September, 1999.

10. Marc Feldman, M.D., Charles Ford, M.D., and Toni Reinhold, *Patient or Pretender: Inside the Strange World of Factitious Disorders.* Toronto: John Wiley and Sons, Inc., 1994.

11. Reuters Health, September 6, 2002.

12. Herbert A. Schreier and Judith A. Libow, *Hurting for Love: Munchausen Syndrome by Proxy.* New York: Guilford Press, 1993.

13. Fred Bayles, Nurse Gets Life In Prison for Killing 4 Veteran's Experts Explore Motives of Medical Murderers. *USA Today,* March 27, 2001.

14. Donna A. Rosenberg, Web of Deceit: A Literature Review of Munchausen Syndrome by Proxy, *Child Abuse and Neglect* Vol. 11, pp. 547–563, 1987.

15. Schreier and Libow, op. cit.

16. Andrew A. Skolnick, Critics Denounce Staffing Jails and Prisons with Physicians Convicted of Misconduct, *Journal of the American Medical Association,* Volume 280(16), pp. 1391–1392, October 28, 1998.

9

Rampage

Interestingly enough, most middle-class people probably think more of the possible serial killer in their midst, when, in reality, the risk of mass murder is much greater. As we suggested in Chapter 7, the victims of the typical serial killer are female prostitutes. By contrast, the victims of the mass murderer tend to be students, teachers, co-workers, friends, and family. Whether a disgruntled former employee or a spouse, an unhappy customer, a client or student, we all bear some risk of becoming a mass murder victim, whether at work and school, eating out, or running errands—not to mention the risk we face when we get home. A significant number of mass killers have annihilated their families.

While the terms mass and serial murder were used interchangeably when research into these phenomena began some 20 years ago, much research has more recently been directed at defining the mass killer as a distinct and separate type. Yet, much confusion remains.

Were the September 11, 2001, deaths a mass murder? If so, then 3,000 people died in a massacre, where the weapon was an airplane. Clearly, we have to make some decisions when creating our mass murder typologies, as there are very different prevention and intervention implications for the workplace shooter, the family annihilator, and the terrorist with an airplane. We have chosen to discuss mass school shootings, hate crimes, and terrorism in separate chapters due in part to their possibly different causal factors and policy implications. In this chapter, we have focused on mass killers who target family, former and current co-workers, and total strangers.

Methodical and Selective

Mark Barton's exit line dripped with evil sarcasm. "I hope this won't ruin your trading day," said the 44-year-old stock investor as he wrapped up his July 29, 1999, bloody rampage at Atlanta's financial district. Armed with two semi-automatic pistols, a Colt .45-caliber and a Glock 9 mm, the gunman had navigated deliberately through two Atlanta investment offices, All-Tech and Momentum Securities, located just across Piedmont Road from each other. The afternoon shooting spree left nine dead and a dozen others wounded. By sundown later that evening, Barton had turned his gun on himself when cornered by police at a gas station several miles northwest of the scene of the crime.

What was it that caused Mark Barton to snap? And, did he in fact snap? The widespread notion that mass gunmen like Barton erupt suddenly into an uncontrollable, murderous rage is deeply rooted in the popular vernacular frequently used to describe these events: expressions such as "going berserk," "going ballistic," or even "going postal" (a code word for workplace massacres coined after a string of post office shootings in the mid-1980s and early 1990s). Psychiatric research has also generally supported the idea that mass murderers "run amok"—they are totally out of touch with reality (i.e., psychotic) and select victims at random who happen to be "in the wrong place at the wrong time."[1]

A more careful examination reveals quite a different picture. On the contrary, most mass killers do not just snap and start shooting anything that moves. Typically, these murderers generally act with calm deliberation, often planning their assault days, if not months, in advance. Their preparations often involve assembling the arsenal of weaponry as well as the most effective means of ambush. In addition, mass murderers tend to be quite selective in targeting their victims. They aim to kill those individuals they are convinced are responsible for their miseries, frequently ignoring anyone not implicated in the plot against them.

Mark Barton surely didn't just wake up on that warm July day and spontaneously decide to perpetrate a bloodbath. His crime spree was hardly sudden and episodic. Two days earlier, Barton had rammed a claw hammer into the skull of Leigh Ann, his 27-year-old second wife, stuffing her body into a closet at their home in the Atlanta suburb of Stockbridge. The next morning, he took his two children, 12-year-old Matthew and 8-year-old Mychelle, to get haircuts. Later that night—the eve of his downtown shooting spree—Barton bludgeoned his son and daughter as they slept in their beds. He then held each child face down in the bathtub to ensure they would not wake up in pain. Once he was certain they were dead, he tucked them both into their beds and placed a favorite toy next to each of them—a gameboy for his son and a stuffed animal for his daughter.

Barton was so deliberate in his actions that he left a note at his home explaining his motives. "I killed Leigh Ann because she was one of the main reasons for my demise," Barton wrote. "I killed the children to exchange them for five minutes of pain for a lifetime of pain. I forced myself to do it to keep them from suffering so much later. No mother, no father, no relatives." He also left several other notes around the house relaying whatever sentiments came to mind. Next to his son's body, Barton placed a brief message to God: "I give you Matthew David Barton—my son, my buddy, my life. Please take care of him."

There is considerable evidence, moreover, that Barton's murder string may have actually started six years earlier. He was a suspect in the untimely death of his first wife and her mother at his in-law's home in Alabama. Not only did this clear the way for him to be with his 21-year-old girlfriend/mistress, Leigh Ann (who later became his second wife and next victim), but the life insurance proceeds became invaluable to him to get a fresh start on his slumping career.

The popular image of a killer who shoots randomly at human targets without rhyme or reason would hardly characterize Barton's crimes or, for that matter, the actions of most mass killers. It was no accident or random choice that Barton selected the location for his vengeful shooting spree. The two day-trading centers were the very places where he had been ruined financially. He had failed miserably in the high-stakes, high-pressure occupation of day-trading in volatile technology stocks.

Barton lost $153,000 in a single day, forcing Momentum Securities to call in his credit. He turned next to All-Tech and pushed his losses to almost a half-million dollars. He also resented those around him who had profited so handsomely on trades of shares of Internet stocks like Amazon and Yahoo. As he wrote in his suicide letter, "I don't plan to live very much longer. Just long enough to kill as many of the people that greedily sought my destruction."

There are, of course, cases of mass murderers who do kill indiscriminately. On October 16, 1991, George Hennard, Jr., rammed his pickup truck through the plate-glass window of the Luby's Cafeteria in Killeen, Texas, and then randomly opened fire on customers as they ate their lunch, killing 23. On April 23, 1987, William Cruse, a 59-year-old retired librarian, went on a bloody rampage in a Palm Bay, Florida, shopping center, killing 6 and injuring another 12. Neither Hennard nor Cruse knew any of the victims nor had anything more than a casual connection to their respective murder sites.

Yet more often, the location and even the particular victims are chosen because the killer sees them as responsible for his misfortunes. In 1989, for example, Marc Lepine burst into a lecture hall at the University of Montreal, commanded the men to leave, and started executing the remaining female students, killing 14. Lepine despised women—especially feminists—and blamed them for all of his problems.

Lepine didn't just pick any place for his vengeful rampage. He didn't choose the nursing program where far more women would literally be under his gun. Instead, he purposely chose the Engineering School, where he saw women pursuing "man's work." In fact, Lepine had been denied admission to the Engineering School and was punishing those who had taken his seat in the class.

There are many mass killers who target whole categories of victims, often expressing their racial, gender, or ethnic hatred. Like George Hennard, 25-year-old Patrick Purdy was a young man filled with resentment. In the end, however, he singled out a particular group—Southeast Asians—as being especially blameworthy. On January 17, 1989, Purdy visited his former elementary school in what had become a predominantly Southeast Asian section of Stockton, California. Purdy killed five and wounded dozens more, before committing suicide just as the police arrived.

Similarly, Michael McDermott, in December 2000, killed seven of his co-workers at Edgewater Technology in Wakefield, Massachusetts, but he hardly shot indiscriminately at anything that moved. Blaming his dire financial position on certain offices of the company, McDermott selectively targeted his fellow employees only in payroll and human resources. Moreover, McDermott's rampage was anything but spontaneous. A day earlier, he had left a cache of weapons and ammunition under his desk, so as to be fully prepared for his murderous onslaught. In court, McDermott tried to convince the jury that he was a victim of severe mental illness—that he had been convinced that he was killing not co-workers but Hitler and six of Hitler's henchmen. Not believing the defendant, McDermott was given a life sentence without parole eligibility.

More often than not, however, mass killers select particular victims to kill in order to avenge perceived injustices. After Ronald Gene Simmons executed 14 family members for insult and insubordination, he then launched a 45-minute shooting spree through the town of Russellville, Arkansas, killing a woman who had spurned his romantic advances and a former boss, and wounding several others at former worksites. As he surrendered, Simmons remarked, "I've gotten everybody who hurt me."

Despite the killer's selectivity, even in the most focused rampage many innocent victims die in the crossfire or because they stand in the way of the killer's murderous swath. Frequently, however, they are killed because the gunman associates them with the primary target. The notion of murder by proxy (described earlier in Chapter 4) explains the carnage in many worksites. On August 20, 1986, the morning after being reprimanded for poor job performance, 44-year-old Patrick Henry Sherrill arrived early at the Edmond, Oklahoma, post office with his mail bag full of guns and ammunition. Sherrill's first victim was a supervisor who had threatened his job. He then opened fire on his co-workers, all associated in his mind with the more amorphous enemy, the unfair postal service.

Losses and Frustrations

Even though mass slaughters may not be sudden, there generally are still clear-cut events that precipitate the bloodshed. The most random crimes are often inspired by small and seemingly insignificant matters, but which in the killer's paranoid and sometimes psychotic view of the world are important concerns. Hennard, for example, was especially irate about the Senate confirmation hearings for Supreme Court Justice Clarence Thomas during which Anita Hill alleged she had been sexually harassed by Thomas, her former supervisor at the EEOC. Hennard watched the televised proceeding in a local bar, yelling and throwing food at the TV.

In more typical cases, the gunman seeks to redress a personal slight, often real, usually involving a catastrophic loss—the loss of a relationship, of a job, or even of honor. Earlier in Chapter 4, we examined certain cases of mass murder within the family. One of the more common forms of mass killing involves a head of household who either decides to punish his wife and children for some transgression or, alternatively, to protect them from the misery of living in a cold, cruel world. However, the most common form of mass murder, particularly in recent years, surrounds employment disputes—a firing, layoff, warning, or losing out on a promotion or award.

As many as 40% of the mass murders in the United States are in the family, as opposed to the random shootings of strangers at a fast-food restaurant or a shopping mall or the targeting of a category of people. There were almost 250 mass slayings from 1976 to 2002 in which four or more family members were killed. In most of these cases, the father murdered his wife (or ex-wife), children/stepchildren, and often times even the family pet. Chapter 4 described the most common types of family slaughter—illustrated by Ronald Gene Simmons' massacre of his wife, children, and grandchildren as punishment for disobedience and disloyalty and John DeLisle's only semi-successful attempt at family murder-suicide to put an end to his personal and financial problems.

While these two prototypes of family mass murder clearly predominate, certainly other motivations arise as well. Using a broad definition of family, in February 1998, Christopher Churchill of Noble, Illinois, a town of about 300 people, bludgeoned to death five people including his half-brother (age 17), his brother's girlfriend (age 35), and her three children (ages 12, 10 and 6). Now serving a sentence of life imprisonment, Churchill was not eligible for the death penalty due to his age at the time of the crimes—16. After the brutal mass slaying, Churchill sexually molested the bodies of the male and female children as well as their mother, both as they were dying and after they were dead. He later said he just "felt like being sick." It was later learned that Churchill had fantasized about the murders for over a year. He was supposedly envious of the relationship his brother had had with his older girl-friend, and was furious when one of the children had broken one of his CDs. Churchill went in and out of the murder scene for days after the killings—showering, molesting the bodies, and taking cash and cigarettes. Teachers finally started asking questions because the slain children had not been to school and neighbors noticed that the house was too quiet.

Following family annihilations, the second most prevalent form of mass killing involves employment disputes. Thirty-three-year-old Paul Calden said that he'd be back, and regrettably for the employees of the Fireman's Fund Insurance Company in Tampa, Florida, he was true to his word. On January 27, 1993, eight months after being fired from his job, he returned to get his revenge. This time, however, he'd be the one to do the firing. Calden sat in the company cafeteria. He was as cool as the ice in the Diet Coke that he sipped while waiting patiently for his victims to arrive for lunch. Calden approached three of his former supervisors as they were seated together at the back of the lunchroom. Standing over the table and taking aim with his 9 mm semi-automatic pistol. Calden announced, "This is what you get for firing me," and calmly started shooting, methodically encircling the table with gunfire. By the time it was all over, Calden had killed his three former managers and had wounded two other employees. His next and final victim was himself.

Paul Calden was the quintessential disgruntled employee—the so-called co-worker from Hell. He had drifted from job to job, causing trouble wherever he worked. Just prior to his employment at Fireman's Fund, Calden had worked at Allstate Insurance where he threatened his supervisor by deliberately displaying the butt of a gun inside his briefcase. This manager was so frightened by Calden that he offered him a severance package that he couldn't refuse.

During his two-year employment at Fireman's, Calden had developed a reputation for being a belligerent hothead. He constantly challenged his supervisors' authority, at one point nearly coming to blows because of a reprimand. He threatened to sue the company for denying him a raise that he felt he deserved. He shouted obscenities at a female co-worker who had taken his favorite parking place. He even filed a harassment complaint because a fellow employee displayed on her car a bumper sticker that offended him.

By contrast to Calden's spotty work record, other vengeful employees come to feel invulnerable to job loss because of their long-term employment with the same company. From their perspective, they have given their best years to the boss, have unselfishly dedicated their careers to the organization, and resent that their hard work and loyalty are not being returned in kind by the company.

Forty-seven-year-old Joseph Wesbecker, for example, was furious about perceived mistreatment by management at the Standard Gravure Printing Company. The Louisville, Kentucky, plant had recently been sold to a new owner, and Wesbecker felt strongly that the new management team didn't appreciate his over 20 years of hard work. By all accounts, he was an excellent pressman, and he always put in long hours of overtime and extra shifts, which had earned him the nickname "overtime hog."

Suffering from depression, Wesbecker sought an exemption from a certain job task that was particularly stressful to him, a request that was endorsed by a government employment arbitrator but resisted by management. Wesbecker was so resentful that he told a co-worker that he was going to get even with the company and even showed him the gun in his lunch bag with which he intended to carry out his plan of action. He also talked about his "hit list" of intended victims.

Months later, on September 14, 1989, while out of work on long-term disability for depression, Wesbecker made an unscheduled visit to work—he had a job to do. Roaming the corridors with an AK-47, Wesbecker systematically sought out his intended targets, killing eight and wounding a dozen others. He was so methodical in his assault that he purposely spared a friend: "Not you, John," Wesbecker said to the fortunate co-worker who was cowered in front of him and sauntered on by.

Profile of the Workplace Avenger

According to the offender age patterns presented in Chapter 3, teens and young adults are overrepresented among all murderers, with a mean age of 29 years old. Workplace murder is a notable exception to the rule of youth, with workplace avengers averaging 38 years of age. As shown in Table 9.1, moreover, well over half are at least 35 years old. Also as shown, whites represent nearly three-quarters of vengeful workplace killers, compared to the more even racial split for homicide offenders generally. In fatal workplace disputes, finally, the gender ratio is even more imbalanced than usual, with nearly 93 percent male perpetrators.

TABLE 9.1 *Characteristics of Workplace Murderers, 1976–2002 Combined (Non-Felony Related, at least one victim)*

Category	Percent
Age of Offender	
Under 25	18.1%
25–34	29.4%
35–44	23.8%
45–54	16.2%
55+	12.4%
Race of Offender	
White	72.6%
Black	24.4%
Other	3.0 %
Sex of Offender	
Male	91.2%
Female	8.8%
Weapon	
Firearm	67.5%
Knife	13.6%
Blunt object	7.7%
Brute force	5.8%
Other	5.5%

The overall profile of the typical workplace murderer is a middle-aged white male, who feels that his employment problems signal the end of the world as he knows it. Despite changing gender roles, men—much more than women—still tend to judge their self-worth by what they do, rather than who they are. If they aren't doing anything, then what good are they? Furthermore, men tend to regard violence as a means for establishing control, as an offensive move, whereas women see it as a last resort, as a defensive move.[2] Thus, men who suffer psychologically because of the loss of a job are more likely to respond violently in order to "show them who's boss." Or perhaps, women are more content to exact their revenge in quieter ways, for example, by means of poisoning, assassinating someone's character, gossiping, or getting others to do their dirty work?

There are relatively few female workplace avengers. While women have been offenders in a number of mass murders, they typically massacre their families. Other women have gone on rampages but have shot to death only one or two victims and thus don't fit the widely accepted definition of a mass murderer. In a rare case of a woman targeting a number of strangers, Sylvia Segrist in 1986 randomly shot to death three people outside a shopping mall in Springfield, Pennsylvania. In 1988, Laurie Dann, a 36-year-old resident of Glencoe, Illinois, went on a shooting spree with a .22 caliber handgun in a Winnetka, Illinois, elementary school. Although she shot several students, only one died. It was later learned that Dann may have also poisoned other children for whom she had babysat. As women begin to focus on their careers the way that men have traditionally done so, they can be expected to face similar disappointments and to become more skilled in the use of firearms. If so, we might reasonably expect to see more female mass killers.

Some workplace murders involve youthful perpetrators, but most do not. To a younger employee, a job is often just a job, certainly not a career, and there is always another opportunity down the road. The middle-aged employee, however, views termination or the threat of termination as truly the end of the road. He sees few opportunities for alternative employment at the same wage, benefit, or status level to which he has grown accustomed. At this juncture, the middle-aged man expects to be at the top of his career, not hitting rock-bottom.

In part, the middle-aged worker responds desperately and violently, not just because of limited opportunities in the future but because of what has transpired in the past. The road to mass murder, particularly at the job site, is a long one, involving a good number of bumps along the way.

Mark Barton, for example, had experienced years of disappointment, which likely eroded his ability to cope and intensified his feelings of persecution. After graduating from the University of South Carolina with a degree in chemistry, he seemed to fail at each and every turn. He was pushed out of an executive position at TLC Manufacturing in Texarkana, Texas, a company he helped to form. Moving next to Georgia, he tried his hand at chemical sales, another dead end financially. Finally, he used the profits from the insurance settlement from his first wife's death to invest in the stock market, a move that ultimately bankrupted him.

Of course, most disgruntled employees and ex-employees don't take out their anger on the company. Some may blame themselves, become depressed, and consider suicide as their only option. Others may take out their frustrations on their family. But for the one who typically externalizes blame, responsibility always lies elsewhere.

When fired from his job as a public parks worker in Ft. Lauderdale, Clifton McCree, a 41-year-old African-American, was unequivocal in his view of whom to blame. In a suicide note written just prior to his February 9, 1996, killing spree that claimed the lives of five former co-workers at the Department of Parks and Recreation, McCree alleged racism to be at the core of his unfair termination by the city over a year earlier:

> None of this would have happened. All the hope, effort, and opportunity at employment only prove to be futile after [being] terminated by the city of Ft. Lauderdale. I felt I was treated very unfairly by the city after 17 years. The malicious and racist nature of how my situation was "set up" and handled. The economic lynching without regard or recourse was something very evil. Since I couldn't continue to support my family, life became nothing. I no longer wanted to live in this kind of world. I also wanted to punish some of the cowardly, racist devils that helped bring this about, along with the system. I'm glad illness did it. It became war. There should have been a more humane system. But NO . . .

On July 8, 2003, a workplace shooting at a Lockheed Martin plant in Meridian, Mississippi, took the lives of 5 employees and injured 11 others. The death toll was actually 6 if you count Doug Williams, the shooter who ended his rampage by killing himself. Whether or not we count the offenders in the body count may be another basis for deciding who makes the mass killer list. Technically the death of the offender is usually either a suicide or a justifiable homicide by police, so their death should not be counted in the mass murder death toll. Ironically, the Mississippi shooter left an ethics and sensitivity training session, went home and armed himself with a shotgun, a Ruger, a derringer, a rifle and scope, an automatic pistol, and lots of ammo.

Many workplace avengers commit suicide, but not until exacting revenge for the wrongs they perceive have been committed against them. Almost without exception, workplace murderers feel as though they are the victim, feeling that others, especially the boss, have treated them unfairly. Were they to trace the job disappointments to their own inadequacies, they might turn aggression inward. Seeing everyone else to blame, however, they choose to execute those responsible, before taking their own life.

On February 25, 1998, 35-year-old Matthew Beck, back to work at the Connecticut State Lottery following a stress-related leave, went on a deadly rampage, killing four of his superiors before turning the gun on himself. Beck had complained to co-workers that his supervisors were stalling on negotiations to pay him back wages and that he was not being assigned any work to do. Months earlier, he had filed a grievance contending that he was being assigned jobs outside of his work classification and that he deserved a raise of $2 an hour. Just a few days before going on his rampage, the gunman spoke angrily of suing the Lottery for job discrimination.

Many Americans, of course, suffer the kinds of catastrophic losses and letdowns endured by Beck, Barton, and Wesbecker, yet they are able to lean on close friends and family to help them deal with life's disappointments. Most of the workplace avengers, however, are socially isolated. Either they are like Paul Calden and live in seclusion or like Barton and don't feel sufficiently connected to family. Socially and psychologically alone, they regard work as the only meaningful part of their lives. When they lose their job, they lose everything. They lack not only the emotional support for their problems but the healthy reality check as their feelings of paranoia and persecution build.

This is exactly how it was for Joseph Wesbecker. He was divorced for the second time, and his relationships with his children were badly strained. For Joe, his job was the only thing in his life that was going well and that gave him some sense of purpose and satisfaction—a reason to get up in the morning. But that was taken away when management forced him to take long-term disability rather than to make a reasonable accommodation for his psychological disability, which was to be exempted from performing a particularly stressful job function.

For the lonely employee, like Wesbecker, termination from a job means not just a loss of his self-esteem, and not just the loss of income. It also means the loss of his only source of companionship—his co-workers. Therefore, job loss carries a double burden: frustration and anger, on the one hand, and a severance of important social anchors, on the other.

Here too there is a trend in society that places more and more middle-aged men at risk. An increased rate of divorce, greater residential mobility, and a general lack of community and neighborliness mean that, for many Americans, work is their only source of stability and companionship. And men, much more than women, often center all of their friendships on the job.

Finally, a worker may be frustrated and angry, lonely and isolated; he may blame the boss and feel that management is corrupt and unfair. But if he doesn't have access to a powerful weapon or know how to use it, the disgruntled employee may not be able to exact the kind of revenge that he seeks.

Firearms play a key role in several respects. Most important, the gun corrects the perceived power imbalance between the employee and his superior—it's "The Great Equalizer" as 28-year-old Gang Lu put it in a letter to the press, just before his 1991 rampage at the University of Iowa in which he sought out and executed three professors who had overlooked him for an important dissertation prize. Actually, over a 12-minute period, the graduate student in physics shot to death five members of the university community. If he had had a knife or had used his hands, there is little chance that Gang Lu would have amassed such a large body count.

The gun, of course, is simply far more lethal, particularly if the avenger wants to kill large numbers. Also, the gun psychologically distances the attacker from his victims. Although full of rage, he might be deterred were it necessary to kill with his hands. By contrast, a gun makes it very easy psychologically . . . and America's gun laws make it very easy for him to acquire what he needs to carry out his act of vengeance. Louisville's Joseph Wesbecker went into a gun shop, pointed to a semi-automatic weapon displayed under the counter, and asked "How much?" Surprised at the price, he responded, "That's all? I'll take two!"

Curiously, most disgruntled workers and other mass killers would not even consider buying a weapon through illegal means. After all, they see themselves as law-abiding citizens, not criminals. They are just looking for some justice. To them, the murder is not a crime; it's simply just desserts. For example, 35-year-old Colin Ferguson, who on December 7, 1993, transformed the Long Island Railroad into a shooting gallery, purchased his gun legally in California. Nine months before going on his killing spree, he checked into a cheap hotel and waited more than the necessary two weeks to qualify for a legal gun purchase.

Nationally, as many as six people are murdered every month at the hands of a co-worker or former co-worker.[3] And for every tragic incident of workplace homicide, thousands of workers are assaulted or threatened by an associate on the job. Even less conspicuous are the countless numbers of angry workers who seek to sabotage their company's bottom line. They may spread ugly rumors to discourage sales or surreptitiously subvert the manufacturing process. In one recent case, an angry worker was caught on videotape as he secretly urinated into the company office coffee pot.

In response to rising levels of violence in the American workplace, a wide range of books and pamphlets, seminars and consultants have surfaced to help companies large and small cope with the growing threat of violence on the job. Some experts focus on security concerns, others on promoting effective EAP strategies. Still others recommend processes to enhance employment screening techniques or channels of communication so as to alert management about troublesome workers before they explode.[4]

While all these approaches may be useful, the overriding goal should be to make civility and decency in the workplace as critical a goal as profit. Companies need to upgrade and humanize the way in which they deal with all employees every day rather than just to focus narrowly on how to respond to the occasional worker who has made threats.[5] Long-term planning to improve employee morale pays off in human terms. A study conducted for Northwestern National Life Insurance concluded that companies with effective grievance, harassment, and security procedures also reported lower rates of workplace violence.[6]

Twenty or 30 years ago, the bond between management and worker was by far stronger. Most Americans believed that bosses had the best interests of workers in mind; managers felt that their workforce was loyal to the company. But the expectation of loyalty between worker and boss has gone the way of the dinosaur and has been replaced with an adversarial perspective on both sides. In an era of corporate takeovers, mega-mergers, and corporate CEO scandals, workers often feel that they are left with nothing while the corporate fat cats have multi-million dollar homes and enormous savings accounts. This represents a lethal mix for disenfranchised, marginalized, mentally ill workers who have been demoted, passed over for promotion, or fired.

Murderous Customers and Clients

It isn't only workers and ex-workers who blame their problems on the company. Disgruntled customers, clients, and even patients sometimes seek to avenge perceived mistreatment by banks, loan offices, law firms, hospitals and clinics, schools and colleges, unemployment offices, courthouses—in short, "the system"—through violence and murder. Each year, several dozen workers are killed at the hands of customers or clients.[7]

For example, 45-year-old George Lott opened fire with a concealed 9 mm semi-automatic handgun during an appellate court proceeding in Ft. Worth, Texas, on the morning of July 1, 1992. It appeared to those present in the crowded fourth-floor courtroom that Lott was shooting wildly at anything that moved. It appeared that two attorneys who were slain and a third attorney and two judges who were wounded just happened to be at the wrong place at the wrong time. Lott escaped through the mass confusion, only to show up six hours later at a local television station to tell his side of the story. Speaking on-air with the news anchor, Lott detailed his deep-seated grudge against the judicial system that he believed had been unfair to him.

Similarly, in July 1993, eight people were slaughtered at a San Francisco law firm by a former client; eight others were shot to death at a Jacksonville GMAC office in June 1990 by an embittered customer whose car had been repossessed. Four public employees were gunned down at the Schuyler County Courthouse in October 1992 by a "deadbeat dad" who questioned the legitimacy of the child support demands. And in 1993, three doctors at the Los Angeles County Medical Center were shot by a patient who believed that the doctors weren't taking his chronic illness seriously enough.

Fifteen years ago, it was virtually unheard of for a dissatisfied customer or client to seek revenge through murderous means. Times have changed, however. "Fighting city hall" has taken a new and ominous meaning. Economic resentment can be felt not only by vengeful employees but also by disgruntled clients and customers who seek to get even with the system—"to win one for the little guy."

In a complex, bureaucratic society, more and more citizens are feeling powerless against the red tape and unresponsiveness of big business and government. Most, of course, will do little more than complain loudly about the injustice. But increasing numbers simply refuse to sit back and take it.

Like the disgruntled employee, the vengeful customer/client is typically an isolated, middle-aged man who, after a prolonged period of frustration, suffers a major financial or personal setback that he views as catastrophic. With no one to turn to for assistance or support, he deliberately decides to punish the institution that has caused him so much grief. Tending to externalize blame, he sees himself as a victim, not a criminal, who seeks justice through killing.

Part of the problem lies in the impersonal or ineffective response of customer relations in both public and private sectors. Increasingly, consumers are frustrated by automated phone systems with endless button-pushes and lengthy holding queues, by poorly trained or overburdened customer relations representatives, and, of course, by computer glitches. In many companies, customer service has become customer disservice.

And now with virtually every company having an Internet site, getting help is even harder. They all have Web pages with "Frequently Asked Questions," but they are never the questions that you seem to have. For that, you have to log on to www.customerservice.com/dont-hold-your-breath.

When customers or clients deal with a small company, they can easily identify the right person to see in order to resolve a complaint. In large, impersonal bureaucracies, however, finding a responsible party is all but impossible. Some customers get mad yet give up in frustration; a few decide to get even through sabotage or, worse, through murder.

Murder by dissatisfied customers or clients will likely never reach epidemic proportions, but these incidents reflect, albeit in the extreme, a more general problem in America today. In the face of growing alienation and cynicism, large companies and agencies must upgrade and humanize their customer relations efforts. They must always remember the adage: "The customer is always right, especially when he's holding a gun!"

Endnotes

1. See Joseph Westermeyer, "Amok," in Claude T. H. Friedmann and Robert A. Faguet, eds., *Extraordinary Disorders of Human Behavior.* New York: Plenum Press, 1982.

2. Anne Campbell, *Men, Women, and Aggression.* New York: Basic Books, 1993.

3. U.S. Department of Labor, Bureau of Labor Statistics, *Census of Fatal Occupational Injuries.* Washington, DC: 1996.

4. Sandra L. Haskett, *Workplace Violence: Before, During and After.* Boston: Butterworth-Heinemann, 1996.

5. Mark Braverman and Richard V. Denenberg, *The Violence Prone Workplace: A New Approach to Dealing With Hostile, Threatening, and Uncivil Behavior.* Ithica, NY: Cornell University Press, 1999.

6. Northwestern National Life, *Fear and Violence in the Workplace.* Minneapolis, MN, 1993.

7. U.S. Department of Labor, op. cit.

10

Hate Homicides

According to the FBI, hate or bias crimes, including homicides, involve "criminal offenses committed against persons, property, or society that are motivated, in whole or in part, by the offender's bias against a race, religion, disability, sexual-orientation, or ethnicity/national origin."[1] Thus, the FBI definition specifies the motivation for committing the offense; it requires that a racial, religious, ethnic, or some other identified difference between victim and offender play at least some role in inspiring the criminal act. For example, an individual who illegally takes money to buy illicit drugs may decide to rob only Asians because of some stereotype he holds regarding this group of people. If part of the motivation for the robbery involves the victim's Asian identity, then the offense can be regarded as a hate crime.[2]

The term "hate crime" was coined in the late 1980s in response to a racial incident in the Howard Beach section of New York City, in which a black man was killed while attempting to evade a violent mob of white teenagers, shouting racial epithets. Although widely used by the federal government, the mass media, and researchers in the field, the term is somewhat misleading because it suggests incorrectly that hatred is invariably a distinguishing characteristic of this type of offense. While it is true that many hate crimes involve intense animosity toward the victim, many others do not. Conversely, many crimes involving hatred between an offender and a victim are not "hate crimes" in the sense intended here. For example, an assault that arises out of a dispute between two co-workers who compete for a promotion might involve intense hatred, even though it is not based on any racial or religious differences between them. Similarly, a love-triangle may provoke intense emotions, having nothing at all to do with race or religion.

Characteristics of Hate Murders

According to the FBI, there were more than 9,222 victims of bias crimes in 2002, including some 5,960 involving some form of violence. Among the victims of hate-motivated violence, 52 percent were intimidated, and 46 percent were assaulted. Less that one percent (11 in actual count) were murdered.[3] Of course, the FBI count is based on a voluntary reporting system to which many local jurisdictions refuse to contribute, causing hate offenses of all kinds to be under-reported. In 2002, almost 12,073 law enforcement agencies representing 247.2 million people or 86 percent of the country's population, reported hate crimes to the FBI. In states such as Arkansas, Alabama, and Mississippi, very few local jurisdictions submitted hate crime data. In fact, these three states combined reported only five incidents. Moreover, an offense may not be recorded as a hate crime because of lack of evidence that it is motivated by bias. The perpetrators may not use a racial slur or write hate graffiti, may not have a history of committing hate offenses, or might never confide their intent to the police or an acquaintance. But even if the FBI statistics vastly underestimate hate homicides, it is still hard to imagine—using the federal criteria—any more than 30 or so committed in the United States in any given year.

National data on hate homicides collected by the Southern Poverty Law Center (SPLC) in Montgomery, Alabama and published in its *Intelligence Report* suggest a much larger number of hate attacks committed in the United States.[4] Based on newspaper accounts, law enforcement reports, and interviews rather than just police reports, the SPLC estimates that in the year 2001 as many as 50,000 hate crimes (in contrast to under 10,000 included in the FBI statistics for the same year) including 21 homicides were committed. During this period, gay or transgendered individuals (or perceived to be gay or transgendered) were murdered more often than any other of the groups studied. Specifically, out of the 21 hate homicide victims killed, 11 were gay or lesbian, six were (or perceived to be) Muslims or Arabs, two were Asian, one was black, and one was Latino. These hate killings occurred in 12 states, including four victims each in California and Florida. The victims ranged in age from 16 to 76.

Judging by the amount of media attention that they typically receive, the influence of hate homicides seems much greater than their relatively small numbers might indicate. Not unlike less serious hate offenses, they impact not just a particular individual, but every member of a victim's group. In June 1998, three white men dragged James Byrd, a black man, to his death behind their pickup truck down a rocky country road in Jasper, Texas. Whether intended or not, the killers sent an unmistakable message to every black person in town regarding their vulnerability.

Similarly, the vicious murder in October 1998 of 21-year-old gay college student Matthew Shepard, by two young men in Laramie, Wyoming, was a warning to every gay person not to exercise their constitutionally guaranteed rights. For his "sin," Shepard was beaten into a coma and left tied to a fence in the desert. He died five days later.

After 9/11, hate crimes targeting Muslims (and anyone who might possibly have been a Muslim) increased some 1,600% from the year 2000, making them the second-most likely religious group (behind Jews) to be victimized. Many were victims of arson, vandalism, or assault. A few were murdered not to rob them, but simply because they wore a turban or spoke with an accent. In Mesa, Arizona, a 49-year-old Sikh Indian wearing a turban was shot down in front of his gas station. In Dallas, a Pakistani Muslim was found shot to death in his convenience store. In San Gabriel, California, an Egyptian Christian was killed in his grocery store.[5]

Perhaps because they target a group of people rather than an individual, hate-motivated murders generally attract tremendous amounts of media publicity. This was certainly true during the summer of 1999 when national attention was given to several hate homicides. In July, a former student at Indiana University, Benjamin Smith, went on a two-state shooting spree resulting in the death of a graduate student from Korea who was studying at Indiana

University and a black man who was formerly the basketball coach at Northwestern University. Driving his blue Ford Taurus through a Jewish neighborhood in Chicago's far north side, the 21-year-old Smith then opened fire on a group of Orthodox Jews, but managed only to injure six of them. Then, he took his own life.

Just weeks later, a 37-year-old white supremacist, Buford Furrow, walked into the North Valley Jewish Community Center in Los Angeles with a semi-automatic, where he fired more than 70 bullets, wounding six people. While attempting to avoid the law, he then approached an Asian-American letter carrier and asked him to mail a letter. Before the postal worker could reply, Furrow had shot him to death. In March 2001, in a Los Angeles courtroom, U.S. District Judge Nora Manella imposed a life sentence without the possibility of parole. "Your actions were a reminder that bigotry is alive," the judge told Furrow. "If you've sent a message, it is that even the most violent crimes can strengthen a community."[6]

Another characteristic of hate homicides is that their perpetrators are more likely than in other bias crimes to be linked with an organized hate group. The three killers of James Byrd had met behind bars where they joined the Aryan Brotherhood, a penitentiary hate group for white inmates who, after serving their time, are frequently recruited by white supremacist groups on the outside. The three perpetrators also had connections to the Ku Klux Klan. Indeed, they had planned to start a local chapter in the Jasper community.

Similarly, Benjamin Smith was a member of the World Church of the Creator, a relatively obscure white supremacist group whose members preach an anti-Christian, anti-Semitic, and racist set of doctrines. Operating out of East Peoria, their inspirational leader and father-figure, 27-year-old Matthew Hale, was denied the ability to practice law by the state board's Committee on Character and Fitness, whose members argued that he had flunked their test of ethics and character. Indeed, there is reason to believe that Hale's rejection by the Illinois bar may have angered his protege, Benjamin Smith enough to precipitate his killing spree. Buford Furrow had connections to Aryan Nations, a white supremacist organization, and to Christian Identity, the theological arm of a number of different hate groups around the country whose members believe that blacks and Latinos are subhuman "mud people" and that Jews are the children of the Devil.

The influence of group membership can hardly be exaggerated in the case of murders inspired by hate. As a cultural phenomenon, there may be literally millions of Americans who have adopted ethnocentric attitudes. They may tell racist jokes, use racial epithets, and verbalize their dislike of immigrants, gays, Jews, or people of color. Most Americans, however—notwithstanding their bigoted beliefs—would never dream of translating their hate into the commission of a crime, especially not murder.

But for someone who is angry and hate-filled, membership in an organized group can make all the difference. For one thing, the hatemonger's group teaches him that he is not alone in his bigotry. He knows, perhaps for the first time, that other Americans share the depths of his concern and his revulsion about the state of the nation and the decline of his "heritage" or race. Joining up gives him the inspiration needed to translate his attitudes into activism, to risk his personal safety in order to take a strong stand against race mixing, communism, the Zionist conspiracy, or the one world order. Second, if a hatemonger works together with other members of a group, then there often is some sharing of tasks that weakens his feeling of personal responsibility. He has only driven the car or gone along for the ride; he only kicked or hit the victim, but never delivered the fatal blow. Moreover, owing to what social psychologists call a group effect, he may also be able to take risks with his personal safety that he would have regarded as unthinkable before taking membership in a group of like-minded comrades. Finally, white supremacist organizations tend to be apocalyptic, preaching to their members that global racial war is inevitable. The battle cry of the World Church of the Creator, for example, is "Rahowa"—standing for racial holy war. The bible for many hate groups is Andrew Macdonald's[7] novel *The Turner Diaries,* a fictionalized account, written by a white supremacist under a pseudonym, in which a bloody racial war is waged and won by the Aryan good guys. The FBI has suggested that *The Turner Diaries* provided the blueprint for the tragic Oklahoma City bombing episode in which 168 innocent people lost their lives.

Types of Hate Homicide

Hate homicides, not unlike hate crimes generally, seem to fall into one of four categories in terms of their perpetrators' motivations: thrill, defense, retaliation, and mission.

Thrill hate crimes are typically perpetrated by groups of teenagers or young adults who, bored and idle, decide to go out together looking for someone to attack. The sadism and excessive brutality involved in many thrill homicides suggest that at least some of the killers—perhaps the leaders of the group—have an excessive need to feel powerful at the expense of their victim. It takes only one sadistic bigot with power to exercise his will in a group of young people who are eager to please their peers and be accepted. Most thrill offenders might easily fit the label, offered by political scientist Meredith Watts, as "fellow travelers."[8] They may not harbor intense hatred toward their victim, but they also cannot bear the idea of being rejected by their friends. These are typically marginalized and alienated youngsters, whose thrill attack gets them little more than bragging rights and a vague sense of their own importance. But that is apparently enough to provide the inspiration for singling out a vulnerable victim. The majority of all hate attacks can be regarded as thrill hate crimes.[9]

Most thrill attacks take the form of vandalism, desecration, and assault. Occasionally, however, a group of young people looking for some excitement will attack their victim with lethal force. Twenty-year-old James Burmeister and his two buddies were soldiers stationed at the Ft. Bragg army base outside of Fayetteville, North Carolina. They were also racist skinheads who hated blacks, Latinos, and Jews. The three friends didn't belong to any nationally organized hate group. By day, they completely immersed themselves in the disciplined military training required of all recruits on base. But, at night, they shed their military uniforms in favor of the steel-toed boots and green jackets associated with the Nazi movement.

During the early morning hours of December 7, 1995, the three soldiers drove their Chevrolet Cavalier into a black neighborhood located in the heart of town. They had spent the night drinking, playing pool, and watching topless dancers at a local sports bar.

All the while, Burmeister had made his intentions clear enough—he talked incessantly to his friends about wanting to find the enemy and have a little fun, about wanting to earn a badge of honor in the form of a spider web tattoo worn only by those members of the movement who had killed in order to further the Nazi cause. He liked the excitement, the thrill, and the bragging rights.

Shortly after midnight, the three spotted the victims, Michael James, 36, and Jackie Burden, 27, who were walking together along a dirt road, totally unaware of the danger lurking just ahead. Burmeister jumped out of the car and, without warning, immediately opened fire on the black couple with his 9 mm Rugar handgun, killing them both. The three then sped away from the scene of the crime, leaving the bodies of their two victims to be discovered by passersby.

In contrast to thrill offenses motivated by a need to be accepted and feel important, *defensive* hate crimes are, from the perpetrators' viewpoint, designed to protect their turf, territory, neighborhood, women, job, reputation, school, or campus—in general, their birthright. In some precipitating episode, the victims are perceived to threaten what the offender regards as belonging to him: members of a black family moving onto a previously all white block, the first Asian student in a college dormitory, a gay man attending a party. The attack is typically aimed at particular victims, those who dare challenge or threaten the security or well-being of the offender. When the threat subsides, so does the attack.

Defensive hate crimes may begin with relatively harmless acts designed to signal the victim that he is trespassing on private property. If, however, the original message is disregarded—if the black family remains on the block, if the gay man refuses to leave the party, if the Asian student fails to change residence halls—then the offense may escalate into violence, until the desired result has been achieved.

Defensive hate crimes are occasionally provoked by a highly personalized threat, especially when it involves a challenge to a perpetrator's sexual orientation. In February 1999, 25-year-old Steven Eric Mullins lured Billy Jack Gaither, a 39-year-old gay man, to a remote area in a small Alabama town for the purpose of taking his life. When Gaither showed up, the 25-year-old Mullins approached his victim from behind, slashing his throat with a long-bladed knife, and cracking open his head with an ax handle. Along with his 21-year-old companion Charles Butler, Mullins then burned Gaither's body and car in order to destroy the evidence.

The defensive motivation underlying Mullins's attack became clear in court. He had decided to eliminate Gaither in order to cover up his own homosexual tendencies, if not the relationship he had had with his victim. According to the testimony of eyewitnesses, the defendant had recently attended a party of gay men and had been observed dancing with his victim. Mullins testified in his own defense that he and Gaither had been drinking partners until Gaither propositioned him. That's when the defendant decided it was necessary to defend his reputation from irreparable damage.

A single hate crime is often followed by a number of *retaliatory* follow-up attacks by members of the victimized group. The month with the most hate offenses in New York City's history, for example, followed the brutal murder of a young black man, Yusuf Hawkins, in the white community of Bensonhurst. Believing that someone should pay, those in the black community who attacked in the aftermath of Hawkins' death were looking for revenge.

Retaliatory attacks tend to have the greatest potential for fueling additional hate crimes on both sides. Unlike defensive hate crimes designed to eliminate a particular "outsider" from a neighborhood, a workplace, or a school, retaliatory offenses often target not the original offender but anyone from the offender's group. Thus, the victim of a retaliatory crime is selected at random, so long as he is perceived to belong to the perpetrator's group.

An important example of how the desire for general revenge can lead to an escalation of violence between groups can be found in an incident that occurred in the Crown Heights section of New York City in August 1991. Seven-year-old Gavin Cato, a black child who lived in the Crown Heights section, was accidentally killed when the car driven by an Orthodox Jewish motorist jumped the curb.

In retaliation, a 29-year-old rabbinical student from Australia who was totally unconnected to the accident was stabbed to death. For almost a week, blacks and Jews exchanged insulting remarks, hurled rocks and bottles at one another, and broke windows in homes and cars. Dozens more were injured.[10]

In Crown Heights, mistrust and suspicion were palpable between Blacks and Jews. Many black residents believed that the motorist who hit the black child would get special treatment from city officials and get off scot free. At the same time, many Jewish residents of Crown Heights were convinced that the black mayor of New York City would rather look the other way than to bring the black murderer of the Australian rabbinical student to justice.

Mission hate crimes are the rarest and also the most dangerous category of offenses. They are the most likely to involve the members of an organized hate group as well as severe mental illness on the part of the perpetrator. They are also the most likely to result in a murder. Mission hate offenses represent no more than five percent of all hate crimes but probably a much larger proportion of hate homicides.[11]

Unlike thrill, defensive, and retaliatory attacks, mission hate crimes tend to be broad in scope and extend over time. Their perpetrators generally have no particular person or persons in mind to victimize; instead, they seek to destroy each and every member of a particular group. As a result, they may kill indiscriminately within a category, targeting a number of people simultaneously or going on a killing spree in a number of venues. For those who have made a career of bigotry, they might continue their killing spree until such time that they are finally apprehended by law enforcement.

In November 1995, four young men affiliated with the Nazi Lowriders of Lancaster, California brutally murdered Milton Walker, a 43-year-old black homeless man in a vacant lot behind a fast food restaurant. While shouting racial slurs at their victim, the young white attackers repeatedly bludgeoned him with a wooden board, kicked him, and then smashed him in the face with a pipe. The assailants were at least partially inspired by a desire to impress other members of their group. But their motivation went far beyond the bragging rights bestowed on those who kill. All of the perpetrators were devoted to the cause of eliminating minorities from their town.

Indeed, the attack resulting in the slaying of Milton Walker was no isolated incident committed by dabblers, but one episode in a much larger series of offenses carried out by the Lancaster Nazi Lowriders whose members had sought for years to eliminate minorities and create an all-white community. Their group had a long record of intimidating and attacking minorities for the purpose of leaving the impression that Lancaster was not safe for blacks, Latinos, and Asians. Members had taken part in a number of racially-motivated beatings, stabbings, and threats.

Not every mission killer is connected, of course, with some organized hate group. Included in the mission category are also the relatively rare individuals who, acting out of severe mental illness, go gunning for victims representative of a group they despise. In 1989, for example, Patrick Purdy murdered five Southeast Asian children as they congregated on the playground at the Cleveland Elementary School in Stockton, California. Having drifted from place to place and unable to hold a steady job, Purdy came to blame the immigrants who had recently moved into his community for all of his personal problems.

Another example of a mission killer operating on his own took place more recently in a Pittsburgh suburb, when Ronald Taylor, a 39-year-old black resident of Wilkinsburg,

Pennsylvania, decided to settle the score with all those bigoted white people he held responsible for his miseries. On March 1, 2000, disturbed that the superintendent of his apartment building had not yet repaired his broken front door, Taylor reportedly first set his apartment on fire and then shot five people, three of whom died. According to investigators, Taylor targeted only whites. At one point in his rampage, while waving his gun and making threatening gestures toward a group of people, he yelled at a black woman, "Not you, sister." In his apartment, the police found letters written by Taylor, in which he expressed anger toward whites, Jews, Asians, Italians, and law enforcement officers.

Organized Hate Groups

Most Americans are at least somewhat acquainted with the objectives of white hate groups like the Ku Klux Klan and neo-Nazis. Those who are familiar with American history know that the Klan has risen and fallen time and time again in response to challenges to the advantaged position of the white majority. During a short period of post-Civil War Reconstruction, for example, many whites were challenged by newly freed slaves who sought some measure of political power and began to compete for jobs with white working-class southerners. As a result, the Klan, responding with a campaign of terror and violence, lynched thousands of blacks. Klan-initiated violence increased again during the 1920s, as Americans sought "protection" from an unprecedented influx of immigrants from Eastern and Southern Europe. During the 1950s and 1960s, uniformed members of George Lincoln Rockwell's American Nazi Party gave the Nazi salute and shouted "Heil Hitler." Over the same period, Klansmen in their sheets and hoods marched in opposition to racial desegregation in schools and public facilities.

By contrast, the newer organized hate groups operating since 1980 aren't necessarily known for bizarre uniforms or strange rituals. Followers of such white supremacist groups as John and Tom Metzger's White Aryan Resistance (WAR) have shed their sheets and burning crosses in favor of more conventional attire. They often disavow the Klan and the neo-Nazi movement in favor of a brand of "American patriotism" that plays better among the working people of America. In 2002 alone, the American Knights of the Ku Klux Klan dropped from 18 to 14 chapters. Its listing of events on the Klan website remains empty.[12]

Tom and John Metzger's suspicion about the declining appeal of the Klan seems justified. They now wear shirts and ties, not sheets or hoods. Some of their most influential followers are former KKK members who recognize the futility of looking deviant, perhaps even anti-American. The new groups talk in code words and phrases about the very issues that concern middle-America. They preach that the heritage (meaning race) of white Christians is being eroded by foreign (meaning Jewish/communist) influence; they lament the rise of government interference (meaning Jews in high places who force racial integration down the throats of white Americans) in the lives of average citizens (meaning white Christians); and they condemn welfare cheating (meaning blacks and Latinos) which they see incorrectly as of overwhelming proportions. In addition to wearing business suits, some get face-lifts (like former Klan leader David Duke did) or don hairpieces (for awhile Tom Metzger had one). Several have run for public office. For example, Duke once ran for governor of Louisiana; Christian Identity's Richard Butler entered the race for mayor of Hayden, Idaho. Even in their support of bizarre-looking skinhead youth, they themselves are more concerned with projecting a respectable public image. They realize that younger people often reject the robes and ritual in favor of paramilitary dress. Concerned with the reaction of both the public and the police, some skinhead groups have recently taken a cue from their mentors by wearing their hair long and getting rid of their black leather jackets.

Even some Klan leaders have changed their tune, at least in the way it is played for recruiting purposes. The leader of the Knights of the Ku Klux Klan in North Carolina, for example, actually barred violent neo-Nazis from its meetings. The head of the Klan in Florida urged its members to become a group "known for hating evil, instead of being a group known for hating Negroes." He has repeatedly suggested that his group does not hate anyone, but "loves the white race."

In 1978, after leaving his position as national director of the KKK, David Duke launched the National Association for the Advancement of White People. More recently, after spending a term of office in Louisiana's House of Representatives, Duke inaugurated a "civil rights group" for the purpose of fighting the "massive discrimination" against "European Americans" and in favor of blacks, Latinos, Jews, and gays. But, according to Ken Jacobson of the Anti-Defamation League, Duke's organization represents nothing more than an obvious attempt on the part of a "leading racist" to pitch himself in a more socially acceptable manner as a civil rights leader.

According to the Southern Poverty Law Center's Klanwatch project, there may be 20,000 and almost certainly no more than 50,000 members of some 708 white supremacist groups across the United States. Considering that the United States is a country whose residents number some 290 million, this is a relatively small total, and it does not seem to be growing.[13]

If anything, the influence of the white supremacist movement seems during the last few years to have declined sharply. Several of the leading organizations in the hate movement— the National Alliance, David Duke's European-American Unity Organization, Matt Hale's World Church of the Creator, and Aryan Nations—all suffered setbacks of major proportions.

In the wake of the death of its leader William Pierce in 2002, the National Alliance's major source of revenue, Resistance Records, a distributor of racist and anti-Semitic white power CDs, took a serious hit. Visits to Resistance Records' website declined substantially. Sales of Resistance Records' CDs plummeted. Many of its younger associates withdrew their memberships in the organization, as followers of Pierce sought to abandon what they saw as a "sinking ship."

In December 2002, after two years in Europe, David Duke plead guilty to embezzling money from his followers in order to support a gambling addiction. Matthew Hale, leader of the World Church of the Creator, was charged with soliciting the murder of a federal judge. And Aryan Nations, formerly one of the most important neo-Nazi groups, was successfully sued by the Southern Poverty Law Center.[14] Although these demagogues of hate may have fallen from grace, surely other hatemongers are waiting in the wings to exploit the irrational fears of certain Americans in order to catapult themselves into positions of power.

Current State of Hate Crime Laws

In 1990, the Congress of the United States passed the Hate Crime Statistics Act which requires the reporting of statistics on hate crimes nationally. When it comes to formulating hate crime legislation, however, the task has been mostly left up to the states. While 49 states (absent Wyoming) presently have some form of hate crime statute, there exists a wide variation among states in the specifics of their laws. For example, in the area of protected groups (i.e., particular groups are designated as protected in the statute), most states list crimes targeted towards individuals because of their race, religion, or ethnicity as prohibited. However, a number of states also include sexual orientation, disability, and age. The implication of this lack of uniformity is that members of a particular group may be protected by a hate crime statute in one community but not protected in a neighboring community in an adjacent state.[15]

Hate crime laws have been recently challenged by legal scholars and social scientists who suggest that by punishing speech, the statutes violate the First Amendment. Yet hate crime laws do not punish constitutionally protected hate speech. Most of these statutes only increase the penalty for behaviors that are already illegal—vandalism, harassment, murder, and the like. Moreover, using the words of a perpetrator who utters racial slurs or ethnic epithets to establish motivation is nothing new or unusual in criminal law. For example, the difference between killing someone in self-defense versus committing first-degree murder may rest largely on what a defendant has said. Criminal law has always taken into consideration the motivation and intent of the offender.[16]

The United States has chosen not to follow the lead of many European countries, where anti-hate speech legislation has been passed. Countries including Canada, France, Great Britain, and Germany have all passed laws prohibiting at least some forms of hate speech. In Germany, these forms of prohibition have been applied most broadly, particularly in the area of Nazi propaganda and symbols which are illegal to own or display. Consistent with its long tradition of free speech protections, the United States has, except on college campuses, decided not to develop similar legislation. Even in the area of campus speech codes, moreover, the American efforts to control offensive speech have been met with significant resistance and debate.[17]

Another argument often espoused in opposition to hate crime laws is that they apply only to "special groups." In reality, however, each and every American potentially receives protection from hate crime statutes that criminalize acts motivated by a characteristic of the victim. Thus, Christians who are targeted are as likely as Jews and Muslims to be protected by the law. Whites are as likely to be protected as blacks, Asians, and Latinos. Straights are as likely as gays and lesbians. In fact, some 20 percent of all racially motivated incidents reported to the FBI involve white victims targeted by members of another racial group.

When a bias crime results in murder, opponents of hate crime laws take the opportunity to emphasize that enhanced penalties are meaningless when applied to a crime for which a life sentence or the death penalty is already the only option. How is it possible, some argue, for hate crime legislation to have deterred the killers of Matthew Shepard or James Byrd?

Actually, the arguments surrounding hate crime legislation are much more complex than some have suggested. First, as noted earlier, most hate crimes do not rise to the level of murder—they are intimidations, vandalisms, and assaults. Second, bias-motivated murders may be committed by several individuals—a leader who possesses sadistic tendencies and fellow travelers who join in because they fear being rejected by their friends. While they may not discourage a sadist who plays a leadership position in a group, hate crime laws might very well dissuade those who are on the fence about going along for the ride and about helping out. In the beating death of Matthew Shepard, for example, the two perpetrators were accompanied by their girlfriends who were accused of serving as accomplices by, among other things, helping to dispose of the killers' bloody clothes.

Finally, even if they fail to deter a single homicide, hate crime laws send a symbolic message of some importance, first, to members of vulnerable groups who are eager to know that not every American is a hatemonger and, second, to good people everywhere who disavow hate and intolerance but are not always so sure that they have company. In sum, from the perspective suggested decades ago by French sociologist Emile Durkheim, hate crime legislation plays a symbolic function by reflecting and reinforcing the values—values of tolerance and respect for diversity—that Americans claim to cherish.

Endnotes

1. Federal Bureau of Investigation, *Crime in the United States—2001.* Washington, DC: U.S. Government Printing Office, 2002.

2. Jack Levin and Jack McDevitt, *Hate Crimes Revisited.* Boulder, CO: Westview Press, 2003.

3. FBI, *Crime in the United States—2001.*

4. "Tolerance in the News," *Intelligence Report,* SPLC, May 23, 2002.

5. Jack Levin and Jack Mcdevitt, *Hate Crimes Revisited.*

6. Associated Press, "Man Gets Life for California Hate Crime," March 27, 2001.

7. Andrew MacDonald is a pseudonym. The author of *The Turner Diaries,* the late William Pierce, was until his death in July 2002 the leader of the white supremacist group known as the National Alliance.

8. Meredith W. Watts, *Cross-cultural Perspectives on Youth and Violence.* Stamford, CT: JAI Press, 1998.

9. Jack Levin and Jack McDevitt, *Hate Crimes Revisited.*

10. Jack Levin and Gordana Rabrenovic, *Why We Hate.* New York: Prometheus Books, 2004.

11. Jack Levin and Jack McDevitt, *Hate Crimes: The Rising Tide of Bigotry and Bloodshed.* New York: Plenum Press, 1993.

12. Mark Potok, "The Year in Hate," *Intelligence Report,* 2003.

13. Ibid.

14. Ibid.

15. Jack Levin and Jack McDevitt, *Hate Crimes Revisited.*

16. James B. Jacobs and Kimberly A. Potter, "Hate Crimes: A Critical Perspective," *Crime and Justice: A Review of Research,* ed., Michael Tonry. University of Chicago Press: Chicago, 1997.

17. Walker, Samuel, *Hate Speech: The History of an American Controversy.* Lincoln, NE: University of Nebraska Press, 1994.

11

Murderous Terror

Some mission-oriented hate homicides can be regarded as acts of terrorism, using the FBI's definition, as "the unlawful use of force or violence against persons or property to intimidate or coerce a government, the civilian population, or any segment thereof, in furtherance of political or social goals."[1] Clearly, there are violent mission hate offenses whose purpose is to send a message of coercion and intimidation. As noted earlier, for example, the Lancaster Nazi Lowriders had sought for years to eliminate minorities from their town and create an all-white Lancaster.

According to specialists on the topic, terrorism is a premeditated act of violence which aims to produce a climate of fear and anxiety. It is aimed then not just at a set of immediate victims, but at a much wider audience. The terrorist attacks are typically random and symbolic, targeting civilians and government officials. Because terrorism is widely regarded by society's members as a deviant act, it causes a general sense of outrage.[2]

The September 11th Attack on America has all of the elements associated with an act of murderous terror. Its perpetrators, the 19 suicide bombers who flew planes into the World Trade Center and the Pentagon, had planned their attack for years, hoping to optimize its impact in spreading anxiety across the United States. Thousands lost their lives in the assault, but almost every American was impacted as secondary or tertiary victims. Afterwards, millions refused to take a plane or travel abroad; for a period of time, they wished to stay close to home. Flag-waving became a national pastime. Almost everyone felt profoundly threatened.

Hate Homicide and Domestic Terrorism

Not every terrorist act is a hate crime; not every hate attack is an act of terror; but the line between hate crime and terrorism is not always clearly drawn. At the Los Angeles International airport on the morning of July 4, 2002, Hesham Mohamed Ali Hadayet waited patiently in line at the El Al airlines second-floor ticket counter, and then, without uttering a word, opened fire with his .45 Glock semi-automatic handgun. Before security guards could wrestle him to the ground, the Egyptian immigrant had managed to spray a dozen bullets into a crowd of people, fatally gunning down two innocent victims, both Israeli citizens.

The 41-year-old assailant was a Cairo-born accountant who had migrated to the United States some 10 years earlier. Unfortunately, his personal life had recently fallen apart. The small limousine service he had been running out of his apartment in Irvine became mired in debt. And a few days before his deadly rampage at LAX, Hadayet's wife and two sons had left him to return to Egypt.

Hadayet's grievances were political as well as personal. He was outraged by the policies of the United States toward Palestinians. He had long argued that the government of his Egyptian homeland be overthrown. He had told an ex-employee that he despised all Israelis. And he had vented his anger at a neighbor for flying an American flag after September 11, 2001. Somehow, Hadayet's political views and personal problems intersected in his mind, as he searched in vain for some reasonable resolution to the circumstances that had left his life in shambles. In the end, however, he solved his problems by committing murder.

From the standpoint of the Israeli government, there was no doubt from the beginning that Hadayet had committed an act of terrorism. Rather than target Aer Lingus, Air Canada, or Alitalia, he had directly and exclusively attacked the Israeli national airline. And Hadayet was an Egyptian who despised Israelis. From the FBI's viewpoint, however, the assailant had more likely committed a hate crime. He had personal problems; his wife and children were gone; he had recently suffered financial disaster; and he hated Jews. What is more, there was no evidence that Hadayet was a member of any organized terrorist group. Almost one year after the assault at LAX, however, the FBI admitted that Hadayet's crime was an act of terrorism, even if it was also a hate crime. The two types of attacks are not mutually exclusive. An individual who for personal reasons incites terror among a civilian population can still be regarded as a terrorist, based on the consequences of his behavior. Moreover, even if he is not a member of al Qaeda, someone who hates Jews, Americans, Muslims, or any other group of people can be regarded as committing a terrorist act. Attacking as an individual rather than a group simply does not disqualify him from fitting the FBI's definition.

International Terrorism

The worst act of international terrorism ever committed occurred in the United States on September 11, 2001. Coordinated by the al Qaeda terrorist network, the attack involved four jet hijackings by 19 terrorists: an American Airlines flight from Boston to Los Angeles that was instead crashed into the North Tower of the World Trade Center in New York City, a United Airlines flight from Boston to Los Angeles that was deliberately flown into the South Tower of the World Trade Center, a United Airlines flight from Newark to San Francisco that crashed in Stony Creek Township, Pennsylvania, and an American Airlines flight from Washington's Dulles Airport to Los Angeles that was guided into the Pentagon in Arlington, Virginia. Some 3,000 people—citizens of 78 nations—lost their lives in these four terrorist attacks.

In response, President Bush sought to eliminate the base of operations and training facilities for worldwide terrorism. On October 7, 2001, he initiated Operation Enduring Freedom, a military maneuver designed to destroy the al Qaeda training camps and Taliban military installations in Afghanistan, where—according to intelligence sources—Islamic extremists from around the globe had assembled. As a result, the Taliban governing body was forced from power and some 1,000 members of al Qaeda were arrested.

Also following September 11th, the Bush administration moved to expand the power of federal law enforcement to detain, investigate, interrogate, and prosecute suspicious individuals in this country. Congress, in immediately passing the Patriot Act, made it easier to conduct searches, wiretap telephones, and secure electronic records. Attorney General John Ashcroft approved of giving FBI agents increased powers to monitor the Internet, political rallies and demonstrations, and mosques. Almost 80 percent of Americans expressed their willingness to forfeit certain of their freedoms for the sake of security.

Hundreds of civilians and government officials around the world are killed each year by international terrorists. In 2002, 725 individuals including 30 United States citizens lost their lives. In January, for example, Daniel Pearl, a reporter with the *Wall Street Journal,* was kidnapped and murdered in Karachi, Pakistan. In June, as Philippine soldiers sought to rescue an American couple being held hostage, Martin Burnham was murdered and his wife injured by members of the Abu Sayyat Group. In October, a car bomb detonated in a crowded resort area of Bali, Indonesia, killing more than 200 people from 24 countries.[3]

Homegrown Terrorism

Largely as a result of the September 11th attack, most Americans, when they envision terrorism, understandably conjure up the name of Osama Bin Laden and fixate on al Qaeda, Hezbollah, and Hamas. To most Americans, terrorist murder arises not out of the warped and perverted psyches of their deranged, vengeful, or sociopathic friends and neighbors, but in the plotting and planning of blood-thirsty groups originating in the Middle East.

Yet in October 2002, 10 innocent people lost their lives, when John Allen Muhammad and Lee Boyd Malvo, two down-and-out criminals—one an American citizen, the other a teenager originally from Jamaica—conspired to hold the Washington, DC area hostage to their demand for $10 million. Their three-week killing spree was meant to "intimidate" or "coerce" government officials. Their targets were not soldiers but civilians. Their motivation was apparently mixed: to extort a fortune from authorities, but perhaps also to get even with Americans for their treatment of immigrants and Muslims after 9/11, and to gain a sense of power by taunting the police and becoming celebrities. The DC sniper episode reminds us, in a particularly chilling manner, that much of the terrorism in the United States is home grown, originating as much in the psychopathology of the perpetrators as in their politics.

According to the FBI, only slightly more than one-third of all terrorist acts in the United States are international in origin.[4] Most are instead perpetrated by Americans who hold a deadly grudge against the federal government, a particular category of people or all humankind. The terrorists see social and political issues in black and white terms and feel frustrated in their attempts to change society. They are self-righteous and utopian in their beliefs about the world. They are socially isolated, having no place to turn when they seek to confirm the validity of their ideas. Finally, they possess a cold-blooded willingness to kill, in order to secure a measure of sweet revenge through the barrel of a gun or a bomb and perhaps also a sense of their own power and importance.[5]

The terrorists may elect to play a cat and mouse game with law enforcement, which they are convinced they will ultimately win. They may hope to terrify the community. They may seek to become big shot celebrities, reading about their crimes in the headlines, on the

11 o'clock news, and on the cover of *People* magazine. Or, they may attempt to play God, by deciding whether, and in what manner, their victims live or die. The terrorists might choose to strangle and mangle, torture and rape, bomb, or spray bullets at random targets. And in the process, they get even with those they hold responsible for their miseries and wreak havoc throughout a community, a region, or an entire nation.

Since 9/11, citizens have felt very vulnerable. Many Americans are completely unaware that they were just as unsafe, perhaps more so, long before Middle Eastern terrorists decimated the Twin Towers in September 2001. FBI data indicate that almost 500 acts of terrorism occurred in the United States between 1980 and 1999. The unprecedented carnage of 9/11 can obviously never be ignored, but there have been numerous acts of terror committed against American citizens long before al Qaeda became a household name. Indeed, the 1993 bombing of the World Trade Center in New York City took the lives of six people, a number that was apparently too small to make Americans pay attention.[6]

Acts of domestic terror have been perpetrated by persons operating on their own, small groups of individuals, as well as the members of highly organized groups. The bombing offensive committed by the Unabomber, Theodore Kaczynski, represents one of the most deadly examples of domestic terrorism committed by a single individual. Not only was the Harvard educated mathematician alone when he perpetrated his 18-year killing spree, but he was also a loner who despised high-tech society and, in order to communicate his message of destruction, decided literally to blow it up through the mail. Injuring 23 and killing 3 was as close as he came.

The Unabomber had spent his days in an out-of-the-way Montana cabin, constructing bombs to be sent to his "enemies" and typing his manifesto, in which he railed against the evils of post-modern, technology-dependent America. Kaczynski's manifesto was printed in its entirety—just as he had demanded—in the *Washington Post,* where it accomplished its twofold purpose. First, from the point of view of the killer, it made the Unabomber into some kind of folk hero—a high-tech Robin Hood, the image of a well-meaning if misguided humanitarian who had dedicated his life to saving us from ourselves. From the viewpoint of the FBI, however, printing the manifesto had a different result—it provided the American people with a set of clues that could be identified with the Unabomber's background and ultimately contributed to his apprehension. In the end, both objectives may have been realized: Americans organized Unabomber fan clubs and defense funds; they wore Unabomber T-shirts and watched as Jay Leno participated in Unabomber skits on his nightly TV show. At the same time, the Unabomber's brother, David Kaczynski easily recognized certain idiosyncrasies in the syntax and substance of the Unabomber's manifesto which, according to the FBI, led to Theodore's arrest. Thanks to a family that turned in one of its own in order to save the lives of people they didn't know, Kaczynski is presently serving a life sentence in a California prison.

In carrying out murderous terrorist acts, the number of perpetrators does not always come close to matching the number of victims. It is ironic indeed that an act of domestic terrorism resulting in a record-setting body count—168—would have been committed by perhaps only two or three individuals who together concocted a plan to retaliate against the United States Government for failing to respect the constitutional rights of citizens by blowing up a federal building and killing large numbers of government workers. But this is precisely what occurred in Oklahoma City in 1995 when Timothy McVeigh and his buddy got even with Uncle Sam.

In a very real sense, students who seek to destroy their schools with gunfire or bombs can be considered homegrown terrorists. Many of the distinguishing features of terrorism (e.g., premeditation, creation of fear and anxiety, victimization of a civilian population larger than the death toll, and outrage) can be seen in episodes of school slaughter like those discussed in Chapter 6. In an odd but telling twist, the diary of Eric Harris, who teamed with his buddy Dylan Klebold to perpetrate the April 1999, Columbine massacre, described their plans to crash a hijacked plane into the New York City skyline. What for millions of Americans seemed after September 11, 2001, to be absolutely unthinkable—intentionally to fly a jet into a skyscraper—had been conceived by a pair of Colorado teenagers more than two years prior to the Attack on America.

Left-Wing vs. Right-Wing Terrorists

Domestic terrorism can also be linked to the operation of organized groups whose members plot and conspire to carry out the objectives of some violent master plan. For much of the 20th century, and especially between 1960 and the mid-1980s, murderous domestic terrorism came for the most part from political extremists on the left—from Marxist-communists, socialists, militant minority groups, and Puerto Rican nationalists. Left-wing terrorists tended to be young, well-educated, upper-middle class, and from urban areas. Many were African- and Latino-Americans; almost one-third were women.

In 1970, a group known as the Weather Underground declared war against the government of the United States. While preparing a bomb in a New York City safe house, three Underground members were accidently killed. They later bombed the U.S. Capitol building, the Pentagon, police stations, and prisons.

Weather Underground members committed a number of murders in a series of bank robberies. In September 1970, campus revolutionary Katherine Ann Powers and three companions set afire a National Guard Armory in Massachusetts, stealing a truck and ammunition which they supplied to the Black Panthers, a group of black militants. Three days later, the same Underground members robbed the Brighton bank in Boston, taking $26,000 with which they hoped to fund their revolutionary army. In the process, they murdered Walter Schroeder, a 42-year-old police officer who had responded to the bank's call for help. Although her four accomplices had long ago been apprehended and convicted, Powers remained a fugitive for 23 years before she surrendered to authorities. For her conviction of armed robbery and manslaughter, she was paroled in 1999 after serving 6 years in prison.

Another member of the Weather Underground, Kathy Boudin, participated in the 1981 robbery of an armored Brink's truck in suburban Nanuet, New York. During the holdup, Boudin and her friends shot and killed a security guard and two police officers. They made off with $1.6 million. For her part in the crime, Boudin was convicted of second-degree murder and served 22 years in prison. She was freed on parole in September 2003.

Most of the terrorist murders committed from 1960 through the early 1980s involved left-wing revolutionaries in groups like the Weather Underground. By contrast, Americans committing murderous acts of organized domestic terrorism since the mid-1980s have tended to represent right-wing extremist causes, often involving white supremacy and/or hatred toward what they regard as a communist-controlled federal government. There continue to be left-wing sources of terror especially in the radical environmental and animal rights movements, but to this point they have not committed murder in pursuit of their objectives—at least not in the United States. In 2003, however, less than two weeks before voters in the Netherlands went to the polls to elect a new government, animal-rights activist Volkert van der Graaf shot to death a right-wing candidate for prime minister who had supported pig farmers in their battle against the animal rights movement. Hopefully, the prime minister's death will turn out to be an isolated incident rather than a trend.[7]

Typically, those Americans reputedly involved in right-wing terrorism are middle-aged, mostly white males who lack college degrees, and are likely to be unemployed or impoverished. In the mid-1980s, a white supremacist militia group known as The Order sought to make good on its promise to spark revolution and to rid the nation of Jews, people of color, and liberals. In 1985, Andrew Macdonald's novel about the inevitability of a global race war came to the attention of the U.S. Department of Justice, when members of The Order committed a number of robberies and murders in an effort to ignite the same kind of bloody war depicted in *The Turner Diaries*. The group committed crimes ranging from robbing armored cars and counterfeiting to gunning down a Jewish talk show host in the driveway of his Denver home.

In 2003, Eric Rudolph was arrested for the deadly 1996 explosion that ripped through Centennial Olympic Park in Atlanta and in 1998 the fatal bombing of an abortion clinic in Birmingham. Hiding in the hills of North Carolina, Rudolph was able to stay on the loose for five years before being apprehended.

Allen Sapp has identified three trends in the right-wing movement beginning in the mid-1980s.[8] The first involves Americans having group affiliations which read like a "Who's Who" of organizations promoting white supremacy—Aryan Nations, Arizona Patriots, Ku Klux Klan, The Order, and Posse Comitatus. Their main objective in perpetrating terrorist acts is to prevent minority Americans from exercising their constitutional rights by sending them a message of fear and terror. The second trend noted by Sapp consists of survivalists who withdraw from conventional society in order to construct armed compounds in rural areas. They build bunkers, in which they can stockpile weapons and food, and await the demise of the federal government. The third and final trend in right-wing extremism, according to Sapp, involves the growth of Christian Identity, a set of religious tenets that provides a theological basis for believing that white Christians are intellectually and morally superior to people of color and Jews. White supremacist organizations now often cloak their hatred in the aura and dogma of religion. Followers of the Identity Church, are only "doing the work of God." At Sunday services, they preach that white Anglo-Saxons are the true Israelites depicted in the Old Testament, God's chosen people, while Jews are actually the children of Satan. They maintain that Jesus was not a Jew, but an ancestor of the white, northern European peoples. In their view, blacks are "pre-Adamic," pre-Old Testament, a species lower than whites. In fact, they claim that blacks and other non-white groups are at the same spiritual level as animals and therefore have no souls.

Members of this movement also believe in the inevitability of a global war between the races which only white people will ultimately survive. The survivalists among Christian Identity followers prepare for war by moving to communes where they can stockpile weapons, provide paramilitary training, and pray. According to a recent Identity directory, there are Identity churches in 33 states, Canada, England, South Africa, and Australia.

Author Kenneth Stern has noted three important events and issues which were responsible for reinvigorating the extremist right beginning in the closing decade of the 20th century.[9] First, federal gun control legislation (especially the waiting period initially included in the Brady law) caused white supremacist organizations to downplay their racist rhetoric in favor of espousing the belief—much more appealing to mainstream America—that the federal government was out to eliminate gun ownership. Second, the mishandled attempt on the part of ATF undercover agents in 1992 to arrest white supremacist Randy Weaver on firearm charges galvanized right-wing forces already convinced that the federal government was their enemy. During a prolonged standoff outside of Weaver's mountain cabin at Ruby Ridge, Idaho, federal snipers killed the white supremacist's pregnant wife and young son. Third, distrust of the federal government was further reinforced by the 1993 FBI siege of the Branch Davidian compound outside of Waco, Texas, which ended in a tremendous conflagration killing some 80 people, including two dozen children. Botched attempts on the part of federal agents to arrest extremists on weapons charges—episodes such as those at Ruby Ridge and Waco—added fuel to the fire of discontent among Americans who already doubted the competence and trustworthiness of government. For a relatively few extremists, such incidents inspired organized efforts to "defend the Constitution" and served to justify their acts of murderous terrorism. Membership in right-wing citizens' militias and survivalist groups together comprising the so-called Patriot movement has been estimated at between 15,000 and 100,000.[10]

Klanwatch suggests that these militia groups have declined every year since 1996, when the militia movement reached its peak with 858 groups. The widespread impression that Timothy McVeigh, just prior to his bombing of the federal building in Oklahoma City, had visited an Arizona chapter of the Patriot movement caused many Americans to turn away from right-wing extremist groups. The enormity of McVeigh's attack—taking the lives of so many men, women, and children—apparently disgusted potential members of the Patriot movement. By 2002, the number of groups in the Patriot movement had dropped to only 143. According to the Southern Poverty Law Center, many Patriot groups simply disappeared. Not unlike international terrorists around the world, Patriots have organized themselves into small "cells" with no centralized leadership.[11]

Though possibly limiting the ability of right-wing groups to amass resources, this lack of structure also restricts the effectiveness of any surveillance efforts on the part of federal security forces in their efforts to track political extremists.

Many members of the Patriot movement are residents of rural and small town America who experienced financial disaster beginning with the deep recession of the early 1980s, when ranchers, farmers, miners, and timber workers suffered profoundly. They were joined by blue-collar workers from major cities, who lost their jobs when the automobile industry went into severe decline.

It should also be pointed out that the militia movement in the United States is diverse. Some members are clearly bigoted in their beliefs and despise Jews and blacks, but there are also Jewish and black militia members.[12] The constitutionality of militia activities has, however, been challenged by observers who regard them as illegal private armies.[13] In addition, there seems to be some degree of overlap in the memberships of white supremacy groups and militias, perhaps accounted for by the fact of their shared conspiratorial thinking and their hatred for the federal government.[14]

The Impact of Murderous Terror

To the extent that a sizable number of Americans remain alienated and marginalized, murderous acts of domestic terrorism cannot be expected to disappear entirely from the societal landscape. Depending on the state of our economy, the effectiveness of our government's foreign policy, and the ability of our society to reach residents who feel angry and ignored, there are bound to be violent and explosive outbursts, from time to time, aimed at terrifying citizens or eliminating government officials.

International terrorism can similarly be expected to continue having an impact not only in the United States but around the world. Wherever the peace process moves forward, extremist groups will predictably turn to violence. So long as terrorists believe that peace only robs them of their political and military clout, they will increase their efforts to destroy prospects for ending armed conflict. This is precisely what has recently occurred between Israelis and Palestinians in the Middle East, between Catholics and Protestants in Northern Ireland, and between Muslims and Hindus in India. As of this writing, terrorist attacks have also erupted in Iraqi cities, where local leaders have cooperated with the American occupation or have sought to restore some semblance of normalcy to everyday life.

Years have passed since the September 11th Attack on America, but we are only now beginning to assess the full impact of this tragic event on our way of life. Thousands lost their lives, including 60 police officers and 343 firefighters. And the Twin Towers were crushed into nearly two million tons of burning concrete and steel.

Most Americans have not put completely out of their minds the pain and suffering experienced by thousands of primary victims at the Twin Towers, the Pentagon, or in a doomed airliner over Pennsylvania, as well as tens of thousands of family members and friends and hundreds of thousands who knew a friend or the relative of a victim. In addition, there were millions of Americans in places like California, Arkansas, Michigan, and Massachusetts, who never had the opportunity of knowing the victims of 9/11, but nevertheless felt as though they had been robbed of a family member or a good friend.

Notwithstanding its horrific carnage, not all of the news about 9/11 has been bad. In fact, only about 15 percent of all Americans still suffer psychologically—depression, anxiety, trauma, and stress. Nearly 60 percent claim that the Attack on America has not made them more pessimistic about our nation's future. More than 80 percent are opposed to singling out Arabs or Muslims for questioning without probable cause. And more than a third of all Americans say that they have coped with the horrors of September 11th, not by purchasing a firearm or hiding in their homes, but by reaching out and establishing a closer relationship, a tighter bond with their families and good friends. Moreover, Americans' naiveté concerning the likelihood of being victimized by international terrorism has been replaced by a new collective awareness—vigilance—regarding the possibility of another major attack.[15]

September 11th has given us new heroes—firefighters, police officers, the former mayor of New York City, the President of the United States, the volunteers at Ground Zero, the family members of victims, the passengers on Flight 93 who refused to allow terrorists to fly into the White House or the Capitol, the police, and our military in Afghanistan and Iraq.[16] Rather than focus so much celebrity on the evil people among us, the Attack on America has changed our thinking—90 percent of all Americans continue to rate firefighters as honest and trustworthy. And after much controversy about whether to feature Osama Bin

Laden as its "Person of the Year" for 2001, *Time Magazine* decided instead to honor Mayor Giuliani of New York City for his heroic efforts in the aftermath of the Attack on America.

September 11th has brought out the generosity and compassion of Americans everywhere. In the months after the attack, much of the anger targeting Arabs and Muslims subsided, and grieving Americans found a more productive and healthier way to mourn our nation's loss—they volunteered at Ground Zero, they donated money, time, or blood, and they prayed for the victims.

Following 9/11, the nation's charities were swamped with checks, cash, clothes, and even frequent flier miles. This was the biggest flood of donations that fund raisers had ever seen. During the first two weeks alone, donations hit $500 million. By August 2002, the 10 largest charities claimed they had collected $2.3 billion.

The sources of charity were so diverse: race drivers donating their helmets, an all-star rock concert at Madison Square Garden, school bake sales in Wyoming, and a Massachusetts congressman's education fund to help the victims' families.

On September 11, 2001, Americans witnessed the most violent single incident of hate-motivated violence in our country's history. The Attack on America was apparently inspired by an intense hatred of America and a desire to eliminate as many American citizens as possible. This horrendous incident demonstrated the power and devastation that hate is capable of generating. One of the important lessons learned from the Attack on America was that to ignore murderous terrorism is to risk the potential for unimaginable tragedy.

Endnotes

1. Brent Smith, *Terrorism in America: Pipe Bombs and Pipe Dreams.* Albany, NY: State University of New York Press, 1994.

2. Paul Wilkinson, "Current and Future Trends in Domestic and International Terrorism," *Violence and Terrorism: Annual Editions.* Guilford, CT: McGraw-Hill/Dushkin, 2004.

3. Federal Bureau of Investigation, Report on International Terrorism, *www.fbi.gov,* 2001.

4. Federal Bureau of Investigation, Report on Terrorism, 1980–1999, *www.fbi.gov,* 2000.

5. Paul Davis, "The Terrorist Mentality," *Violence and Terrorism: Annual Editions.* Guilford, CT: McGraw-Hill/Dushkin, 2004.

6. Federal Bureau of Investigation, 2000, op. cit.

7. Heidi Beirich and Bob Moser, "From Push to Shove," *Violence and Terrorism: Annual Editions.* Guilford, CT: McGraw-Hill/Dushkin, 2004.

8. Allen Sapp, "Basic Ideologies of Right-Wing Extremist Groups in America," paper presented at the annual meeting of the Academy of Criminal Justice Sciences. Las Vegas, NV: 1985.

9. Kenneth S. Stern, *A Force Upon the Plain: The American Militia Movement and the Politics of Hate.* New York: Simon and Schuster, 1996.

10. Jonathan Karl, *The Right to Bear Arms: The Rise of America's New Militia.* New York: Harper, 1995.

11. Klanwatch Intelligence Report, "Two Years After: the Patriot Movement since Oklahoma City," Spring, 1997; pp. 18–20.

12. Jack Levin, "Visit to a Patriot Potluck." *USA Today,* March 1, 1997, p. 6A.

13. Thomas Halpern and Brian Levin, *The Limits of Dissent: The Constitutional Status of Armed Civilian Militias.* Amherst, MA: Aletheia Press, 1996.

14. Karl, op. cit. Levin, 1997, op. cit.

15. Gallup Organization, *www.gallup.com,* December 2001–January 2002.

16. Gallup Organization, *www.gallup.com,* February 2001.

12

Cult Killings

In popular culture, almost any bizarre or esoteric group one can imagine has been considered a cult. In this broad view, tens of millions of Americans have been involved for varying periods of time in one or another "cult," whether organized around neo-Christian religious beliefs, Hindu and Eastern religion, the occult, witchcraft or Satanism, Zen and other Sino-Japanese philosophical or mystical orientations, race, psychotherapy, politics, or self-improvement. Even broader in scope, the term "cult-like following" has been applied to include the inspired fans of certain rock groups, rap artists, movies, and sports teams, as well as the zealous followers of exercise or diet regimens. Similarly, referring to the "cult-like" characteristics of a group stretches the scope of inquiry to encompass almost any group—a gang, a fraternity, even a business enterprise—to which members are "slavishly devoted."[1]

In this chapter, we have adopted a more limited view of what constitutes a cult, defining it as a loosely structured and unconventional form of religious group, whose members are held together by a charismatic leader who mobilizes their loyalty around some new religious cause. Typically this cause is at odds with that of more conventional religious institutions. Using this definition, almost any new religious group that hasn't yet become institutionalized or widely accepted—whether benign or dangerous—could be regarded as a cult. From this perspective, then, early Christianity during Roman times was a cult; but so were the Branch Davidians who in 1993 perished in the flames of Waco orchestrated by their leader David Koresh. Our definition would, at the same time, exclude from consideration here a wide range of groups that might have a strong influence on their members, but are essentially secular rather than religious in their objectives.

As a force for social change, the cults or new religious groups of one generation may represent the conventional religious institutions and traditions of another. For example, the Church of Jesus Christ of Latter-day Saints (a.k.a. the Mormons) began in 1830 as a small cult in an upstate New York village, but now numbers more than 10 million Church members around the world. Similarly, recently established cultural ideas and practices such as gender equality on the job, shelters for victims of domestic violence, and healthier diets all began as heretical or pioneering cult concepts (in this case, from the Oneidas, the Holy Order of MANS, and the Seventh-Day-Adventists, respectively).

Dangerous Cults

Of course, many people nowadays restrict the use of the term cult to refer only to new religious groups that they regard as destructive or dangerous. And there are many cults that give anti-cultists plenty of reason to despise them. Some cult members recruit in a deceptive way—they might, for example, lure unsuspecting students by promising them a party or a get-together at some out-of-the-way retreat while they fail to inform the students of their true intent—which is to convert them; other cults are said to use methods of mind control or thought reform. And many groups regarded as cults require their members to become totally dependent on some authoritarian group leader who claims to have a special knowledge, gift, or talent. In extreme cases, the recruit is no longer allowed to make any important personal decisions of his or her own and must give up all relationships with old friends and family. The cult becomes a total and tyrannical institution.

Cult specialist Margaret Singer defines dangerous cults in terms of characteristics of its leaders, its leader-follower relationships, and its programs of persuasion. Based on these dimensions, she suggests that cults exhibit the following characteristics: (1) authoritarian leaders who claim a special mission and/or knowledge; (2) a charismatic, dominant leadership style; (3) leaders' claims to total allegiance; (4) claims to an innovative and exclusive answer to individual and societal problems; (5) an "ends justifies the means" logic that justifies manipulation of outsiders; (6) totalistic ideological and behavioral control over members; and (7) a major transformation of lifestyle.[2]

Most traditional religious organizations don't have a pressing need to use such tactics; established Christian churches may, for example, recruit, but they can also depend on the process of socialization to attract new members—generation after generation—grandparents to parents to their children who carry on the religious traditions they have been taught at home. The last thing desired by conventional religious groups, in most cases, is to separate family members from one another—they are the most effective recruiters.

But new religious groups typically don't have the luxury of being able to count on their beliefs and rituals being passed from parents to children in their congregations—not unless, of course, they are successful enough to stick around for more than one generation. And most of them don't. So its either recruit from the ranks of the non-believers, or perish as a religious group. As a result, the pressure for deception and unethical tactics of persuasion (also known as brain washing) can become fierce. In addition, the extreme dependency often found among cultists can force members of a cult to abandon their relationships outside—relationships that might otherwise reduce their loyalty to their fellow cultists, to their cause, and to their charismatic leader as well. So, there may be considerable pressure to give up old friends and reduce contact with family members. There are powerful forces within the cult to conform, comply, go along with the program. At the extreme, such forces have occasionally been harvested by a deranged but convincing father-figure who seeks to persuade his flock to follow him like sheep into practicing human sacrifice or committing murder.

It should be noted that the all-encompassing popular culture definition of cults, while too broad for our purposes, also makes an important point. Even though gangs, fraternities, and exercise groups are not cults, their appeal may depend in part on certain of their cultish features—for example, their ability to isolate new members from former friends and relatives and an authoritarian decision-making structure.

Writing about the success of the Microsoft Corporation, reporter Bob Weinstein recently asked: "What do the Branch Davidians and Microsoft have in common?" His answer was: "Both organizations are cults. No joke. The only difference is one is religious (Davidians), while the other (Microsoft) is corporate. . . . Both are classified as cults because the members of these organizations are cut off from the real world and are obsessed with achieving the mission of their leaders. . . . Just as religious cults revolve around the lofty mission of their leaders, work cults center around the rules, regulations, and culture of the organization."[3]

The Appeal of Cults

Cults seem to become more attractive to the members of society during periods of rapid social change, at times when individuals are feeling a lack of structure and belongingness in their lives. Such new religious groups reflect tensions in society which make many citizens receptive to ideas originating outside of the conventional culture. In the second quarter of the 19th century, for example, as new technologies began having an impact throughout American society, there was a dramatic upsurge in evangelical and communal organizations. During the tumultuous 1960s, as social and cultural change quickened its pace, cult activity once again swept across the country. These tend to be periods during which the credibility of traditional institutions suffers.

The rise of marginal groups such as cults also has at least something to do with the calendar. At the end of every century (not to mention every millennium), organized groups emerge to prophesize the end of the world. This millennial myth can be traced back to ancient Biblical writings which predict that a cosmic cataclysm orchestrated by God will destroy the ruling powers of evil and raise the righteous to a new existence in a messianic kingdom lasting 1,000 years. This is the prophesied millennium.[4]

But not all contemporary millennialists sit back and wait for God to destroy the old system and usher in the new. Their vision of apocalypse goes far beyond any vision of a spiritual New Age metamorphosis. For some of these new apocalyptic thinkers, increasing income inequality since 1970 is the result not of abstract forces such as global competition and automation, but of active behind-the-scenes covert manipulation by human beings with a purpose—international bankers, the United Nations, the federal reserve system, and one world order types who benefit at the expense of the average American. Their notion of apocalypse is just as active and just as physical—all out war, nothing more, and nothing less.

Some apocalyptic thinkers have given death a helping hand. In April 1999, 39 members of the Heaven's Gate cult committed mass suicide in their rented mansion in Rancho Santa Fe near San Diego. Marshall Applewhite, the cult's leader, had convinced his followers—20 women and 19 men ranging in age from 26 to 72—that a spaceship traveling behind the Hail Bopp comet was coming to pick them all up soon after they had shed their vehicles or containers (also known as bodies). They were totally convinced that civilization on Earth was about to end, but that they could enter a higher life form by getting rid of their bodies and boarding a spaceship to travel to what they called the next level. So they killed themselves and then their corpses were positioned in a ritualistic way—the lower half of the bodies were dressed in black pants, dark socks, and new Nike sneakers; the top of each body had been covered by a purple sheet which was neatly folded to resemble a diamond. When the bodies were found, each had a five dollar bill and several quarters in their pockets.

Not only did the Heaven's Gate suicide victims represent both genders and a wide range of ages, but they also consisted of blacks, Latinos, and whites who had come from all over the country—from New Mexico, California, Texas, Utah, Colorado, Florida, Minnesota, Washington, Ohio, Massachusetts, Arizona, Missouri, Iowa, Wisconsin, New York, Idaho, and Nebraska. And these were not stupid or uneducated people. They were computer-skilled, musically-talented, and scholarly—but they were also needy, lonely, and depressed. Many had abandoned their families and friends months or years earlier and were completely on their own.

The Heaven's Gate cultists were hardly the first to commit mass suicide by poison. Over a 15-month period, beginning in October 1994, the bodies of 69 members of the Order of the Solar Temple were discovered in Switzerland, Canada, and France. Most of the charred bodies had been ritualistically positioned in a star formation and burned, with their feet facing the ashes of a campfire. Several handwritten notes found in homes and meeting places used by the cult suggested mass suicide. In one letter, the doomsday cultists explained that they were "leaving this Earth to find a new dimension of truth and absolution, far from the hypocrisies of this world." However, it was determined upon closer inspection that most of the members of the Solar Temple had died methodically planned deaths—by shooting, poisoning, stabbing, or asphyxiation. Even if all of the adult members had consented to be killed, it would be hard to argue that the many children (as young as age 2) were anything more than murder victims. Incredibly, many of the Solar Temple cultists who died were wealthy, well-educated, and respected members of their communities—architects, nurses, and celebrated police officers—who were philanthropic, owned expensive property, or were regarded as intellectuals.

Charismatic Leaders and Their Followers

The body counts amassed by Heaven's Gate and the Solar Temple cultists are bad enough, yet they pale by comparison with the November 1978, mass suicide in Jonestown, Guyana, in which 913 Americans, all members of the Peoples Temple, perished. The complete domination of the Peoples Temple leader, 47-year-old Jim Jones, had a great deal to do with the effectiveness of the mass suicide. He had brought his followers from the United States to their new home in an isolated area in the jungle, thousands of miles from the influence of family or friends. Jonestown was located literally in the middle of nowhere.

Indeed, the one and only reality for the followers of Jim Jones was the power of Jones himself, whose charismatic sermons and rantings and ravings were the means by which he exercised control. Jones was convinced that the FBI and the CIA were closing in on him and his flock. He decided to take everyone to a better life in the hereafter.

The hundreds of Jonestown cultists were rehearsed in the collective suicide procedure whereby they would take their turn to willingly drink a lethal dose of cyanide-laced Kool Aid. Men, women, and children stood in long lines, awaiting with faith and confidence their chance to sip the Kool Aid and die with their comrades. But those who resisted and tried to escape were instead shot to death by Jones' armed guard. Others knew they had no realistic options, and died taking the path of least resistance. During the mass suicide he had orchestrated, and knowing the end was near anyway, Jim Jones raised a pistol to his head and fired a single bullet through his brain.

It is relatively easy to explain why a reportedly psychotic individual like Jim Jones might turn his paranoia and delusional thinking into destructive behavior. It is more difficult to understand how apparently normal, intelligent people can buy into a philosophy promising that they would achieve a better life in the hereafter or even that human sacrifice would miraculously protect them from harm. As illogical and immoral as such beliefs may seem, however, many people could be made to accept these promises given the right set of circumstances. Abnormal situations can make normal people do "crazy" things, especially if they perceive a strong self-serving purpose in doing so, such as profit, power or protection.

On April 12, 1989, the Mexican police unearthed a mass grave containing 15 victims including many Americans, on an isolated ranch some 20 miles west of Matamoros, Mexico, just south of the Texas border. Within 24 hours, police had arrested four young men and sought several others, all members of a major drug ring, who allegedly were involved in the killings.

The police identified the spiritual ringleader of the drug smuggling cult as Adolfo de Jesus Constanzo, a 26-year-old native of Cuba. His loyal followers called their charismatic leader "El Padrino"—the Godfather. Because of his spellbinding influence over his devotees, Constanzo allegedly was able to convince them that their drug activities could never be touched by the law so long as they obeyed his command to, among other things, kill for survival. His band of drug smugglers practiced Palo Mayombe. This black-magic derivative of Santeria ("the way of the Saints"), a Caribbean voodoo belief, was blended with both Satanism and Bruja, a form of witchcraft practiced by 16th-century Aztecs. Human and animal sacrifice was thought by the group to bring them immunity from bullets and criminal prosecution while they illegally transported 2,000 pounds of marijuana per week from Mexico into the United States.

Just as the disciplines of Jim Jones and Marshall Applewhite seemed within the range of psychological normality, the followers of Constanzo were hardly the crazed lunatics that many people associate with ritualistic slaughter and human sacrifice. Most of the cult members grew up in relatively affluent families and did not have histories of violence. Believed to be the high priestess or witch of the operation, for example, 24-year-old Sara Maria Aldrete Villareal was an honor student at Texas Southmost College, where she was listed in the college's "Who's Who" directory.

In a sense, Constanzo was the "Hitler" of his cult. Adolf Hitler, as a charismatic leader, had transformed ordinary German citizens into brutal SS killers through constant marches, all-day group singing of the Party's anthem, and required cheering. Hitler capitalized on the promise of turning around Germany's terrible economy to help convince his followers of the urgency of his grand plan. Constanzo similarly capitalized on a powerful economic incentive, as well as on group pressure in order to foster obedience to his command. Like Hitler's marches and chants, Constanzo involved his followers in the elaborate and mysterious rituals—animal sacrifices and demonic incantations—in order to achieve in his flock selfless devotion to the cause. Over time, they came to believe that they had been privy to a secret wisdom revealed only to their leader's disciples.

Constanzo's final command was to perform a death ritual—this time his own death. Several of his followers obediently shot Constanzo to death as police authorities closed in on them in Mexico City. Apparently, the practice of Palo Mayombe couldn't really protect Constanzo from bullets, nor could it immunize Aldrete and other cult members from prosecution for murder.

Needs Filled by Cults

Cults have historically had much drawing power with alienated youth. Teenagers who join satanic cults often suffer from mood disorders (e.g., depression and bi-polar disorder), post-traumatic stress disorder and other personality disorders (including antisocial personality disorder).[5] Moreover, cults have a long history of recruiting lonely college students. Away from home for the first time and trying to make friends and fit in, they may be particularly vulnerable to the psychological manipulation of "cultivation." Colleges across the U.S. have banned from campus some of the more extreme religious groups known to prey on students (e.g., the International Churches of Christ and their sister group, HOPE Worldwide, University Bible fellowship, Hare Krishnas, and the Boston Church of Christ). Like many of the hate groups discussed in Chapter 10, cults often hide behind a façade of Christianity. Other life stressors—a divorce or break-up, job loss or deterioration in mental health—may all act as risk factors for the charismatic lure of a cult. Like serial killers, cult killers prey on the vulnerable. Although fortunately the Elizabeth Smart case did not result in a homicide, she fell under the spell of a crazed, cult-like husband and wife who were masters of religious persuasion. There now exists a new hunting ground for cults—the Internet. A perusal of virtually any chat room finds the cult-recruiters proselytizing via instant messages.

Adolescence is a stage of development frequently marked by a profound sense of marginality and powerlessness. Teenagers are neither children nor adults; they are expected, at the same time, to remain submissive to the demands of the older generation and to achieve some sense of independence. For a youngster troubled in his search for belonging and personal meaning, a group that promises to provide both friendship and a sense of importance can be extremely attractive. As a result, cults organized around themes of vampirism and Satanism may be particularly appealing to teenagers who feel thwarted in their quest for power and who are dissatisfied with their conventional peer relations.

In November 1996, a group of youngsters from in and around Murray, Kentucky, all members of a self-described "Vampire Clan," traveled to Eustis, Florida, and the home of Richard and Ruth Wendorf, where they bludgeoned the couple to death with a crowbar. The victims were the parents of one of the murderous cult disciples—a 15-year-old girl who claimed to have been a demon in past lives. Along with her four fellow cultists, she fled the bloody scene in her parents' 1994 Ford Explorer, inside of which police later found a credit card belonging to the dead couple, a blood-drenched sheet, and books on ancient spells and vampirism.

The youthful members of the cult all believed they were vampires who possessed supernatural powers and who communicated with spirits while engaging in rituals in which they drank their own blood and that of mutilated animals. According to the 17-year-old leader of the cult, Rod Ferrell, as he gave his confession in court, slaying the Wendorfs was a necessary act that would "open the gates to Hell."

As vulnerable to cult influence as adolescents may be, alienation and marginality are hardly peculiar to the teenage years. Individuals from all age groups may be persuaded to commit even the most evil acts if they are also convinced of the righteousness of their cause. Those cults whose members are intensely hostile to conventional institutions have a potential for espousing and practicing violence.

According to Lifton, this potential for violent behavior has recently taken a much more dangerous turn for the worse.[6] In fact, weapons of mass destruction in the hands of apocalyptic, paranoid cults pose a new—perhaps unprecedented—form of danger for citizens of countries around the world.

The doomsday cult known as Aum Shinrikyo (Supreme Truth) is a case in point. In March 1995, its members killed 12 people and injured 5,500 more in a sarin nerve-gas attack in the Tokyo subway system. The cultists left packets of frozen sarin on the trains, timing their assault so that the nerve-gas thawed just in time to poison the rush-hour commuters.

Orchestrated by its 41-year-old charismatic leader Shoko Asahara, the subway mass murder was part of a vastly larger plot designed to overthrow the Japanese government, establish a kingdom ruled by Asahara, and then ultimately to initiate a world-wide nuclear disaster which only he and his disciples would survive. Along the way, the cultists had committed murder and kidnapping, had smuggled in firearms and had produced the Nazi-era nerve gas. Their deadly subway attack was designed to divert the attention of the police from an imminent raid on the cult's headquarters in the village of Kamikuishiki near the foot of Mt. Fuji. By the time they perpetrated the subway assault, the cultists were already under suspicion in a wave of violent acts including the murder of a local lawyer and his family, the kidnapping and killing of a notary public, the explosion of a letter bomb in City Hall, and the shooting of the Chief of Police. Their ultimate objective was world annihilation.

Yet many talented and wealthy people were attracted to the cause of Supreme Truth including physicians and scientists who sincerely believed that Asahara possessed supernatural powers. In total, there were more than 9,000 members of Aum Shinrikyo including 500 who lived in centers around Japan, many of whom donated their entire life savings and personal property to the cult. They were attracted by Asahara's Hindu and yogic teachings and powerful presence and were convinced by his promise to develop their supernatural talents.

First of all, distraught or troubled people have an amazing capacity to rationalize their dangerous behavior. They don't need Satanism or Vampirism or even Heaven's Gate or Jim Jones, although such influences make a difference. At the same time, troubled people can take the most benign, even honorable idea, and twist it into something hideous and evil.

In 1992, for example, five middle-class suburban New Jersey high school students murdered one of their classmates for kicks. The five youngsters ranged from 14 to 18 years of age; one was an altar boy and an Eagle Scout; another was a high school dropout who worshiped the Mafia. The victim, Robert Solimone, Jr., was a perpetual outsider, a young man with a reputation around school as nothing more than a nerd. Then, one night, the victim sat with his buddies in the front seat of a car parked next to their high school. Everybody in the car convinced him to recite Hail Marys and then suddenly, without warning, he was taken from behind and strangled to death with an extension cord. These youngsters had used religious ideas to give their evil deeds an aura of morality. They never constituted a cult in any formal sense, but they practiced a perverted version of mainstream religion which permitted them to commit murder with moral impunity.

As in the murder of Robert Solimone, it is sometimes difficult to conclude that violence is a consequence of participating in a cult. Both cult membership and homicidal (or suicidal) behavior may be a result of another set of factors—personality and mood disorders, sociopathy, etc. So when cult membership and homicidal behavior occur in the same people, one of the factors is not necessarily a cause of the other.

Normal People in Abnormal Situations

It is all too easy to regard all cultists as crazy or naive. As we have seen, the truth is that normal but vulnerable individuals can do abnormal, even insidious things. In August 1969, a number of young people under the guidance and direction of Charles Manson brutally murdered seven people in Beverly Hills. Manson was a charismatic leader who convinced his followers of his great power. If Manson had killed alone, it would have been understandable; he had grown up in the most horrific circumstances imaginable and had spent most of his life behind bars.

But his followers represented something else. Members of the so called Manson family sincerely believed that Manson was Jesus Christ. Most of the Manson family members were white and middle-class. Many were well-educated; in high school, one had been voted most likely to succeed. Another had a master's degree in social work. You see, Manson's followers were given a cause—they really believed that through the race war they hoped to precipitate that they would assume the leadership of the country. This objective more than justified their staying together.

In fact, being part of the family and serving its cause were seen by the Manson cultists as the ultimate solution to all of their problems. The Manson followers were as active as Manson himself in committing murder. None of them had been brainwashed into joining the family. Each was attracted to Manson by the promise of becoming a very important, extremely special person who was destined to make a mark on the world.

At various times in their lives, many people can fall into vulnerable states—they may be lonely, hurting, having a hard time socially, having academic problems, or feeling overwhelmed or confused. During such temporary periods of misery and loss—for whatever reason—another person can have a great deal of influence—especially another person who promises to point the way out of misery. Vulnerable people tend to be especially suggestible when they are flattered, deceived, lured, enticed, are feeling very needy.

Under such conditions, many people are more suggestible, more malleable, and more likely to be deceived. After all, when people are miserable, they are looking to change. Conformity and obedience become powerful forces under such conditions.

Psychologist Stanley Milgram long ago demonstrated that normal Americans from a broad range of occupations and social classes, both men and women, are willing to administer a severe electrical shock to a stranger, simply because they have been told to do so by an authoritative leader.[7] We shouldn't be surprised that vulnerable people are especially responsive to the demands of an authority figure—someone who is treated by fellow cultists as possessing special—perhaps even supernatural—knowledge, powers, or talents.

Once an individual joins a group—perhaps any group—there are strong pressures to conform to its norms. Few people want to be left out, to be rejected by one's peers, to look different in a negative way. Numerous psychological studies have shown that many otherwise healthy and normal individuals will give an incorrect answer to a simple and obvious question after observing other people give an incorrect response—not because they are confused but because they don't want to look different even if it means being wrong.[8]

In most live-in cults, just about every detail of everyday life comes under the scrutiny of the group. In many, there are dress codes, restrictions on what the members can eat and drink, and enforced marriages and relationships. Most of the members work for cult-owned businesses. Of course, there are also cults whose members seem to belong on only a part-time basis. For example, they might work outside of the cult. But even when the control of a cult seems less than total, members are often restricted in terms of their friendships, what happens to the money they earn, where they are permitted to live, and whether they are allowed to raise their own children.

Because society romanticizes the teenage years, it may not be obvious that there are probably numerous students who are miserable enough to want to make profound changes in their lives. They hope to feel a sense of power and control; they want very much to be accepted, to have a sense of belonging. Some will lower their level of aspiration, others will change their goals to those that do not require an advanced degree, still others will find a source of satisfaction outside of their jobs, school or family. A few who cannot adjust and remain miserable, in their quest for acceptance and success, may even choose an illegal alternative. Others will continue ritualistically to go through the motions of getting an education without knowing why.

Once a student is motivated to accept an alternative approach, however, instructors, advisors, friends, clergy, family members, resident assistants, and counselors have a special opportunity to become agents of change. This is when they ought to intervene to provide structure and support and, in some cases, to avert disaster. Students need inspired mentors and role models. Instead, they may seek peer counseling and involvement and perhaps an alternative point of view. Some will look for tutoring and advice. Others will want support and encouragement. If they find what they need, they may become productive, happy citizens. If not, they may remain miserable, whether or not they join some dangerous cult.

Suicide or Homicide?

Because of the tremendous influence of cult leadership, there can be a fine line between mass homicide and mass suicide. At the very least, the ritualized act of self-destruction of the Heaven's Gate cultists, for example, was *encouraged* by their charismatic leader. It is reasonable to speculate that most, if not all, of the 39 Heaven's Gate victims would still be alive today, if they hadn't met up with Marshall Applewhite. The same probably applies to members of the Solar Temple. Out of loyalty to their spiritual mentor and to one another, cultists are especially vulnerable to commandments for self-destruction. The last thing they want is to be rejected by their deified leader and their cherished fellow cultists. The strong group processes in a cult—conformity, suggestion, obedience to authority—make it all but impossible for dedicated cultists to defy the collective will of the group and ignore an order, even if it means dying for the cause. This was apparently true of the Heaven's Gate victims.

Suicide bombers in the Middle East have been similarly encouraged to take their own lives. In some extremist Islamic groups, martyrdom is taught as a technique for furthering their religious and political agenda. Dedicated members are urged to strap on an explosive device and become a human bomb, killing as many civilians as possible. Recruits are typically young men and women who have been taught that self-sacrifice in the struggle against the infidels will assure them a place of honor on earth as well as in the hereafter. To encourage suicide, the photographs of bombers are placed on a wall of honor, in the way that the pictures of sports heroes and entertainment celebrities are featured in the Western world. They receive the respect and admiration of the people who mean the most to them—their fellow cultists. Much the same logic seems to motivate the suicidal attacks perpetrated by a terrorist cult known as al Qaeda. On September 11, 2001, this religious and political group perpetrated the most deadly incident of mass murder in American history, killing some 3,000 people at the World Trade Center in New York City, the Pentagon in Washington, DC, and a crash-site in rural Pennsylvania.

If we claim that people under duress should not be held to the same level of responsibility for their criminal behavior, then people who have fallen under the "spell" of a tyrannical cult leader can be regarded as incapable of making a decision about taking their own lives. The abduction of 14-year-old Elizabeth Smart by a self-styled cultist and his wife has provided a recent illustration of this point. Smart was snatched from her bed in the middle of the night and held captive for more than a year, during which time she may have had, but didn't take, opportunities to escape her kidnappers. In a sense, she was a "prisoner of war" whose very survival depended on the mercy of her captors. Her life was constantly threatened, as were the lives of her family members. Fear was a powerful motivator. It eventually forced Smart to believe that her abductors had absolute control over her fate and the fate of her loved ones.

Basing his notion of cultic persuasion on the experiences of prisoners of war, Lifton has identified a number of characteristics of a thought reform (a.k.a. brainwashing) environment: (1) *milieu control,* which involves control over all communication and information, to prevent doubt about the omnipotence of the group from arising; (2) *mystical manipulation,* which involves a claim of higher authority that morally elevates the group's ends, justifies its practices, and undermines the individual independence of its members; (3) *demand for purity,* which involves a black and white world view that allows leaders to control members through inculcation of guilt; (4) *sacred science,* which involves defining group ideology as ultimate truth and inhibits individuality of members; (5) *loading the language,* which involves use of insider jargon that constricts members' capacity for independent thought and feeling; (6) *doctrine over persons,* which involves denial of any self and reality that is independent of the group; and (7) *dispensing of existence,* which involves degrading outsiders and creating an us versus them mentality.[9]

According to the American Family Foundation, destructive cult characteristics include the following: (1) a polarized world view that defines inside as good and outside as bad; (2) feeling over thought to make emotions more credible than rational conclusions; (3) manipulation of feelings by the leader; (4) denigration of critical thinking such that rational processes are defined as extraneous or evil; (5) salvation, fulfillment, and/or self-realization only through conforming to the group; (6) ends justify the means; (7) group concerns supercede individual concerns; (8) secrecy, elitism, guarded initiation rites; (9) warnings of severe or supernatural sanctions for defection from the cult, severing of ties with outsiders; (10) group beliefs constitute absolute truth and are above the law; and (11) group membership conveys access to special powers and privileges.[10]

Both Lifton's and the American Family Foundation's lists of persuasive techniques and beliefs operate only to the extent that a recruit is virtually a prisoner whose total environment has been modified and controlled by his cult membership. In most cases of cultic influence, by contrast, it is pure myth to suggest the image of a totally passive recruit who lacks any power to resist while under the spell of a madman. Some social scientists have argued instead that cult recruits possess an element of free will that can only be manipulated so much.[11] They regard affiliation with cultists as fundamentally voluntaristic. Some even refer to the groups not as cults, but as "new religious movements," because they do not conclude that the group structure of recruitment processes undermine individual autonomy and voluntarism.[12]

As suggested by Bromley and Shupe, moreover, what appears to be extreme behavior may not actually represent a personal transformation but rather conformity to expected role behavior.[13] Even extremely vulnerable individuals possess an *active self*—they are typically not brainwashed into misbehaving, but comply willingly to the requirements imposed on their membership. From this viewpoint, there is a definite limit to the power of a charismatic leader to mold or shape the behavior and beliefs of his disciples. Most cult leaders are not in the category of a Jim Jones or Marshall Applewhite, even if they are extremely persuasive. When they do harm to others, cult followers are therefore responsible for their criminal behavior.

Endnotes

1. Nicole Biggart, *Charismatic Capitalism.* Chicago: University of Chicago Press, 1989.

2. Margaret Singer, *Cults in Our Midst.* San Francisco: Jossey-Bass, 1995.

3. Bob Weinstein, "Be Wary of the 'Corporate Cult.'" *Newsday,* March 5, 2000, 12B.

4. Philip Lamy, *Millennium Rage.* New York: Plenum Press, 1996.

5. Margaret Singer and Richard Ofshe, "Thought Reform Programs and the Production of Psychiatric Casualties." *Psychiatric Annals* 20, 1990: 188–193.

6. Robert Jay Lifton, *Destroying the World to Save It.* New York: Metropolitan Books, 1999.

7. Stanley Milgram, "Behavioral Study of Obedience," *Journal of Abnormal and Social Psychology* 66, 1963: 371–378.

8. Solomon Asch, "Effects of Group Pressures Upon the Modification and Distortion of Judgement," In George Swanson, Theodore Newcomb, and E. Hartley, eds., *Readings in Social Psychology.* New York: Holt, Rinehart and Winston, 1952.

9. Robert Jay Lifton, *Thought Reform and the Psychology of Totalism.* Chapel Hill, NC: University of North Carolina Press, 1989.

10. American Family Foundation, *Cults: What Parents Should Know.* Weston, MA: American Family Foundation Press, n.d.

11. James D. Tabor and Eugene Gallagher, *Why Waco?* Berkeley, CA: University of California Press, 1995.

12. Eileen Barker, *The Making of a Moonie,* Oxford: Blackwell Press, 1984.

13. David Bromley and Anson Shupe, "Affiliation and Disaffiliation: A Role Theory Approach to Joining and Leaving New Religious Movements." *Thought: A Review of Culture and Ideas* 61: 197–211.

13

Catching Killers

If one were to judge solely from television crime dramas like *Law and Order, CSI: Crime Scene Investigation,* and *Crossing Jordan,* crime doesn't pay. Almost without exception, TV criminals, and murderers in particular, are identified, arrested, and convicted, all in under an hour (unless it's a "two-parter," of course). Although these shows may frequently feature real stories that are "ripped from the headlines," the lesson that virtually no one gets away with murder is obviously more than a slight exaggeration. After all, this is television-land, and the good guys usually prevail.

Hollywood distortion aside, the idea that murderers are typically apprehended is actually not so out of line with the facts. Of the seven so-called "Index offenses" that comprise the FBI's collection of serious crimes, homicide has the highest clearance rate—that is, the percentage of offenses known to the police that are cleared or solved by law enforcement authorities. As shown in Figure 13.1, violent crimes (murder, forcible rape, robbery and aggravated assault) have clearance rates that exceed those of the three property offenses (burglary,

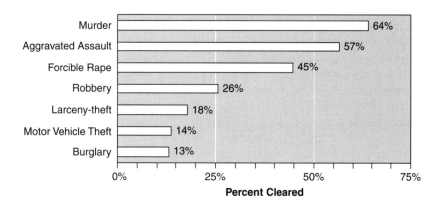

FIGURE 13.1 *Offense Clearance Rates, 2002*

Source: Federal Bureau of Investigation, *Crime in the United States—2002,* Washington, DC, 2003.

larceny-theft, and motor vehicle theft), and murder ranks at the top of the clearance rate list. In 2001, over three out of five homicides reported to the police were cleared by an arrest or some other exceptional means (e.g., suspect flees the country or commits suicide).

Science of the Lambs

The greater success that police enjoy in working murder cases may at first appear a bit surprising. After all, the victim isn't able to identify the perpetrator in a police line-up or describe to the detectives exactly what transpired leading up to the attack. Yet, the victim—or at least the corpse—does "speak" in a sense through the wealth of forensic clues left under fingernails, on the skin, or within vital organs, all available to lab experts and medical examiners to exploit in their investigation. Indeed, it is the uniquely violent nature of the homicidal act which tends to produce a large volume of physical evidence for forensic specialists. In addition, many homicides are preceded by a sequence of events—an argument, a challenge, a business dispute, marital infidelity—which often allow the police to identify the perpetrator.

The work of forensics units begins as soon as the homicide (or suspicious death or disappearance) is discovered. The first officer to arrive at the location protects the crime scene, cordoning the area off in yellow police tape and keeping it free of intruders (including other police personnel) until a systematic search and record can be constructed. Photographs and videotapes of the area are taken as soon as possible so that the body can then be sent for an autopsy before certain transient evidence (e.g., stomach contents) becomes compromised.

One of the first objectives for the medical examiner or coroner is to determine the time of death—a window of time when the murder would have occurred that helps ultimately to assess which possible subjects could or could not have had contact with the victim during this time frame. A rough estimate of time of death can be derived from the body temperature. A dead body cools at a rate that can be modeled mathematically, factoring in climate and atmospheric conditions. This process yields an interval of hours when death would likely have occurred. In addition to body temperature, the presence of rigor mortis (stiffness in the muscle tissues) can help narrow down time estimates. Rigor first appears in the small muscles of the hands and jaw within two to four hours, progresses to larger muscle groups within four to six hours, and becomes fully developed in about 12 hours. This stiffness then begins to taper off as the body starts decomposing.

Victims discovered after several days, if not longer, pose greater challenges. For forensic entomologists, the human corpse is viewed as a welcoming host for insect ecosystems or life-cycles that are governed by predictable time patterns. A variety of flies are attracted quickly to moist areas of a cadaver (e.g., open wounds, mouths, nostrils and eyes) as a place to deposit their eggs. In about a day, the eggs hatch into maggots and begin feeding off the human remains. During this process, the maggots shed their casings (pupae) and eventually transform into flies. By examining the type and progress of insect infestation and the presence of pupae the entomologist can assess time of death and possibly location (if the body was moved).

Just as critical, if not more, the medical examiner attempts to isolate the cause of death—to discern if in fact the case is a homicide, rather than an accident or a suicide. The presence of lividity (or livor mortis) often yields clues about the final moments surrounding death. Once the heart stops functioning to circulate blood throughout the body, blood cells pool and settle by force of gravity to the lowest points of the body as it rests against the floor or other objects. A purplish discoloration of the skin at the low points sets in within 30 minutes and becomes fixed in about eight hours. Furthermore, the shade of discoloration can help to indicate cause of death. For example, carbon-monoxide poisoning results in a cherry-red hue to the skin affected by livor mortis. On the other hand, death resulting from heart failure or asphyxia causes a particularly deep purple tinge. In addition, if lividity is at all visible upon discovery of the corpse (that is, not face down), then the body would have to have been moved or turned after death. Examination of the skin also reveals much about the assault. The extent of bruising around injuries can suggest whether they were inflicted pre- or post-mortem, because bruising can only occur while the heart is pumping blood to the affected area.

The medical examiner routinely performs toxicological tests to identify poisonings and drug overdoses. Also, the examiner relies on a range of circumstantial evidence, such as the kind of ligature used and the absence or presence of a note, to distinguish a suicidal hanging from an auto-erotic asphyxiation fatality (accidental death while inducing suffocation to enhance sexual arousal). Inspection of knife wounds, blunt trauma, lacerations on bones and organs, as well as gun-shot wounds all offer clues, not just to cause of death, but often the exact nature and size of the weapon and possibly the stature and approach of the assailant.

In attempting to establish cause of death, recent medical advances help coroners discern purposeful acts of infanticide (e.g., shaken baby, or suffocation) from crib death or accidental falls. Until recently, medical professionals were easily fooled by deceitful parents and caretakers who attempted to cover-up a baby murder by claiming SIDS (Sudden Infant Death Syndrome). At the astonishing extreme, Marybeth Tinning of Schenectady, NY, killed nine of her own children, not all at once in a murderous fit, but one at a time, over the course of more than a decade, in a deliberate and selfish maneuver to win attention and sympathy. Even though suspicions mounted following each infant fatality, it was not until the death of her ninth child, a healthy four-month-old baby girl named Tami Lynne, in December 1985 that Marybeth's pathetic crime spree was fully exposed. With improved methods for distinguishing SIDS from induced asphyxiation, it was determined through a careful autopsy that Tami Lynne had not died of natural causes, but instead had been suffocated. Despite the fact that implicating evidence from earlier deaths had long since been buried, there was enough direct and circumstantial evidence to charge and convict Marybeth with murder. In 1987, she was sentenced to prison for 20 years to life.

Bodies that are not discovered for weeks, or even longer, pose additional problems for forensics specialists to determine time and cause of death, as well as the identity of the victim. A body left exposed to the elements starts the long process of decomposition or putrification. After death, bacteria begin to escape from the gastrointestinal tract, specifically the bowel, compromising the entire vascular system. The body swells from internal gasses and the skin discolors. Putrification distorts facial features and fingerprints, often complicating identification of the deceased.

Depending on atmospheric conditions, the corpse will experience additional kinds of transformation. If lying in a damp area, a greasy soap-like substance—known as adipocere—will form on the skin as body fats go through chemical changes. In especially dry and airy conditions, however, the corpse will mummify rather than decompose as the skin darkens and hardens to a leathery texture.

Corpses undiscovered for longer time spans, particularly when exposed to carnivorous animals, eventually dissolve to skeletal remains. Even then, certain markers may be helpful for identifying the victim. A forensic anthropologist can not only discern whether or not bones are human in origin, but also the age, race, and sex of the victim. The size, development, and wear of bones indicate certain age ranges. Additionally, race can often be classified based on the shape of the skull. Gender may be evident from the structure of hip, pubic, and other bone structures. If all else fails, of course, teeth are often the sole means of identifying victims through comparison with dental records. These and other means of victim identification (including DNA described below) may only provide an answer to the victim's identify, yet say little about who the perpetrator was.

DNA (short for deoxyribonucleic acid), the genetic basis for all inherited traits, has undoubtedly been the single greatest advance for law enforcement in solving cases and bringing criminals to justice. There is a unique DNA blueprint for everyone, except identical twins, that can be extracted from samples of human cells in saliva, skin, sweat, bone, and follicles of hair, but especially blood and semen. DNA typing can be used, therefore, not only to implicate a suspect, but also to exclude someone who's DNA does not match that found in crime scene evidence.

DNA molecules contain a genetic code, consisting of a lengthy sequence of four letters—A, T, C, and G, representing the four nuclear types (Adenine, Thymine, Cytosine, and Guanine). The letters occur in pairs—A is always associated with T and C with G, and the pairs are arranged along a spiral shaped structure known as the double helix.

A genetic code or "genetic fingerprint" present in DNA can be determined from small amounts of bodily tissue or fluid. Enzymes are used to cut the DNA into fragments or segments of the genetic code. These segments are separated and sorted by a lab process to form a pattern that looks like a grocery store bar code used for scanning prices. Currently, DNA analysis is of two types. The older method, RFLP, requires large amounts of genetic material to establish a clear-cut DNA code, and works poorly on partially degraded samples. For example, seminal fluid extracted from a victim's rectal canal is often genetically compromised by fecal bacteria. Its forensic value would be akin to a partial fingerprint. A newer approach, PCR, requires far less genetic material, as available samples can be replicated as needed. This approach still is sensitive to contamination of sample at a crime scene or even in handling at the lab.

Finally, genetic samples come in two types: nuclear and mitochondrial DNA. The former, from the nucleus of human cells, provides the unique genetic code, but cannot be extracted from certain human matter, such as hair. Mitochondrial DNA, from the surface of human cells, may not be unique but is rarely duplicated in large samples of individuals.

The probative value of a DNA match is unparalleled, especially in the opinions of jurors who give great weight to its scientific authority. Of course, this has also meant that scores of falsely-convicted defendants have been freed upon retesting old crime scene evidence with new technology. The ability genetically to identify an unknown killer through DNA left at the murder scene does not, of course, guarantee that the "donor" will be identifiable from available records and DNA databanks. Launched in 1990, the FBI has maintained a computerized DNA database, known as CODIS (Combined DNA Index System). With virtually all states submitting information to the national DNA index system, as of June 2003, genetic profiles of more than 1.3 million convicted offenders were included in the database. Nearly all states have passed legislation permitting DNA data storage associated with convicted murderers and sex offenders; some states have broadened the guidelines to include other violent felons and even non-violent criminals. Although expanding rapidly in scope, the database is far from complete in covering the entire offender population, not to mention those who have never been previously convicted of a crime.

Despite its singular value, there remains a danger to civil liberties that will play out in years to come. The appellate courts will need to deliberate on constitutionally acceptable methods for using this compelling evidence. Investigating the murders of five women between 2001 and 2003, for example, the Baton Rouge police performed a rather controversial DNA dragnet in an attempt to locate the unknown serial killer. Hundreds of potential suspects were asked "voluntarily" to allow a swab to be taken from the inner cheek for the purpose of comparison with DNA recovered at the crime scenes. They were advised of their right to decline, of course, but also were informed that such refusal would result not only in a court order for the sample but public notification of their failure to cooperate. In addition, even after Derrick Todd Lee was arrested and charged with the crimes, at least one innocent subject sued the police in attempt to have his DNA returned rather than have it saved in the state police DNA data bank.[1]

While the scientific theory underlying DNA is unimpeachable and the methods of extracting genetic material from limited trace evidence is improving every year, the testing process is still performed by human beings who are not exactly infallible. Overburdened labs, poorly trained technicians, as well as mistakes in maintaining the integrity of DNA samples and record-keeping have unfortunately resulted in more than a few erroneous results, from mislabeling of samples in Kansas to falsified records at a Florida lab. Errors and false reporting uncovered in 2003 at the overloaded and understaffed Houston crime lab were so bad that several employees were suspended or terminated and hundreds of tests were ordered to be redone.

Clearance Rates

Despite the rapid improvement in forensic techniques, the success rate in clearing homicide cases has dropped in recent years, a trend that has put law enforcement under a certain degree of scrutiny from politicians and the media alike. As shown in Figure 13.2, whereas in the mid-1970s, four out of five homicides were solved, this rate has dropped steadily through the mid-1990s, reaching its current low-point at 62.4%.

Some observers have questioned whether police personnel are doing a poorer job today or if they are just overwhelmed by a rising case load. The slippage in clearance has, however, much more to do with the changing nature of the case load, not the sheer number. As discussed in Chapters 4 and 5, there have been dramatic shifts in the pattern of homicide during the past quarter century—specifically fewer spousal homicides, and more murders involving younger assailants as well as strangers. Within the mix of cases that detectives must confront each year, there are simply fewer easy cases and more challenging ones.

While surely there are exceptions, spousal murders are frequently solved as soon as the perpetrator himself or herself calls the police to report the incident and often times to surrender. Or, if there is any attempt to escape justice, typically a telltale pattern of precipitants

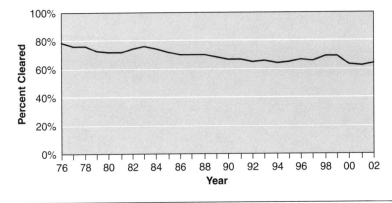

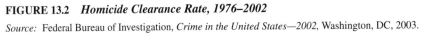

FIGURE 13.2   *Homicide Clearance Rate, 1976–2002*

Source: Federal Bureau of Investigation, *Crime in the United States—2002,* Washington, DC, 2003.

points directly to the current or former spouse or lover—a history of abuse or recent conflicts that friends and neighbors report. There may be a recent affair or a newly secured life insurance policy that gives the police all they need to determine the motive and thus the suspect.

When 27-year-old Laci Peterson of Modesto, California, eight-months pregnant with her first child, disappeared on Christmas Eve, 2002, many of these same suspicious factors prompted the police, as well as a fascinated nation, to look squarely at her husband Scott as the prime suspect. The 30-year-old fertilizer salesman had been romantically involved with a blonde and attractive massage therapist from whom he had concealed his marriage. In addition, Peterson had recently purchased a $250,000 life insurance policy on his wife, and was away alone on an all-day Christmas Eve fishing trip, without an alibi witness, when his pregnant wife reportedly vanished. Each of these implicating factors in isolation could be explained away as innocent; after all many men have extra-marital affairs without resorting to murder, and many decide to upgrade their insurance policies right before the birth of a child. But the confluence of these and other circumstantial factors were just too much for law enforcement authorities to ignore. Even without a "smoking gun," Scott Peterson was arrested in April 2003 and charged with double homicide as soon as DNA testing on the remains of a woman and a baby that had washed ashore in San Francisco Bay, not far from the location of his Christmas Eve fishing jaunt, were positively identified as Laci and her son Conner.

At the other extreme, murders committed by strangers frequently have no clear-cut motive. If there are no witnesses to the attack, the pool of potential subjects of an investigation can be hopelessly endless. In addition, the gang-related and drug-related crimes among youthful offenders and victims, the kind which surged in the early 1990s, were shrouded within a code of silence. Although there may have been many accomplices and witnesses who knew exactly the one responsible for a drive-by shooting or a "sending a message" execution-style slaying, no one was talking to the police. Moreover, the notion that snitches would be dealt with tended to limit the cooperation that the police could expect.

Not only are the old and infirm particularly vulnerable to the malicious and self-serving misdeeds of murderous caretakers, as described in Chapter 8, but medical murders and hospital homicides pose special problems in terms of detection of foul play, suspect identification, and collection of probative evidence. Death among the elderly and terminal patients is more the norm than the exception, and so suspicions are slow to surface. Moreover, should an unusually high volume of deaths occur in a particular ward or on a particular shift, hospital administrators—charged with managing not just the well-being of patients but the financial health of the institution—are in a quandary. They may be reluctant to blow the whistle prematurely and without sufficient cause, not so much out of concern for a staff member whom they might suspect is up to no good, but out of fear of a lawsuit against the facility for negligence or just reluctance to stir up doubts surrounding the management of the hospital or clinic. Furthermore, when there is sufficient cause for an investigation, the physical evidence may be long buried, requiring the delicate task of seeking family permission for exhumation without any certainty that a criminal act had occurred. In addition, some of the remains may have been cremated and along with it any evidence of poisoning.

One particular class of offenders, featured in Chapter 7, which has challenged the skills of homicide detectives, is the serial killer. It is not that these murderers are particularly intelligent—as suggested in the fictional characters like Hannibal Lector in *Silence of the Lambs* or Patrick Bateman in *American Psycho*. It is more a certain degree of cunning, cleverness and carefulness, rather than brilliance that distinguishes these repeat and often prolific murderers from the rest.

A long-standing myth, commonplace in popular films and mystery novels, holds that serial murderers, at least at some level, wish to get caught. According to this view, serial killers—even the most sociopathic—actually do have a conscience strong enough to affect their behavior; they subconsciously leave clues to their crimes in order to get punished for their transgressions against humanity. This popular themes dates back years, at least to the 1946 case of William Heirens, the so-called "lipstick killer," who scrawled a message for the Chicago police on the apartment wall of one of his victims, "For Heaven's sake, catch me before I kill more. I cannot control myself."

Unlike Heirens, most serial killers do everything they can to avoid getting caught. They are clever and careful—when it comes to murder they are fiercely resourceful. They methodically stalk their victims for the best opportunity to strike so as not to be seen, and they smartly dump the bodies far away so as not to leave any clues. The cool and calculating manner in which many sociopaths cover their tracks arises out of the fearlessness which typifies this personality type. They respond unemotionally and without panic to the prospect of capture, undeterred by the risk of apprehension. A self-selection process—a survival of the fiercest—operates to separate the cool-headed men from the hot-tempered boys. If sexual predators like Jeffrey Dahmer or Theodore Bundy were not so good at killing and covering their trail, they would never have remained on the streets long enough to qualify as serial killers.

Murders committed by a serial killer, at least the methodical ones, are typically difficult to solve because of lack of motive and useful evidence. Unlike the usual homicide which involves an offender and victim who know one another, sexually-motivated serial murders are almost exclusively committed by strangers. Thus, the usual police strategy of identifying suspects—boyfriends, neighbors, or co-workers—by examining their possible motive, be it jealousy, revenge or greed, generally helps very little. With no such clear-cut motive, there are no immediate suspects.

In Gainesville, Florida, for example, a large task force investigating the murders of five college students in August 1990 had a wealth of crime-scene evidence for the lab to analyze, including pubic hairs and semen. For months, the task force operated a "pubes and tubes" strategy, collecting hair and blood samples from hundreds of "donors," just about anyone who possibly could have had a connection to the crime. But when seeking a stranger who had no prior relationship to the victims, this hunt for a killer was like searching for a needle in a haystack. The high-profile character of the Gainesville murders, furthermore, made for a particularly huge haystack of "suspects," as well-intentioned citizens from around the country phoned in the names of unscrupulous or sleazy people they thought might be involved.

While the Gainesville investigation team was fortunate to have plenty of clues—perhaps more than they needed, other serial murder investigations have very little evidence of a tangible nature to go on. The more successful serial killers transport their victims from the scene of the murder to a remote dumpsite or makeshift grave. The police may never locate the body and thus never determine that a homicide has occurred. Even if the bodies of the victims do eventually turn up at a dump site, most of the potentially revealing forensic evidence remains in the killer's house or car where the victim was slain; but without a suspect, the police do not know its location. Moreover, any trace evidence, such as semen within the vagina and skin beneath the fingernails, left on the discarded body tends to erode as the corpse is exposed to rain, wind, heat, and snow.

In 1988, for example, the police in New Bedford, Massachusetts, were stymied by a profound lack of physical evidence in their hunt for a killer of at least nine prostitutes and drug users. The unidentified predator had abducted his victims from the crime-ridden Weld Square area of town and discarded their remains along highways in southeastern Massachusetts. By the time the decomposed bodies were finally discovered, the police had enough trouble identifying the skeletal remains, much less the killer. After 15 years, this case remains unsolved; with the trail growing colder with each passing year, it likely will remain unresolved permanently.

In Gainesville and New Bedford, like many other serial murder sites, the police have little difficulty detecting the work of a serial killer from an alarming increase in similarly-patterned murders or disappearances. Despite the fact that the police, alerted to a serial murder operating in the area, may heighten levels of surveillance, the killer may continue to tempt fate, believing arrogantly that he can outsmart the police. He persists in killing close to home or his workplace, staying within his "comfort zone," knowing where he best can find and dump his victims as well as the best escape routes to avoid detection.

Many other serial killers, however, are able to obfuscate the serial pattern underlying their attacks by spacing them over time and distance. They can kill and dump one victim in Ohio, and then be in Indiana stalking the next victim by the time the police uncover any evidence of the previous murder. With the murderous carnage distributed far and wide, law enforcement, by virtue of its decentralized nature, may never discern the wide-ranging work of a single murderer. Even if the killings are consistent in style (similar victim type or method of killing), so-called "linkage blindness" becomes a significant barrier to solving serial homicides.[2]

VICAP and Profiling

To aid in the detection of serial murder cases—and specifically to address the linkage blindness problem, the FBI's Behavioral Sciences Unit in 1985 launched its Violent Criminal Apprehension Program (VICAP). VICAP is a computerized database for the collection and collation of information pertaining to unsolved homicides around the country. It is designed to flag similarities in unsolved homicides that might otherwise be obscured.[3]

VICAP was used successfully, for example, in identifying unsolved homicides linked to Rafael Resendez-Ramirez, the "FBI's Ten Most Wanted" fugitive who in 1999 traveled state-to-state by train committing robbery-murders along his route. Once it was determined that two Texas cases were linked to the same serial offender, the VICAP database was searched for similar incidents in other jurisdictions, leading analysts to a two-year-old Kentucky case which was eventually tied to the "railway killer" by DNA tests.

While an excellent idea in theory, VICAP has encountered significant practical limitations over the past two decades. According to former VICAP manager Gregory M. Cooper, "[the system is] potentially a very effective tool . . . as in any database, it's only as good as the amount of information in it."[4] Because of complexities in the lengthy and detailed data collection forms, cooperation from local law enforcement in completing VICAP questionnaires has been far less than satisfactory. Only three states—Alaska, New York, and New Jersey—mandate that police submit unsolved murder cases; overall, only about 500 of 17,000 local law enforcement agencies participate in the VICAP initiative.

In addition to the missing data problem, pattern recognition is not as easy or straightforward as some may believe, regardless of how powerful the computer or sophisticated the software. Serial killers often vary their targets or method of killing, sometimes just to experiment with new approaches or even purposely to throw off the authorities. Because of these factors and despite a healthy dose of funding from the U.S. Congress, VICAP has failed to reach its potential. For example, of the 20 murders and assaults associated with the 2002 shooting spree committed by John Allen Muhammad and Lee Boyd Malvo—attacks in Washington, Arizona, Louisiana, Georgia, Alabama, Maryland, Virginia, and the District of Columbia—none was linked to the crime spree by VICAP.

The VICAP model rests on the assumption that offenders follow a specific pattern or signature—consistency in victim type, sexual rituals, style of killing, etc.—and that this can be discerned from a pre-set list of categories describing the victim, offender and crime scene. Case similarities, however, cannot necessarily be adequately reduced to a set of questionnaire-type items.

During the 1990 investigation of the five grisly slayings in Gainesville, the task force was forced to look out of state for help in solving a murder case that dragged on for months without any of a large pool of potential subjects successfully tied to the crime scene through lab tests of blood and hairs. The critical lead eventually came from 800 miles away when a Shreveport, Louisiana, detective alerted the task force to a potentially related triple murder that occurred almost a year earlier. On November 4, 1989, 55-year-old Tom Grissom, his 24-year-old daughter Julie and her 8-year-old nephew Sean were found bound and stabbed to death. Julie Grissom, a brunette college student, had been raped and her body posed in a sexually provocative manner possibly for shock value. Her body was washed with vinegar, and the killer had apparently spent considerable time cleaning the crime scene of potential evidence.

Many experienced investigators inside and outside the task force discounted this lead, focusing on certain dissimilarities. To them the cases were as different as day and night, literally: the Grissom murders in Shreveport had occurred in the late afternoon, unlike the early morning hours of the Gainesville attacks. Also, the Grissom murders did not reveal anything close to the level of brutality found in the mutilation and decapitation of the Gainesville victims.

Based on visual comparison of the crime scene photos, however, the Grissom murders appeared like they very well could have been committed by the same assailant as the Gainesville slaughters. The task force was impressed with the similarities—the use of duct tape to control the victims, cleansing of victims following sexual penetration, attempts to destroy evidence, similar provocative posing of bodies. As it happened, it was this link that directed the task force to consider 36-year-old Danny Rolling, hometown Shreveport, who was jailed in Ocala, Florida, on a robbery charge.

Needing more than just a Shreveport address to elevate Rolling to a high priority suspect, the task force sought physical specimens to compare with evidence recovered from the Gainesville crime scenes. Because Rolling was in custody, however, rules pertaining to search and seizure prohibited him from consenting to investigators' requests for blood and hair samples. By virtue of the coercion implicit by their confinement, jail and prison inmates cannot consent to searches. Further complicating matters was that the Shreveport address was insufficient to convince a judge to issue a warrant for a body search. By a stroke of good fortune, however, Rolling needed to have an impacted wisdom tooth removed by the dentist. The bloody tooth, once discarded as trash, was no longer Rolling's possession and could be submitted to the lab for DNA testing, an analysis that ultimately implicated Rolling as the Gainesville murderer.

Despite the problems encountered by the VICAP initiative, computers are clearly an indispensable tool in managing homicide investigations. Large-scale investigative task forces rely on them for information storage and retrieval. In a case that drags on for weeks or months, particularly when there are multiple victims and multiple crime scenes, the volume of information is unmanageable without the use of technology. This is especially true in high profile cases when the public is encouraged (often with promise of reward) to call information into a tip line.

The annals of law enforcement reveal so many instances in which a large-scale investigation failed because certain key pieces of information were difficult to access, lost, or not relayed to the appropriate detectives. In recent years, software for indexing investigative data (including witness statements, tips, and field reports) allows detectives to query a database to link, for example, forensic analysis of tire tracks with a witness's statement about observing a truck leave the scene of a crime.

Of course, the computer is really only doing what police ordinarily do—tracking down leads and comparing information—but at lightening fast speed. Recent advances in information data base matching and artificial intelligence have assisted law enforcement in drawing critical clues from seemingly disparate and incomplete sources. Designed by an Arizona-based software firm, a program called "Coplink," for example, searches and matches arrest records, emergency calls to 911, motor vehicle registration files, and other existing data bases to help police track down information in a timely fashion. Coplink was installed late in the DC sniper investigation; in fact on the very day when the police closed in on the two suspects while they slept in their blue Chevrolet Caprice in a rest stop off Route 95. A query about any person or vehicle identified within an hour of the shooting sites, Coplink flagged the fact that the same blue Caprice was stopped by police in multiple post-shooting roadblocks.

In addition to the VICAP clearinghouse, the FBI provides technical assistance to local law enforcement in attempting to solve open cases of suspected serial murder and other extraordinary crimes. Upon request, FBI assembles an investigative profile of the unknown killer based on psychological clues left at crime scenes, autopsy reports, and police incident reports. Typically, these profiles speculate on the killer's age, race, sex, marital status, employment status, sexual competence, possible criminal record, relationship to the victim, and likelihood of committing future crimes.

At the core of its profiling strategy, the FBI distinguishes between "organized nonsocial" and "disorganized asocial." Based on an FBI study of 36 killers, 25 serial and 11 nonserial, the organized killer typically is intelligent, is socially and sexually competent, is of high birth order, is a skilled worker, lives with a partner, is mobile, drives a late model car, and follows his crime in the media, whereas the disorganized killer generally is unintelligent, is socially and sexually inadequate, is of low birth order, is an unskilled worker, lives alone, is non-mobile, drives an old car or no car at all, and has minimal interest in the news reports of his crimes.[5]

According to the FBI analysis, these types tend to differ in terms of crime scene characteristics. Specifically, the organized killer uses restraints on his victims, hides or transports the body, removes the weapon from the scene, molests the victim prior to death, and is methodical in his style of killing. In contrast, the disorganized killer tends not to use restraints, leaves the body in full view, leaves a weapon at the scene, molests the victim after death, and is spontaneous in his manner of killing. The task of profiling involves, therefore, drawing inferences from the crime scene to the behavioral characteristics of the killer.

The profiles are intended as a tool to focus on a range of suspects rather than to point precisely to a particular suspect. Even in meeting this limited objective, the profiles are not always successful. In Baton Rouge, months after the police had linked several murders to a serial killer, the task force released details of an FBI profile of the unknown assailant. The profile described the killer as a strong, 25–35-year-old man who would be awkward in interacting with attractive women. The task force also speculated that the killer would be white or Hispanic because of the race pattern in his victim selection. Derrick Todd Lee, a muscular 34-year-old, was eventually arrested for the crimes. Friends and neighbors described him as "disarmingly charming" and "easy to get along with." And, Lee is black.

The FBI's Unabomber profile, which guided the investigation of a series of bombings during the 1980s and 1990s, suggested that the perpetrator was in his mid-30s or early 40s, was a blue-collar worker with possibly some college education, and had resided in or around Chicago and later San Francisco. When Theodore Kaczinski was eventually captured, he was in his 50s, held a doctorate degree, and lived as a hermit in Montana.

Profiling is more an imprecise craft than an exact science. Behavioral inferences from the crime scene can not be made with substantial reliability. An FBI reliability study revealed a 74 percent agreement rate in classifying crime scenes as organized or disorganized.[6] While this may seem impressive on the surface, it is actually deficient in view of the base rate of organized killers in the sample. Of 64 crime scenes classified in the FBI reliability study, 31 were organized and 21 disorganized, while nine were mixed and three indeterminable. Thus, the 74 percent agreement rate is not much better than a fixed "organized" response.

More to the point, the profiles have a very low rate of success in leading to the identity of a killer.[7] Thus, while psychological profiles work wonderfully in fiction, they are much less than a panacea in real life, even when constructed by the most experienced and skillful profilers like those at the FBI unit. Nevertheless, profiles are not designed to solve a case but simply to provide an additional set of clues in cases found by local police to be unsolvable. Moreover, one should not expect a high success rate in any event; only the most difficult and "unsolvable" cases ever reach the attention of the FBI unit.

It is critical, therefore, that we maintain some perspective on the investigative value of psychological profiles. Simply put, a psychological profile cannot identify a suspect for investigation nor can it eliminate a suspect who doesn't fit "the mold." Rather, a profile can assist in assigning subjective probabilities to suspects whose names surface through more usual investigative strategies (e.g., interviews of witnesses, canvassing of neighborhoods, and "tip" phone lines).

The craft of profiling came squarely under the spotlight during the fall of 2002 when full attention of the print and electronic media was focused on the DC area snipings. While all media outlets monitored the unsolved case, the cable networks in particular covered the case virtually around the clock, examining every possible angle in excruciating detail. Each network had their team of experts—criminologists, psychologists, former law enforcement personnel, etc.—to speculate, pontificate, and interpret each new wrinkle of the unfolding real-life murder mystery.

Among the many topics examined on-air was what kind of person could carry out the deadly assaults and so successfully evade the police. Unlike the usual process of profiling in which a wide variety of information is examined (crime scene photos, autopsy reports, investigative reports, etc.), for the TV profilers there was very little on which to base their speculations. The on-air profilers were not privy to much of the actual evidence that the task force kept under wraps; yet there were certain statistical patterns among snipers generally that helped to shape their speculations. While each of the analysts had their own unique perspective, there were some strong commonalities to their assessments. According to the experts, the shooter was likely a middle-aged, white male, possibly with a military background, and likely a loner. With no connection to the victims, targeted only because they happened to be at the wrong place at the wrong time, the sniper was likely expressing a grudge against all of society.

When finally the sniper case was solved, the media had a field day in scoring and second-guessing the accuracy of the very hunches they had solicited. While many features of the statistical profile were accurate, one glaring error was scrutinized. Not only were there two snipers, not one, but they were black, not white.

Some critics even suggested that the task force and the public at large were misled by the speculations of TV commentators.[8] "The important question is, was the orgy of speculation harmless—or was there a very dangerous undercurrent to it?" questioned *Washington*

Post reporters Paul Farhi and Linton Weeks following the suspects' arrest. "By saturating the public's consciousness with phantom images of thirtyish white men, did the media profilers distract attention from a more general and possibly open-minded search for the perpetrators? ... If so, the media's performance raises a chilling possibility: that the suspects might have evaded detection for so long because witnesses were focusing too intently on media-created 'profiles' that didn't come close to the real thing."[9]

At no time, of course, did the profilers rule out the possibility of the killer(s) being black. In fact, one analysis of statistical patterns published in *The New York Times* noted that even though a majority of snipers are white (55%), as many as 43% are black.[10] Thus, statistically it was more likely that the sniper was white than black, but hardly a certainty. More important, there is no evidence whatsoever that the task force focused only on white suspects or that the public in any way patterned their daily lives avoiding white men. If anything, it was the white van theory, not the white man theory, which slowed and sidetracked the hunt for the DC sniper.

For weeks the police had alerted the public to a white van driven by the sniper, even distributing and posting on the Internet composite sketches of a white panel truck. Given the power of suggestion, eyewitnesses to subsequent sniper strikes reported seeing white van speeding away following the attacks. Of course, there are so many such vehicles on the road that it is hard not to see one in any finite span of time. Plus, the mind can easily be tricked by preconceptions and prejudices—in the moonlight, gray, tan, yellow, and beige can all appear white when expecting to see white.

The FBI no longer prefers the term profiling to identify their serial offender tracking positions. The Bureau has had to contend with the negative connotation associated with racial profiling—e.g., getting pulled over by the police because of "driving while black," Hollywood's distortion of the job of a profiler (e.g., in *The Silence of the Lambs*) and perhaps most importantly with the fact that an analyst cannot offer expert testimony in court as a profiler. Agents can, however, offer expert testimony regarding crime scene staging; hence, the new moniker—Criminal Investigative Analysts (CIA)—who identify the personality and behavioral elements of the individual killer by looking at the crime scene. More often than not, elements of the crime scene are present in a killer's lifestyle (soliciting prostitutes, patronizing gay bars).

Also, contrary to some media portrayals of profilers/CIA, they typically work as a team, not as individuals. To build a profile, their analysis will include a visit to crime scenes (or photographs since, at the actual crime scene, law enforcement may not recognize the work of a serial killer), autopsy and crime lab results, investigative interviews and reports, descriptions and maps of the area around the killing, items taken by the killer, and dump sites. Adding to the tools that can be used by the crime scene analysts are fairly recent geographic profiling techniques that can identify a killer's home base by the addresses of the crimes.

Sightings and Visions

The fallibility of eyewitnesses has been the subject of much research. Seeing may mean believing for the eyewitness, but one must always take the accuracy of these observations with a healthy grain of salt. In an emotional state of panic, expectations and prejudices about what criminals look like can color perceptions. The mind tends to fill in missing information using whatever is available—what others at a crime scene report (collective recollections), what the police suggest through their questions, what the papers publish, etc.

As an experiment of the effect of external validation on eyewitness confidence, Luius and Wells asked a group of subjects who had witnessed a staged theft to identify the perpetrator in a photo line-up.[11] After their identification, some of the eyewitnesses were told that another witness to the crime had picked out the same perpetrator; some were told that another witness had identified a different individual; and some were told nothing about the other witness. As expected, the degree of confidence that subjects claimed to have about their line-up identification was greatly impacted by the positive, negative or neutral feedback they received. More surprising is that those subjects whose confidence in their ability to identify the thief was enhanced or diminished by learning about another's recollection maintained their position even after being told that the information about the second eyewitness was incorrect because of a recording error. That is, their belief in what they saw conditioned in part by external validation or invalidation persisted even after learning that the validation was itself groundless.

At times, the technique of hypnosis has been used in an attempt to improve memory and recall, particularly when a traumatic experience of witnessing a crime may have compelled the mind to repress memory. That is, while hypnosis may be able to uncover recollections shrouded in pain, it cannot improve the lighting, line of sight, or even remove prejudice and bias in stored images.

While the therapeutic uses of hypnosis are well-documented and widely accepted, forensic applications are much more controversial. Research on hypnosis indicates that the so-called "hypnotic trance" is little more than accepting the suggestions of a highly credible source. More important is that hypnosis increases the level of confidence but not accuracy in recalling events. For example, under hypnosis, witnesses to a crime involving a masked gunman have been asked to remove mentally the criminal's disguise and describe his face. Filling in the details on their own, these hypnotized subjects become convinced about the description they give. It may be a figment of their imagination, but one of which they are absolutely sure. In the same way, psychologists studying hypnosis have compared age regression with age progression. After first taking their subjects back several years in life to recall events at that time, they then take them forward into the future and ask them to describe what they are doing. Subjects tend to recollect the future in as much detail and certainty as they recall the past.

While the use of hypnosis to enhance memories of eyewitnesses, victims, and even perpetrators remains controversial, so does the use of psychic visions in homicide investigations. Rarely do investigators like to admit seeking or relying on the input of psychics, but in more than a few instances their input has been valuable.

Perhaps owing to the high profile nature of the case, the Gainesville student murder task force received more than a few tips from self-professed psychics, most of which were delegated with great skepticism to the lowest priority level. Early on in the investigation, the police received a call from a resident of Harrisburg, PA who claimed that she had had a powerful premonition, prompted by a television report of the crimes, that the killer's name was "Rollings." It wasn't until months later, when Danny Rolling catapulted to the top of the suspect list because of a DNA match between his blood and semen at the crime scenes that the investigators, tracking back through their computerized records for any mention of the suspect name, took note of this lead.

"I literally jumped up and said I know who it is," recalled Sharon Carroll, a 45-year-old office manager. "I really don't think they believed me." Carroll was later investigated for any possible connection to the murders. But no alternative explanation for her uncanny accuracy was ever found.

The Gainesville case notwithstanding, the investigative value of psychic visions is more the material for fictional accounts (as in the Johnny Smith character in the TV series *The Dead Zone,* adapted from the Stephen King novel with the same title), than reality. A number of self-styled crime psychics have made exaggerated, if not outlandish, claims of being able to locate missing bodies or help solve major crimes. Yet upon close scrutiny, many of their correct insights about various crimes appear to be a retrofit of vague psychic clues to actual details.[12]

Working a Homicide in the Media Spotlight

As noted early on in Chapter 1, homicide cases receive an inordinate amount of attention in the mass media, especially so when a killer, possibly "armed and dangerous," remains at large. Growth and competition in the news industry has caused media saturation of certain breaking or continuing crime stories. At the extreme, during the nearly month-long investigation of the DC area sniper case in October 2002, the task force headquarters in Montgomery County, MD became a makeshift media village. Virtually every major news organization was "in residence," equipped with satellite trucks, tents, power generators as well as reporters and technicians, ready to go "live" with each new development in the case.

The task force, headed by Chief Charles A. Moose, obliged the information-hungry reporters and an anxious public with routine news conferences about the progress of the sniper manhunt. Not only was this relationship between the media and the investigation extraordinary in its closeness, but it marked a significant break for the usual guarded interactions between police and journalists.

Much of the time, exchanges between law enforcement handling a high profile case and the media attempting to respond to public fear or fascination are strained, if not distrustful. The police typically attempt to control the spread of information, especially certain details of the crime that are withheld for the purpose of validating confessions or interrogations of suspects. Seeking an advantage in covering a major story, reporters have been known to cultivate and even bribe inside sources in order to scoop the competition, although these scoops often turn out to be lacking in accuracy. The much maligned police investigation into the death of five-year-old Jon-Benet Ramsey, found on the morning after Christmas, 1996, in the basement of her Boulder, Colorado, home suffered significantly from constant pressure of politics and publicity. As Colorado and national media speculated endlessly about the case, and especially the role of her parents John and Patsy Ramsey, the local authorities had great difficulty managing the investigation under the constant media spotlight.

Notwithstanding the often contentious relations between cops and reporters, the media has on more than a few occasions been exploited by police to their advantage. In Sarby County, Nebraska, for example, the sheriff was able to challenge the killer through the media. Talking to reporters about the murders of two local boys, Sheriff Pat Thomas referred to the unidentified killer as "sick, spineless, a coward" who didn't have the guts to pick on someone his own size. Little did Sheriff Thomas realize that the killer was closely following the progress of the investigation in the newspaper. Insulted by the Sheriff's remark, 19-year-old John Joubert decided to prove he was more of a man than the sheriff had surmised. His next victim was a female adult who managed to break away from her assailant, take note of his license plate, and thereby help the police in making an arrest.

In the DC sniper investigation, the use of the media to further the police effort was a lot more purposeful. Chief Charles Moose spoke directly to the perpetrators through his televised press conferences. At one point, he attempted to earn the trust of the killer by slamming the media for printing part of a note left at one of the shooting sites. Actually, his outrage was a good job of acting designed to make him appear like the killer's ally.

For their part, killers oftentimes reach out to the police and public through the mass media. Son of Sam frequently sent letters to *New York Daily News* columnist Jimmy Breslin which would then be printed in the newspaper. The Zodiac killer, who terrorized the citizens of San Francisco during the 1960s and 1970s and was never caught, sent dozens of taunting letters to the police.

The police have often published written or verbal communications from an unknown perpetrator in the hope that someone will recognize the author. The most dramatic case was the Unabomber.

After more than a dozen years of serial bombing, the Unabomber went public. Perhaps feeling invincible after fooling the police for so long, the unknown bomber apparently wanted to send a message that would advance his anti-technology agenda. It began with letters sent to *The New York Times,* which were eagerly excerpted in the paper.

Emboldened by his continuing elusiveness, the Unabomber then sent to the press a 35,000 word manifesto, entitled "Industrial Society and the Future," insisting that it be published in a prestigious paper worthy of its content—*The New York Times* or *The Washington Post.* If his demand was not met, he would strike again: an odd and literal twist on the academic phrase "publish or perish."

Much hand wringing ensued at the *Times* and the *Post* about how to respond to the bomber's threat. Ostensibly for the purpose of public safety, the joint decision of the editors of the two papers, in consultation with the FBI, was to start the presses. On September 19, 1995, *The Washington Post* published a special section with the document in full. This set a potentially dangerous precedent. Would others in the future decide to threaten violence unless their letters or manuscripts were published? Of course, reasoned the paper, this was not the typical offender, but someone who has terrorized the nation for almost two decades. They only hoped that someone would read the text and recognize its author.

The curious, if not hypocritical, decision was to print the manifesto in the *Post,* attempting to satisfy the killer's demands in the most minimal way. The *Post* has far less circulation than the *Times,* and the daily substantially less than the Sunday edition. However, in the early-Internet days of 1995, the choice of location virtually guaranteed that no one in the San Francisco or Chicago metropolitan areas—where the FBI believed the Unabomber had lived—would get hold of the daily edition of the *Washington Post.*

As the story unfolded, David Kaczynski did notice some similarity between the manifesto and his brother's ranting and raving about the evils of modern technology. Kaczynski contacted the FBI, leading to the eventual arrest of Theodore Kaczynski for the serial bombings. In the minds of many observers, the happy ending justified the controversial means. But David Kaczynski was actually tipped off long before the *Post*'s publication of the manifesto by reading the letters excerpted earlier in *The New York Times*. Even had the *Post* not published the manifesto, David Kaczynski would, in all likelihood, still have responded to the FBI's invitation for anyone to examine the manifesto, denying the killer his undeserved platform.

While forensic investigation, psychological profiling, and VICAP all play integral roles in trying to apprehend killers, there is no substitute for old-fashioned detective work and a healthy dose of luck. In some cases the police do get lucky because the killer slips up. He may begin to feel after awhile that he is invincible and that the cops cannot match his skill or cunning. By becoming complacent, lazy, and sloppy, he starts to cut corners and take chances, which leads to his ultimate demise.

In June of 1993, the police in Mineola, Long Island, indeed got lucky. Stopping a motorist in the middle of the night because of a missing license plate, state troopers discovered a woman's body in the back of the grey pick-up truck. The driver, 34-year-old Joel Rifkin, was on route to dump the body of his 17th victim.

London's Colin Ireland thought he had all the bases covered, but ultimately he too hadn't worked out every important detail. Spanning several months in 1993, the 39-year-old Briton stalked and killed members of London's gay community without leaving so much as a clue. All of his five victims were gay men who engaged in sado-masochistic sex, enabling Ireland to bind and gag them at will. Hence, they were completely at his mercy.

Ireland was methodical. Before each and every murder, he emptied his pockets so that nothing would fall out and implicate him. Afterwards, he spent hours wiping away the evidence, even destroying the clothes he wore at the scene of the crime. Despite his preparation and planning, however, Ireland made a major blunder. A security camera captured his presence as he walked behind his fifth and last victim at a subway station just prior to the murder. Seeing his photo reprinted in the newspaper, Ireland panicked and came forward to confess.

Frequently murderers are apprehended after being linked to crimes or violations having little apparent connection to their killings. Serial killer Theodore Bundy was captured after being stopped in Florida on a traffic violation and New York's "Son of Sam" killer, David Berkowitz, was identified on account of a parking ticket tagged on his car near one of his shooting sites. While in these and other cases the police appear to have capitalized on some degree of luck, they benefited because of their attention to detail. Bundy's arrest resulted from the officer doing his job correctly and being alert. Similarly, the lucky ticket associated with Berkowitz's vehicle would not have been surfaced had the detectives not decided to track down all violations issued near each of the "Son of Sam" homicides. As in many areas of life, you make your own luck.

Endnotes

1. Susan Finch, "Baton Rouge man sues for his DNA," *Times-Picayune,* New Orleans, LA: June 3, 2001, p. 1.

2. Steven A. Egger, "A Working Definition of Serial Murder and the Reduction of Linkage Blindness," *Journal of Police Science and Administration* 12 (1984): 348–357.

3. J. B. Howlett, K. A. Haufland, and R. K. Ressler. "The Violent Criminal Apprehension Program—VICAP: A Progress Report." *FBI Law Enforcement Bulletin* 55 (December 1986):14–22.

4. Steve Ritea and Stephanie A. Stanley, "Why didn't they put the pieces together sooner?," *Times Picayune,* New Orleans, LA: June 1, 2003, p. 1.

5. Robert K. Ressler and Ann W. Burgess, "Violent Crime," *FBI Law Enforcement Bulletin,* 54 (August 1985).

6. Robert K. Ressler, Ann W. Burgess, and John E. Douglas. *Sexual Homicide: Patterns and Motives.* Lexington, MA: Lexington Books, 1988.

7. Institutional Research and Development Unit, "Evaluation of the Psychological Profiling Program," FBI Academy, Quantico, VA, 1981.

8. Rachel Smolkin, "Off Target," *American Journalism Review,* December 2002.

9. Paul Farhi and Linton Weeks, "A Surprise Ending," *The Washington Post,* October 25, 2002, p. C1.

10. Jeffrey Gettleman, "The Hunt for a Sniper," *The New York Times,* October 15, 2002, p. A19.

11. C. A. Elizabeth Luius and Gary L. Wells, "Eyewitness Identification Confidence," in David Frank Ross, J. Don Read, and Michael P. Toglia, eds., *Adult Eyewitness Testimony: Current Trends and Developments.* New York: Cambridge University Press, 1994.

12. Joe Nickell, ed., *Psychic Sleuths: ESP and Sensational Cases.* Buffalo, NY: Prometheus, 1994.

14

Getting Away with Murder, or Not

"Prison is too good for them." "He'll be out on parole before the victim's body is cold." "The juvenile courts let kids get away with murder."

These are just a few of the kinds of allegations about the failures of the American justice system that not only have become frequent fodder for radio talk shows, but are used by aspiring politicians who wish to characterize their opponents as soft on crime. Apparently, the public seems to agree. According to a 1998 poll conducted by the National Opinion Research Center, three-quarters of Americans feel that the courts are too lenient on criminals.

At times, of course, the "getting away with murder" perception may indeed be accurate. In an effort to protect the rights of the accused, criminals have on occasion received unreasonably lenient treatment from the courts, including the acquittal of apparently guilty defendants because of procedural irregularities. The important question, however, is whether this is the exception or the rule.

It is undeniable that public attention is drawn to the absurd. When the criminal justice system fails, it becomes a big news story and an opportunity for millions of Americans to stand in righteous indignation and to demand reform. It is not so newsworthy when cases follow the course that is intended by lawmakers. Yet one can surely trace the development of criminal justice as a piecemeal effort to respond to the latest high-profile cases, regardless of how common or representative they are.

The Insanity Defense

Many of the recent legislative changes in the criminal code have surrounded an attempt to prevent criminals from "getting away with murder." On occasion, these reforms have enabled the law to stay in touch with a fast-changing society. For example, the historical traditions of English common law could hardly have anticipated regulations needed in the area of drunken driving or even cyber-crime. Similarly, allowances for conditions like posttraumatic stress disorder or the battered woman syndrome have been responses to medical and sociological knowledge as well as public opinion.

Unfortunately, in many aspects of the criminal law, legislative reforms have come in response to perceived loopholes or deficiencies, which in fact were imagined or exaggerated. The law pertaining to the insanity defense and the associated not guilty by reason of insanity (NGRI) plea is surely a leading case in point.

Most people would agree that certain criminal acts committed by deeply impaired individuals may indeed be beyond their responsibility. If a parent stabs an infant daughter, acting under an hallucination that she is being smothered by the family dog (which is actually a stuffed animal), then the parent clearly lacks any intent to kill nor is he or she a negligent caretaker. The homicide is excusable because it arises from a diseased state of mind.

Even English common law recognized "madness" as a defense against criminal responsibility. The first actual insanity trial occurred in 1724 England when Edward Arnold was charged with shooting Lord Onslow whom Arnold had perceived was inside his "belly and bosom" and causing imps to keep him awake at night.

Over the past 200 years, legislatures and appellate courts have struggled with the meaning and definition of "madness" and have attempted various solutions to this elusive issue. Much of the time, however, these changes have been motivated by a perceived injustice in which insanity is seen to have allowed a defendant to get away with a crime. Perhaps it is more in theory than in practice that most people accept the validity of the insanity defense.

The historic McNaughtan rule, still to this day used in some form in a majority of American states, was more a response to public outcry than an attempt to fine-tune the law. In 1843, Daniel McNaughtan, a Scottish wood burner who was overwhelmed by delusions of political persecution by the Tory Party, attempted to assassinate English Prime Minister Robert Peel, instead mistakenly shooting his secretary, Edward Drummond. McNaughtan was found insane and thus not criminally responsible for the homicide, which so incensed Queen Victoria that she formed a panel of experts to rewrite the insanity law. The McNaughtan rule was designed to narrow the defense, especially for use by political "crazies" like McNaughtan.

The McNaughtan rule is often called the "right-wrong test." In order to be criminally responsible under this standard, a defendant must both understand the nature of his act and also know that it was wrong. Despite its widespread adoption, many legal experts were uncomfortable with the strictly cognitive dimension of the McNaughtan defense. That is, McNaughtan considered exclusively what the defendant was thinking, but nothing of his or her affect or emotional state.

As an alternative, the "Irresistible Impulse" test considers whether the defendant was deprived of the mental power or capacity to control his actions. This approach was developed in 1883 and first used in Alabama three years later.

During the 20th century, significant advances were being made in the development of psychiatry and the understanding of human behavior (and misbehavior). Recognizing that mental illness could potentially affect the control mechanisms in ways poorly captured in existing definitions of legal insanity, the federal courts adopted the broadest definition embodied in the Durham rule, first formulated in New Hampshire in 1871. According to this approach, a defendant is not responsible if his or her criminal conduct was the product of a mental disease or defect. This rule was so broad and poorly defined that the number of insanity claims, including successful ones, rose precipitously. Defendants were alleging that their conduct resulted from such disorders as depression or even character disorders.

The turning point in American public opinion arguably came on March 30, 1981, when 25-year-old John W. Hinkley, Jr., attempted to assassinate President Ronald Reagan as he exited the Washington Hilton Hotel, a shooting that was captured on videotape and replayed on TV for weeks. Hinkley was so obsessed with actress Jodie Foster that he contrived the assassination plot to get her attention and win her affection for his courage. Just prior to taking a taxi cab to the assassination site, Hinkley mailed a letter to Foster outlining his plans and motivation:

> I will admit to you that the reason I'm going ahead with this attempt now is because I cannot wait any longer to impress you. I've got to do something now to make you understand, in no uncertain terms, that I'm doing all of this for your sake! By sacrificing my freedom and possibly my life, I hope to change your mind about me. This letter is being written only an hour before I leave for the Hilton Hotel. Jodie, I'm asking you to please look into your heart and at least give the chance, with this historical deed, to gain your love and respect.[1]

Perhaps because of the patent absurdity of his motivation, John Hinkley was successful in raising an insanity defense. Yet an ABC poll taken the day of the NGRI verdict found that 76 percent of Americans felt that justice had not been served by the outcome. The U.S. Congress and many state governing bodies apparently agreed and moved quickly to reform the law of insanity. Many legislatures adopted an approach contained in the American Law Institute's Model Penal Code, which took the best elements from both the McNaughtan and Irresistible Impulse rules and explicitly excluded character disorders.

The Model Penal Code definition of insanity states that "A person is not responsible for criminal conduct if at the time of such conduct as a result of mental disease or defect he lacks substantial capacity either to appreciate the criminality of his conduct or to conform his conduct to the requirements of law." The Model Penal Code approach was used in a majority of American states until the late 1980s, since which time the narrower McNaughtan definition has returned to favor.

More important, through recent reforms to federal and many state statutes, the burden of proof was transferred to the defense. Rather than forcing the prosecution to prove the defendant sane, the defense would have to demonstrate insanity with clear and convincing evidence.

These changes have severely limited the scope of the insanity defense, although many Americans still fear that legal insanity is a gaping loophole through which thousands of cunning criminals walk their way to freedom. This perception could not be further from the truth, nevertheless. For example, a 1991 study funded by the National Institute of Mental Health of felony cases in eight states determined that fewer than 1 percent of defendants attempted the insanity plea as a defense, and only 26 percent of these were successful.[2] In addition, in those rare instances when "Not Guilty by Reason of Insanity" pleas are successfully invoked, most of the time they occur through a plea agreement between the prosecution and defense counsel, not from a jury verdict.

Juries are extremely reluctant to return an insanity verdict. To some extent, this may reflect the difficulties that some jurors have in understanding much of the complex and jargon-filled testimony delivered by psychiatric expert witnesses. Unable to weigh intelligently the conflicting conclusions reached by prosecution and defense experts, jurors may simply vote with their gut feelings and prejudices: "He did the crime, so how can he be not guilty even by reason of insanity?" Furthermore, laboring under the false notion that the insanity defense is tantamount to a pardon, juries are reluctant to return this verdict even in cases that most observers declare "open and shut."

In 1994, for example, John Salvi murdered two receptionists during armed assaults on two Brookline, Massachusetts, abortion clinics in what appeared initially to be a politically motivated crime. Yet as his trial approached, it became clear to virtually everyone that Salvi's motivation for murder had more to do with mental illness than with any real desire to save the lives of unborn infants. He sincerely believed that he was the victim of a large-scale conspiracy to destroy Catholics. He told his parents that he had seen an evil bird in the family room of their home, and that he would stay up all night guarding against the presence of evil. He claimed to have watched a friend turn into a vampire. He ranted and raved about international plots to rob Catholics of jobs, to commit genocide against white people, and to destroy the Catholic Church. Despite the rather compelling evidence surrounding his severe illness, the jury was unwilling to acquit by reason of insanity. After his conviction, Salvi was sent to state prison where he later committed suicide apparently by asphyxiating himself with a plastic trash-can liner.

It is quite possible for a person to be truly mentally ill yet legally responsible. That is, legal and medical definitions are not consistent in defining the forces that influence behavior. Kip Kinkel, who killed both his parents before his shooting rampage at Thurston High School in Springfield, Oregon, was, according to psychiatrists, deeply disturbed and possibly psychotic. The young murderer left this note near the bodies of his parents:

> I have just killed my parents. I don't know what is happening. I love my mom and dad so much. I just got two felonies on my record. My parents can't take that. It would destroy them. The embarrassment would be too much for them. They couldn't live with themselves. I am so sorry.
>
> I am a horrible son. I wish I had been aborted. I destroy anything I touch. I can't eat. I can't sleep. I didn't deserve them. They were wonderful people. It's not their fault or the fault of any person or organization or television show. My head just doesn't work right. Fuck these voices inside my head.
>
> I want to die. I want to be gone. But I have to kill people. I don't know why. I am so sorry.
>
> Why did God do this to me? I have never been happy. I wish I was happy. I wish I made my mother proud, but I am nothing. I try so hard to find happiness, but you know me: I hate everything. I have no other choice. What have I become? I am so sorry.

In his taped confession to the police, Kinkel described voices in his head that encouraged him to kill. He was also suicidal, having taped a bullet to his chest just in case he needed one more round to take his own life. Shortly after his arrest, Kinkel rushed a police officer in a failed attempt to provoke him to shoot ("suicide by cop").

Kip Kinkel initially entered an insanity plea but then withdrew it in favor of a plea of guilty as charged. During sentencing hearings, a defense psychiatrist testified that Kinkel had heard voices imploring him to kill. A neurologist also testified that Kinkel had holes in his brain, consistent with research findings into schizophrenic children. Notwithstanding the medical evidence, Kinkel was given a life sentence.

Perhaps the insanity defense is infrequently attempted because defense attorneys are well aware of what the public likely misunderstands: that is, that a NGRI verdict, whether negotiated by opposing sides or determined by judge or jury, is hardly a "free walk" for the defendant. In fact, defendants committed to a psychiatric facility for an indefinite period of time following an insanity finding tend to spend longer in confinement than they would have had they been convicted of the criminal charge. Though avoiding prison (where they don't belong), they don't "get away" with anything at all.

John Hinkley, Jr., for example, remains institutionalized, more than two decades after his unsuccessful assassination attempt, despite several attempts to win his freedom by claiming he is no longer ill. This is not the kind of lenient treatment that many ill-informed citizens screamed about following his trial. As an historical note, moreover, the infamous Daniel McNaughtan didn't get off easy as the Queen of England had suggested. He died in an asylum some 20 years after he was spared the death penalty for his crime.

Finally, the insanity plea is also eschewed by some defendants because it stigmatizes them as crazy. Some offenders would far rather be considered bad than mad. This is especially true for criminals who act to further their own political cause. Being labeled insane signals that their point of view has no credibility and is just the product of a diseased mind. This is the reason perhaps that Theodore Kaczynski rejected his attorney's attempts to plead insanity. He may have felt that a claim of insanity would negate his anti-technology ideology, articulated in his lengthy manifesto that was published in the *Washington Post* under threat of continued bombings.

Despite its limited usage, many Americans call for the total elimination of the NGRI defense, and some state legislatures have complied. Three states (Utah, Idaho, and Montana) have abolished the defense. Thirteen states have instituted the guilty but mentally ill (GBMI) alternative. The GBMI option ensures that the defendant is confined in custody, yet because of the mental illness, he or she serves time in a psychiatric facility rather than a correctional facility.

Some legal scholars have also argued for the elimination of NGRI, but not for the same knee-jerk emotional reasons that seem to underlie the popular viewpoint. According to Norval Morris, for example, the not guilty by reason of insanity defense is simply unnecessary. If a mental disease is so profound that the defendant cannot form criminal intent, then he should not be convicted of a crime but should instead be civilly committed to a psychiatric facility.[3]

The problems associated with using hypnosis to improve the recall of eyewitnesses to crimes, described in Chapter 13, are compounded when applied to defendants in trials involving the question of legal insanity. The fact that hypnotized subjects can confidently recall, create, or alter their biographies casts doubt on the accuracy of memories. On the one hand, it is quite possible that a hypnotized subject will reveal painful yet accurate memories. On the other hand, subjects can fabricate events in their past if it suits the occasion, the context, or some ulterior motive.

Forensic psychiatrist Dorothy Otnow Lewis, for example, was hired by defense counsel in the Arthur Shawcross case to reveal his motivation and to support a plea of insanity in his trial for the murders of prostitutes in Rochester, New York. Based on sessions of hypnosis in which she age-regressed Shawcross for early memories of mistreatment, Lewis testified that Shawcross suffered from post-traumatic stress disorder brought on in part by experiences of abuse during his childhood. At first, he recalled having a normal upbringing and failed to reveal any abusive experiences. After lengthy and persistent probing under hypnosis, however, Shawcross finally "remembered" being sodomized by his mother with a broomstick and being forced to perform oral sex with her.

Did Lewis's discovery of suppressed and painful memories of abuse in Shawcross's background reflect an uncompromising effort to uncover the truth about deeply hidden secrets? Or did Shawcross finally give his examiner exactly what he figured she expected to hear? Either way, Shawcross's mother called her son a liar; and, given his attempt to save himself through the insanity plea, he certainly had very good reason to fabricate or exaggerate bad childhood experiences. We really can't know for certain, however.

In forensic work, the hypnotist deals with a subject who may have a stake in faking a hypnotic trance and divulging inaccurate information about himself and his past. The hypnotist can actually create the information through subtle and perhaps not-so-subtle suggestions to the subject. Thus, it is possible for an individual who may indeed have felt intimidated as a child to recall under hypnosis experiences of abuse, particularly if the hypnotist solicits such recollections and the subject has a self-serving interest in providing them.

The case of serial murderer Kenneth A. Bianchi provides another revealing example of how hypnosis has been exploited to find support for the child abuse explanation for murderous impulses. In 1977 and 1978, Ken and his cousin Angelo Buono abducted, tortured, raped, and murdered 10 young women, whose bodies they dumped along roadsides in the Los Angeles area.

Kenneth Bianchi's insanity defense was centered on the theory that he suffered from a multiple personality disorder (MPD), a psychiatric illness characterized by the presence of two or more distinct personalities sharing the same body. MPD, it is believed, stems from a history of severe child abuse. An abused child escapes from cruel parental treatment by developing a fantasy world of pleasure and kindness. At the same time, the angry and hateful feelings toward the abusive parent are stored in a reservoir that the child suppresses. In later life, the two perspectives—the loving and the hateful—split into their own personalities which compete for control. The angry "person" takes turns with various alter-egos for dominance over the same body.

If Bianchi was in fact a multiple personality, this could easily explain and reconcile how someone as seemingly nice as Ken could also commit the heinous crimes with which he was charged. Through hypnosis, a second personality surfaced, that of "Steve," a hostile, crude, impatient, and sadistic character who proudly claimed responsibility for the slayings. "Killing a broad doesn't make any difference to me," bragged Steve. Everything now made sense to the psychiatrists.

Bianchi was advised by his hypnotist that his medical history failed to include the kind of documentation of child abuse that would be needed to support his defense based on the Multiple Personality Disorder (MPD). Hypnotized once more, Bianchi then recalled a dream about "a woman putting his hands over a kitchen stove fire while he was young." Finally, the psychiatrists had the evidence of abuse that was lacking!

As the court hearings on Bianchi's sanity approached, the MPD theory and the hypnotically-included evidence began to crumble when subjected to external validation. Bianchi's mother did confess that she had threatened her boy, "See this fire? If I catch you stealing once more, I'll hold your hand over this stove." Moreover, there was no evidence of burns or scaring in Bianchi's detailed childhood medical file. At best, the hypnotically-included recollection was just a fearful memory transformed into an imagined event. At worst, it was the attempt of a pathological liar to escape justice.

Justice for Juveniles

Another gaping loophole, at least according to public opinion, surrounds the legal defense of youthfulness. From the English common law's "infancy defense," persons under the age of 7 could not be charged with crimes because of a irrefutable presumption that they lacked the ability to form criminal intent. For children between the ages of 7 and 14, the same presumption held, but it could be challenged or refuted based on evidence to the contrary. In common law, defendants older than 14 were considered, however, no different from adults in terms of culpability or responsibility.

By the end of the 19th century, children's advocates in America had become deeply disturbed about the treatment of minors by the criminal justice system, and understandably so. Adolescents and youngsters were being prosecuted, convicted, and imprisoned in the same manner (and in the same institutions) as adults. Wanting to provide an alternative approach not just for young criminals but for incorrigible children as well, the so-called child saving movement successfully pushed for the nation's first juvenile court.[4] Established in Chicago in 1899, the new juvenile court was designed to take a therapeutic rather than punitive approach to handling youthful delinquents and status offenders. The process was to be paternalistic rather than adversarial.

The new approach to juvenile justice spread quickly, and through much of the 20th century the juvenile court movement appeared to fare quite well. Over time, juveniles were afforded expanded rights (e.g., the right to an attorney), just like adults in criminal courts. By the 1980s, however, as rates of juvenile violence and murder, in particular, began to surge, politicians and the public alike questioned the role and appropriateness of juvenile court for these dangerous offenders of tender age.

When adjudicated delinquent for committing a homicide or another serious crime, a child would generally serve time within a juvenile detention facility until the age of majority (generally 18 years of age), or in some states a few additional years at the discretion of the judge. Under the assumption that wayward youth could be rehabilitated into law-abiding adults, juvenile sentences even for serious crimes were, for the most part, relatively short.

Even from the earliest years of the juvenile court system, the criminal courts were not completely willing to give up jurisdiction over all crimes committed by children. In part, the battle between the "kiddie courts" and the more prestigious and powerful adult courts was a political one over authority and turf.[5] More generally, in response to concerns that some youthful offenders were simply not amenable to treatment (as well as doubts about the efficacy of rehabilitation itself),waiver procedures allowed juvenile court judges to transfer particular defendants over to criminal adult court for prosecution and punishment. On a case-by-case basis, certain repeat, chronic, violent youth were appropriately removed from the jurisdiction of juvenile court.

As the pressure upon the juvenile court to take a harsher stance toward murder and other serious offenses mounted, however, judges began deciding the transfer question even for first-time offenders, less on the basis of treatment amenability and more to satisfy public opinion. In 1986, for example, 14-year-old Rod Matthews of Canton, Massachusetts, was arrested for the murder of his classmate Shaun Ouillette; and, because of widespread outrage over the shocking and senseless crime, he became at that time one of the youngest children tried for murder in adult court.

Apparently Matthews had made a hit list of possible victims, huddled with two buddies to determine the most deserving target, and then led his unsuspecting victim into the woods where he bludgeoned the boy with a baseball bat. Afterwards, Matthews brought his friends to view the body and to show off his courage. Despite his young age and lack of any criminal record, the juvenile court judge waived jurisdiction over to the adult court in the face of intense pressure from the victim's family and the local media.

In March of 1989, nine-year-old Cameron Kocher shot and killed his seven-year-old neighbor as she rode on the back of a snowmobile. Kocher pled guilty to a first-degree misdemeanor of involuntary manslaughter and was on probation and court supervision until he turned 21. More recently, several Florida juvenile murders have been tried and sentenced as adults. Derek King, 14, and his brother Alex, 13, received eight and seven year prison sentences for beating their father to death with a baseball bat. Lionel Tate, 14, was sentenced to life in prison for the beating death of a six-year-old (but after a subsequent appeal was plea bargained down to second degree murder with a three year sentence) and Nathaniel Brazill, also 14, received a 28-year prison sentence for the shooting death of his middle-school teacher.

Unlike the judicial waiver strategy that Massachusetts and many other states employed, the New York state legislature, reeling from a brutal double murder committed by a 15-year-old, decided to take matters into its own hands. In 1978, after 15-year-old Willie Bosket was sentenced to a maximum term of five years in Family Court for killing two men on the subway, the legislature passed the New York Juvenile Offender Law (also known as the "Willie Bosket Law") mandating that all youth as young as 13 who are charged with murder shall be processed in adult court and receive adult sentences unless there was compelling reason to move the case down to juvenile court.

In the years since the Matthews and Bosket cases, juvenile murder rates have risen, and state legislatures have responded with harsh measures. Rather than leave the waiver decision up to the judges, the wisdom of whose judgment was being questioned in the appellate court of public opinion, lawmakers have generally proposed two alternative strategies: prosecutorial discretion and statutory exclusions. In the former, the determination as to whether to charge a youngster in juvenile or adult court is made by the prosecutor under the logic that this public official, elected by the citizenry, is more responsive to public mood than are judges appointed to the bench for extended terms. Alternatively, some state legislatures have opted to write into the law exactly which offenses (e.g., homicides by offenders ages 13 and over) are excluded from juvenile court jurisdiction. Some states simply lowered the age of majority below the traditional 18 years old for all offenses.

The 1990s saw rapid change in transfer laws across the country.[6] Between 1992 and 1997, 17 states expanded the range of offenses and lowered the eligibility age for judicial waiver. During these same years, 27 states expanded the list of crimes that were excluded from juvenile court jurisdiction, and 7 states reduced the age when these exclusions kicked in. Eleven states increased the range of crimes and reduced the age limits when prosecutors could opt to file charges in either juvenile or adult court.

These changes have opened wide the floodgate for juvenile offenders to be charged and prosecuted in adult criminal courts. From 1985 to 1996, for example, the number of juvenile delinquency cases waived from juvenile to adult court, generally through decisions of the juvenile court judges, rose 47 percent, from 6,800 to about 10,000 annually. For violent offenses specifically, including homicide, the number of waivers more than doubled, from about 2,000 per year to over 4,000 per year.[7] In addition to these more traditional transfers, many times more youngsters are being tried as adults arising from decisions by prosecutors to file cases in adult court or from statutory exclusions of cases away from juvenile court jurisdiction. As a consequence of the movement to prosecute juveniles as adults, the number of offenders under age 18 sentenced to serve time in an adult correctional facility has also climbed, from 3,400 in 1985 to 7,400 in 1997.[8]

Not only have the number of juveniles appearing in adult court increased, their ages have decreased. In 1999, for example, Nathaniel Abraham of Pontiac, Michigan, was tried as an adult for murder surrounding an incident that occurred on October 29, 1997, when he was just 11 years old, making him one of the youngest children ever charged as an adult. Abraham reportedly shot a gun into some trees, hitting and killing 18-year-old Ronnie Greene, Jr., Despite testimony from a defense witness that the defendant had the mental capacity of a 6-year-old at the time of the killing, Abraham was convicted of second-degree murder.

It is likely that the jurors had at least to some extent sympathized with the victim's family. To Ronnie Greene's relatives, in terms of their loss and anguish, it is largely irrelevant that the person who shot and killed him was a diminutive 11-year-old. To the families who lose a loved one, it matters not whether the perpetrator was 11 or 41; the victim is just as dead. In terms of this retributive notion of justice, juveniles and adults should arguably be treated no differently.

Furthermore, there are indeed certain repeat, violent, chronic, ruthless juveniles who have proved through their recidivism that they are not amenable to treatment. They may have been through the juvenile justice system on occasion after occasion, but with little or no improvement in their character or behavior. As juvenile justice failures, these offenders can and perhaps should be sent to the adult system.

It could also be argued that not all juvenile offenders deserve adult-like punishment, even though they may commit an adult-like crime such as murder or rape. The inspiration for their vicious crimes often stems from their immaturity—for example, kids committing murder in order to impress their peers or even to fulfill a dare. We must fully consider the special nature of youthful offending—even murder. Teenagers may look like adults, dress like adults, act like adults, even shoot like adults, but they reason like children.

Some recent evidence from neurological studies supports the view that juveniles have a limited capacity for understanding consequences. According to Deborah Yurgelun-Todd, director of Neuropsychology and Cognitive Neuroimaging at McLean Hospital, the frontal lobe portion of the brain, which controls the ability to think things through fully, does not tend to develop until late adolescence or young adulthood.[9] Indeed, it has long been true that teenagers are often impulsive—in a sense "temporary sociopaths." Thus, leaving aside the purely retributive notion of justice, teenagers may not deserve the same punishment as adults given their limited capacity for considering consequences. Diminished capacity should mean diminished punishability, especially for non-habitual offenders.

Making the juvenile justice system more just and punitive is one thing, but eliminating it, as some have proposed, is quite another. Expanding juvenile penalties and blending juvenile and adult sanctions for the most serious offenders will go a long way toward addressing public concern without entirely sacrificing young lives that could be salvaged. We need to be selective in how we prosecute juveniles, even juvenile murderers.

Most surprisingly, Judge Eugene Moore, upon sentencing Nathaniel Abraham following his adult conviction on a second-degree murder charge, chose not to follow through with an adult punishment. Rather than hand down a protracted term of incarceration, Moore sent the boy to a juvenile facility until the age of 21, at which time he would be released. The judge also boldly articulated his concern for the snowballing trend in America toward trying juveniles as adults as well as his view that we should not forsake the rehabilitative goal, particularly when children are involved.

Quite apart from the question of rehabilitation, many proponents of the movement to try serious juvenile offenders as adults are hoping to send a strong deterrent message to other youngsters who might contemplate attacking a classmate or neighbor. Yet, we cannot deal effectively with teen violence through the threat of the criminal justice system. The threat of punishment, no matter how harsh, frequently fails to deter kids who face the threat of violence and death every day in their classrooms and their neighborhoods. As far as they are concerned, the criminal justice system can just take a number and wait in line with all the other enemies out to get them.

Often these are juveniles who think little and care even less about the future, who don't expect to live past their 21st birthday. The prospect of a long-term prison sentence or even the death penalty will not dissuade them in the least. Criminologists Simon Singer and David McDowall, for example, conducted an assessment of whether the landmark and widely publicized New York Juvenile Offender Law of 1978 (the "Willie Bosket Law") had any impact on deterring youthful offenders. By comparing trends over time both in New York and, as a comparison, Philadelphia, they found that the threat promised by the tough New York law did not have any impact in lowering rates of serious juvenile offending.[10]

Not only does the wholesale transfer of juveniles into the adult court make little sense theoretically, but on a practical level it does little good in reforming offenders. Criminologists Bishop, Frazier, Lanza-Kaduce, and White compared a sample of Florida juveniles who were tried and sentenced as adults to a control group of juveniles retained in the juvenile system, matched on a variety of offense characteristics and risk factors. Upon follow-up, Bishop and her colleagues found that those who had passed through the adult system actually had a higher rate of recidivism than the control group offenders.[11]

Although there are some special, atypical cases in which the crime is so heinous that the likelihood of release is remote, most juvenile offenders, even young killers, do get released from prison eventually, better or worse than when they entered. Several states utilize an alternative approach to just punishing children as adults by combining juvenile and adult punishments. In a so-called blended sentence, a youthful offender serves the first portion of his or her term in a juvenile institution and then, upon reaching an appropriate age, is moved to finish out his or her term in an adult correctional facility.

The Unites States continues to stand with Somalia as one of only two countries that have not signed the United Nations Convention banning capital punishment for those under

18. Although the offenders are not juveniles when they are executed, the U.S. is one of only four countries in the world that since 2000, have executed juveniles (Iran, Pakistan, and the Democratic Republic of Congo are the other three). The U.S. has executed 13 juvenile offenders since 1998, including three juvenile offenders in 2002 and one in 2003. There are currently approximately 80 juvenile offenders on U.S. death rows. Since 1977, the United States holds the title of having executed more juveniles than any other country in the world.

The U.S. Supreme Court decisions in *Thompson v. Oklahoma* and *Stanford v. Kentucky* forced states to set a minimum age of eligibility for the death penalty at 16 (sparing the life of 15-year-old Paula Cooper of Gary, Indiana). Although 22 states permit the execution of 17- and 18-year-olds, the remaining 26 have set their minimum execution age at 18. States like Indiana, whose minimum was 10 at the time of the *Thompson* decision, were forced to raise the bar.

Capital Punishment

For many Americans, the critical question is not so much whether a juvenile or adult penalty is involved, but whether the penalty is substantial enough, regardless of age. Many critics are especially incensed that murderers, whether they are 14 or 44, can ever be paroled because for the victim, of course, there is no parole from death.

The debate over the appropriate penalty for those who take a life often fails to distinguish, unfortunately, between the various kinds of homicides that we discussed in Chapter 1 (that is, first- and second-degree murder, voluntary and involuntary manslaughter). Although most states do indeed allow parole, early release, good time, furloughs, etc., for lesser forms of homicide, statutes on first-degree murder are in most jurisdictions hardly lenient.

Table 14.1 summarizes the penalties available state by state for first-degree murder convictions. As shown, three-quarters of the states currently have a death penalty in place, a matter that we will discuss more below, and as many as 44 states can and do incarcerate first-degree murderers for life without the possibility of parole.

The public is grossly misinformed about the life without parole (LWOP) sentence. Citizens hear about killers released on parole (generally those convicted of manslaughter or second-degree murder) and assume that this is the norm for all convicted killers, even first-degree murderers. Northeastern University criminologist William Bowers, for example, conducted a telephone survey of 603 residents of Massachusetts, a state that has mandatory life without parole for first-degree murder. Only 3 percent of those interviewed were aware of the lack of parole eligibility for first-degree murder.

A U.S. Department of Justice study of sentencing patterns in 1996 for felony defendants provides some information on how homicide defendants are handled by the state criminal courts.[12] For homicide defendants sentenced to parole-eligible terms, the average sentence length was 257 months (or about 11½ years), of which slightly more than half was expected to be served before release. Importantly, however, as many as a quarter of defendants charged and convicted of criminal homicide received either life terms without parole eligibility or death sentences. These offenders are not released, except in the unusual instance of a commutation or pardon.

Fueled by a widespread misunderstanding of the penalty structure for murder convictions as well as by concern over rising homicide rates, public support for the death

TABLE 14.1   *State Murder Penalties*

		Life without Parole	
		Yes (N = 46)	*No (N = 4)*
Death Penalty	Yes (N = 38)	AL, AZ, AR, CA, CO, CT, DE, FL, GA, ID, IL, IN, KY, LA, MD, MS, MO, MT, NB, NV, NH, NJ, NY, NC, OH, OK, OR, PA, SC, SD, TN, UT, VA, WA, WY	KS, NM, TX
	No (N = 12)	HI, IA, ME, MA, MI, MN, ND, RI, VT, WV, WI	AK

Source: Death Penalty Information Center, Washington, DC.

penalty mounted steadily over the final quarter of the 20th century. With this encouragement from the populace, the number of prisoners put to death has grown as well. As shown in Figure 14.1, the number of executions has risen fairly steadily since 1980. Whereas in the mid-1970s, the public opinion in this country was virtually evenly split on the appropriateness of capital punishment, by the end of the 1990s, support for the death penalty was overwhelming, with as many as three-quarters of Americans in favor of it. Apparently, some citizens simply view an execution as the only absolute guarantee against a convicted killer being released on parole, being commuted, or even escaping over the prison walls. In one

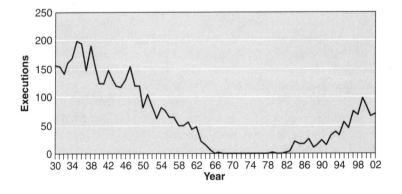

FIGURE 14.1   *Executions in the United States, 1930–2002*

Source: Bureau of Justice Statistics, "Capital Punishment," Washington, DC, 2002.

recent national poll, only 4 percent of respondents believed that criminals sentenced to life incarceration would actually spend their lives in prison.

Arguably, no other aspect of the criminal law receives so much attention as capital punishment, despite its relatively minimal utilization. Even at its peak level of use in 1935 when nearly 199 convicts were put to death, murderers under a death sentence represented a tiny fraction of convicted killers and an even smaller portion of criminals generally.

Notwithstanding its limited application, capital punishment is an issue that has been used as a litmus test for what kind of public officials we elect to office. For example, a case can easily be made that Democratic presidential nominee Michael Dukakis lost to Republican George Bush in the 1988 campaign because of his stand on capital punishment. Even though most death penalty cases (nearly 99 percent) fall within state, rather than federal, jurisdiction, the voting public was concerned about Dukakis's liberal anti-death penalty ideology.

Bill Clinton eased his way into the White House with a pro-death penalty stand. As the Governor of Arkansas, Clinton signed the death warrant for an inmate executed under less than ideal circumstances. Candidate Clinton left the Presidential campaign trail in 1992 to be present in Arkansas for the execution of Ricky Ray Rector, a severely brain-damaged black man who had killed a white police officer (and then shot himself in the head). Rector was obviously mentally retarded and/or mentally ill. He routinely howled like an animal in the days leading up to his execution, and did not understand what was about to happen to him. Rector even saved the cake from his last meal to have later. Although a decade too late to spare Rector's life, the U.S. Supreme Court in 2002 ruled unconstitutional the execution of mentally retarded prisoners.

As shown in Table 14.2, a majority of every socio-political segment of the population supports the use of the death penalty. No wonder that very few politicians who are opposed to the death penalty can get elected to public office, regardless of the strength of their record in other areas.

It is important to view these opinion levels with a whole shaker of salt. Although the sampling and data collection approaches are quite sound, the wording of such questions as "Do you favor or oppose the death penalty for first-degree murder?" may not fully elicit an accurate picture of public sentiment. First, public opinion varies considerably based on the exact nature of the first-degree murder. Whereas the rape, torture, and murder of a child may fully arouse the public's thirst for the supreme penalty of death, felony murders in which robbery victims are shot to death do not quite spark the same level of vehemence and vengeance.[13] More important, Americans may change their opinion depending on the alternatives—that is, the death penalty compared to what other punishment? Several polls have shown that when presented a choice of death penalty or life without parole, public support is almost evenly divided.[14]

Curiously, whereas much of our criminal law pertaining to homicide developed 200 years ago in an attempt to limit those offenders who could face the penalty of death, in recent years most changes in homicide statutes have been introduced to expand the number of capital crimes. Following years of protest and disfavor during which time a majority of Americans actually opposed the death penalty, a virtual moratorium on capital punishment started in the late 1960s and was formalized in 1972 when the U.S. Supreme Court struck down the death penalty. Based on arguments that minorities and the poor were more likely

TABLE 14.2   *Public Opinion on the Death Penalty for Murder, 2003*

	Favor	Oppose	No Opinion
Overall	70%	28%	2%
Sex			
Male	74%	24%	2%
Female	65%	32%	3%
Race			
White	75%	23%	2%
Nonwhite	50%	46%	4%
Black	35%	58%	7%
Age			
18 to 29 years	65%	34%	1%
30 to 49 years	68%	29%	3%
50 to 64 years	75%	24%	1%
50 years and older	73%	25%	2%
65 years and older	71%	26%	3%
Education			
College post graduate	57%	41%	2%
College graduate	72%	24%	4%
Some college	71%	27%	2%
High school graduate or less	72%	26%	2%
Income			
$75,000 and over	69%	29%	2%
$50,000 to $74,999	68%	26%	6%
$30,000 to $49,999	72%	27%	1%
$20,000 to $29,999	66%	34%	0%
Under $20,000	70%	27%	3%
Community			
Urban area	62%	36%	2%
Suburban area	70%	27%	3%
Rural area	76%	23%	1%
Region			
East	62%	34%	4%
Midwest	68%	30%	2%
South	76%	23%	1%
West	70%	28%	2%
Politics			
Republican	85%	14%	1%
Democrat	58%	40%	2%
Independent	67%	31%	2%

Source: Kathleen Maguire & Ann J. Pastore, Sourcebook of Criminal Justice Statistics, Online Edition. Washington, DC: Bureau of Justice Statistics, Table 2.65, Sept. 1, 2003.

to be sentenced to death, the Court held (in *Furman v. Georgia*) that the death penalty was being applied in a capricious, arbitrary, discriminatory, and therefore unconstitutional manner. Importantly, the Supreme Court did not hold that capital punishment was inherently cruel and unusual but set out a process for how the death penalty could be administered in a fair and constitutional manner.

The Supreme Court also added in a later decision that the application of the death penalty must be in proportion to the seriousness of the crime: only the most grievous acts should qualify for the supreme penalty. Because of the proportionality notion, it is now unconstitutional to execute rapists. There is another more practical reason for eliminating rape as a capital crime. Despite the historical practice, executing a rapist may even encourage murder by removing any disincentive for the offender to kill his victim in order to prevent her from testifying against him.

In the wake of this landmark 1972 *Furman* decision, more than three dozen states hurried to redraft their murder statutes to include a death penalty consistent with the Court's framework. To pass constitutional muster, the guidelines for sentencing a defendant to death would have to be clearly defined. A first-degree murder conviction was not sufficient. In order to limit the potential for bias, states had to identify those aggravating factors that would warrant it and mitigating factors that would disqualify it. In addition, the trial would need to be bifurcated so that the fact-finding guilt phase of the trial would be separate from the penalty phase. Thus, should a jury find a defendant guilty of capital murder (murder in the first degree with one or more special or aggravating circumstances), the trial would then proceed to hear testimony about the most appropriate sanction, usually either death or life imprisonment.

Volumes have been written debating the utility and appropriateness of the death penalty. One controversy that has received the most attention is that of its general deterrence—that is, whether or not the existence of the death penalty discourages potential murderers from following through with the act. Could life be so precious even to hardened criminals that the ultimate penalty might dissuade them more than any other sanction?

Much of the early research on this topic, conducted through the mid-1970s, suggested that the deterrence argument was little more than wishful thinking. Comparative studies showed that death penalty states did not have lower homicide rates than similar neighboring states without such a law.[15] In 1975, however, economist Isaac Ehrlich surprised the criminological community and changed the legislative debate by claiming to have demonstrated through a sophisticated statistical analysis that each execution deters about eight homicides.[16]

On the wings of Ehrlich's provocative study, several states rushed to enact death penalty legislation. Death penalty supporters seemed finally to have some hard evidence with which to defend their point of view. It was not until several years later that critics of Ehrlich's research were able to identify the fatal flaws in his work. The most important was that Ehrlich's analysis mainly hinged on the fact that during the late 1960s and early 1970s when the death penalty was rarely used (only three executions were staged from 1966 to 1976), the homicide rate soared. Yet other crimes soared as well, even those such as auto theft that had little to do with capital punishment. Clearly, other factors were responsible for the growth in crime during the 1960s and 1970s, including a homicide rate that doubled from 1963 to 1973.

By the time that Ehrlich's work and a few similar studies by a handful of his disciples were refuted, America had seen renewed support for capital punishment. By then, the pro–death penalty movement had gained so much momentum that the deterrence argument was no longer vital to undergird the pro–death penalty position.

On balance, therefore, the scientific evidence is fairly clear that the death penalty fails to deter murderers, that is, any more than life imprisonment does. Those offenders who are not dissuaded from committing a murder by the prospect of being locked up for life also are not likely to be discouraged by the prospect of death. That is, while the death penalty may deter in an absolute sense (even murderers fear death), in a relative sense it is no more of a deterrent than the life imprisonment alternative. The key term is prospect, or the perceived probability that the penalty will be applied. Those who act with deliberation, planning, and premeditation generally view their risk of apprehension as low. If one is not caught, there can be no punishment, regardless of what penalty is on the books.

Although life imprisonment may be virtually as powerful a deterrent, many Americans are concerned about their tax dollars being used unnecessarily and wastefully to house and feed convicted murderers for the rest of their lives. Yet, economic analyses have shown that the cost savings associated with removing a prisoner from a cell and executing him or her has been grossly exaggerated. Given the fixed overhead costs of incarceration—utilities, salaries, and maintenance, relatively little is saved by staging an execution. On the other side of the fiscal ledger, moreover, the cost of capital trials tends to be rather high. Given the life-and-death stakes, the necessary procedural safeguards in place in some states in an attempt to avoid a wrongful execution provide capital defendants with the best defense that the taxpayers can buy. Capital murder trials tend to be many times more costly than non–capital murder trials, given the complexity and length of these prosecutions. The process could be streamlined, of course, but at a very different cost—increasing the possibility of executing an innocent person.

Of course, for most people, according to polls, the defining issue is justice or vengeance—an eye for an eye, a tooth for a tooth. According to a 1991 Gallup poll, half the supporters of capital punishment indicated retribution as the primary reason for their position, well ahead of any other justification.[17] Many supporters insist, despite the lack of deterrence and the costliness, that it is the just punishment, not to mention a surefire way of preventing the offender from repeating his offense, outside or even inside prison.

The concern for racial discrimination, which motivated the 1972 moratorium on executions, no longer appears to sway public opinion or even today's conservative Supreme Court. Despite statistical evidence alleging discrimination based on the race of the victim, the Court held that defendants may appeal on the issue of racial discrimination but only based on evidence of bias in their own particular trials. The Court appears satisfied that the statistical trends no longer disadvantage minorities.

Under current operating procedures, there are indeed more whites sentenced to death—in absolute numbers and in comparison to the murder rates—than blacks (see Figure 14.2). But the pattern of racial discrimination is subtler.

Figure 14.3 shows the probability of execution by comparing victim/offender race combinations among solved homicides for the years 1976–2002 with executions through the end of 2002. Overall, regardless of race, 0.12 percent (or 1 in every 850 known murderers) are executed. The differences according to race are, however, quite provocative and give different inferences once probed below the surface. White killers have twice the likelihood of being executed as blacks. Furthermore, those who kill whites are six times as likely to be executed as those who kill blacks.

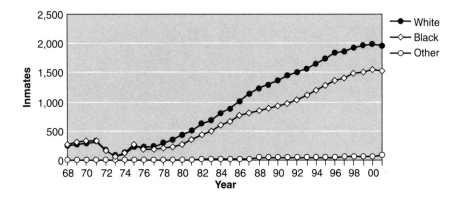

FIGURE 14.2 *Death Row Inmates by Race, 1968–2001*

Source: Bureau of Justice Statistics, "Capital Punishment," Washington, DC, 2002.

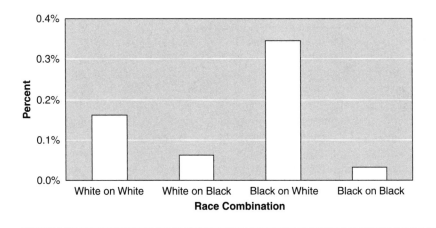

FIGURE 14.3 *Probability of Execution by Race of Victim and Offender, 1976–2002*

But when examining the race combinations of offenders and their victims, an apparent injustice emerges. Blacks who kill whites have the greatest chance of being executed (.35 percent), twice as high as when whites kill whites (.16 percent), 6 times higher than when whites kill blacks (.06 percent), and 11 times higher than when blacks kill blacks (.03 percent).

Thus, although it may appear that black murderers are less likely to receive the death penalty, this is a function of the intraracial nature of homicide and the racism of a criminal justice system that places less value on black murder victims. When blacks kill whites, they are more likely than any other victim-offender dyad to receive the death penalty. Indeed, a long history of scientific research has exposed the racial bias associated with the use of capital punishment.

The death penalty is also less likely to be carried out against women than men. Since 1977, 866 men and only 10 women have been put to death. As an oddity of recent history, an Alabama woman may be the last person to be executed in the electric chair.

Recent advances in DNA technology have had a tremendous impact on the criminal justice system. Police investigators have found in DNA a significant forensic tool for their attempts to solve homicide cases, and prosecutors have been able to offer definitive proof of a defendant's guilt, placing him or her at a crime scene by linking samples of the defendant's blood with various genetic evidence (e.g., blood, saliva, semen, etc.) left at the crime scene.

The value of DNA has not just been for the law enforcement community in trying to catch and prosecute criminals. Not only has DNA excluded certain suspects because of genetic code mismatches, but many previously convicted prisoners have been exonerated by this new evidence that had been unavailable at the time of trial. Most critically, many death row inmates have been saved from a potentially wrongful execution by DNA technology.

Growing awareness of overturned capital cases has made many observers extremely nervous about the finality of the death penalty. Lifers, such as ex-boxer Hurricane Carter, can be released from custody once exculpatory evidence surfaces, but those who were executed have no reprieve. Governor George Ryan of Illinois, a state that has traditionally been willing to execute murderers, made history and headlines by calling a moratorium on executions until the reliability of capital prosecutions could be determined. Upon announcing this move, he noted that the 13 condemned prisoners removed from death row in recent years based on innocence was 1 more than the number of executions that the state had performed since the restoration of capital punishment. Then, just prior to leaving office, Governor Ryan commuted the death sentences of all 156 inmates on the Illinois death row (along with 11 others). Most of the sentences were reduced to life without parole.

Ryan's discomfort surrounding the possibility of egregious error in the application of capital punishment likely reflects why death penalty support has softened in this country since the late 1990s. The receding tide of support may not just be the result of plunging homicide rates, which helped make the public feel more secure. More fundamentally, in a nation whose system of jurisprudence honors and protects the rights of the innocent over all else, growing concern for wrongful executions may signal that the days of the death penalty are numbered.

Epidemic Thinking and Over-Response

For years, the United States has stood alone amongst Western nations in the practice of executing murderers. Our foreign peers—countries such as Australia, Canada, Finland, France, Germany, Italy, Netherlands, New Zealand, Norway, and the United Kingdom—have abolished capital punishment. Others, such as Mexico and Greece, have retained the penalty of death, but only for military crimes and high treason. Even the Russian Federation has imposed a moratorium on executions, although the provision for capital punishment remains on the books. Meanwhile, the United States is conspicuous among the list of nations imposing the death penalty for common murderers, a collection that includes countries like Afghanistan, China, Cuba, Iran, Iraq, and Saudi Arabia.

The rapid growth in the number of executions performed in this country during the 1990s has been followed by a modest short-term downturn at the start of the new millennium. In part this may reflect strategic decisions in states like Illinois where in 2002 then Governor Ryan commuted the sentences of all death row prisoners and Maryland where a temporary hold was placed on scheduled executions while the fairness of the death penalty was reviewed. It may also signal a shift in public mood prompted by recurrent revelations about innocent defendants who had been convicted and sentenced to die (e.g., Illinois's Governor Ryan had granted clemency to 13 death row inmates after further investigation into their cases exonerated them). Whereas in 1994, three-quarters of Americans were in favor of the death penalty for convicted murderers, this figure declined to 62.4% by 2001.

The shrinking support for capital punishment may also reflect a more general shift away from get-tough approaches as crime rates have dropped precipitously. Figure 14.4 compares the ebb and flow of death penalty sentiment concomitant with the rise and fall in the U.S. homicide rate. While it may be difficult to establish any firm causal connection between murder rates and death penalty support, it does appear that the passion for capital punishment may have cooled somewhat as the murder toll has diminished.

Whatever the connection between opinion poll results and murder rates, public perception and attitude is quite volatile, and can easily be altered by high profile events, regardless of their statistical prevalence. Crime rates may be at their lowest point in three decades, yet a particularly heinous episode of senseless violence, if covered extensively by the mass media, can quickly renew demands for tougher sanctions for criminals.

To suggest that the news media is over-reactive to extraordinary episodes is perhaps an understatement. Constantly seeking to increase their market shares, local and syndicated news outlets often treat the latest shocking murder case like a national catastrophe. Moreover, there is a clear tendency to hype their coverage by declaring the crime as the latest epidemic to confront the American public. The logic seems to be that if it isn't a raging epidemic, then no one will pay attention.

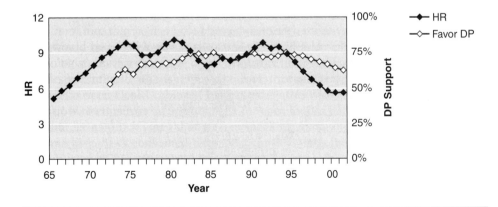

FIGURE 14.4   *Trends in the U.S. Homicide Rate and Public Support for the Death Penalty*

Sources: Federal Bureau of Investigation, *Crime in the United States,* Washington, DC, various years; National Opinion Research Center surveys, various years.

Virtually ever year, the news media contributes to constructing a new crime growth curve. Very few Americans realize that the current crime rate is lower than it has been in 30 years.The mid-1980s witnessed a serial murder panic fueled by outlandish reports that as many as 5,000 Americans were killed annually by these sexual predators. Next came a media-hyped scare in relation to carjackings, then home invasions, then sexual molestation in day care centers, then workplace killings, then road rage, then school shootings, then child abductions. Many of the episodes on which the media focused their attention and their cameras were real in their impact on victims, yet statements concerning the risk to others were often exaggerated.

Recent cases of missing children illustrate exactly how these so-called epidemics are invented. In February 2002, seven-year-old Danielle van Dam was snatched from her bedroom during the middle of the night, prompting a massive search of her San Diego neighborhood as well as a nationwide appeal by her parents on the *Today Show* pleading her safe return. Three weeks later, however, the girl's charred and decomposed body was found near a small grove of trees east of San Diego. She had been abducted, molested, and murdered by her neighbor, 50-year-old David Westerfield.

"Bad things come in threes," it is said, and numbers two and three came in quick succession. In June, 14-year-old Elizabeth Smart was abducted from her bedroom while her younger sister watched in horror; nine months later, Smart resurfaced alive and well after having roamed with a nomadic husband and wife team of religious zealots. Her abductor, who called himself "Emmanuel" was a self-styled prophet with a long history of delusions that included fantasies of multiple child brides. In July 2002, a month following Smart's disappearance, five-year-old Samantha Runnion was kidnapped as she was playing with a friend in the yard next to her home; her body was found the following day with evidence that she had been sexually molested and asphyxiated. Alejandro Avila, age 27, was arrested and charged with Runnion's murder.

Eager to jump on the latest and scariest crime trend, the news media declared kidnapping the newest epidemic. One media outlet dramatically labeled the long steamy months of 2002 as the "Summer of Abduction." Having considered the possibility that these abductions signaled a new and ominous trend, journalists and news directors began searching news wires far and wide for any story of a disappearance or attempted abduction to fit and confirm the epidemic theory.

On Fox television, Bill O'Reilly, host of *The O'Reilly Factor,* cited an erroneous statistic that 100,000 children are abducted each year by strangers. Hurriedly doing the math, he also miscalculated there to be more than 30 such kidnappings a day. Actually, the mathematically correct calculation would place the daily count at about 300 children, the host being off by an "O'Reilly Factor" of 10. If it were indeed the case that 100,000 children annually fall victim to stranger abduction, we would all likely be personally familiar with at least one such unfortunate child. Among a national population of 50 million youngsters under the age of 13, this prevalence of stranger abduction would translate to one out of every 500 children. At this rate, an average size grade school would endure one stranger abduction each year. Stated in this way, the statistics seem more than a bit preposterous. Unfortunately, once these blatant exaggerations are stated as "facts" on one of the many 24 hour news channels, they are repeated and continue to contribute to uninformed policymaking.

Amidst the tremendous media hype about stranger-child abductions, some sober perspective on the scope of the problem would surely have calmed some nervous parents and outraged politicians. The most reliable and trustworthy estimates of stranger-child abductions are in the hundreds, not hundred-thousands. The national organization Child Find, for example, estimates that after removing parent abductions arising out of custody battles (the most common form) as well as attempted kidnappings, fewer than 600 children are abducted by strangers each year. Furthermore, the majority of these youngsters are eventually found alive. The less fortunate victims who are slain by their abductors number about 50 per year.

Of course, the thought of any child being kidnapped, raped, and murdered is horrible, but in statistical terms it is hardly one of the greatest perils that children face on a daily basis—even if and when a serial predator is operating in the neighborhood. A child is more likely to be killed in a fall off a bicycle than by being grabbed off the bike by a rapist/murderer; still, some parents are more apt to keep their children at home in "protective custody" than to enforce the use of the helmets. More children are killed each year by playing with their parents' loaded gun; yet, some parents are more apt to lock up their children for safekeeping than their firearms.

With 50 million children in the United States under the age of 13, the likelihood of any one ending up like Samantha Runnion is literally one in a million. For Samantha's family, of course, it matters not that her case is statistically exceptional. But for the rest of us, it matters a lot.

For the well-being of children, it is important that parents not pass along a sense of paranoia to their kids. Youngsters should not be made into prisoners of fear, constantly looking out for the boogeyman in a parked car. For society, it also matters—it matters that we resist the temptation to rush to enact legislation and public policy that is not well-conceived.

Like other imagined epidemics, attention to the problem of child abductions waned by the close of 2002, as Americans moved on to the next issue of the day. But in so many of these instances, also left behind is some poorly-conceived policy response hurriedly crafted amidst a climate of hysteria. Talk of an epidemic of workplace homicide with scores of disgruntled employees "going postal" may have enhanced efforts to support laid-off workers, but it also led to misguided efforts to profile unhappy workers rather than respond to their grievances. Widespread concern that our schools were populated by armed misfits who might "do a Columbine" may have forced educators to take seriously such as issues as bullying, but it also resulted in serious infringements upon the rights of many innocent students caught up in zero-tolerance policies. In the final analysis (literally for this book at least), the important lesson is to view with healthy skepticism any public policy proposed in the wake of extraordinary and ghastly episodes of murder and mayhem.

Endnotes _____

1. http://www.law.umkc.edu/faculty/projects/trials/hinckley/letter.htm.

2. L. A. Callahan, M. J. Steadman, M. A. McGreevy, and P. C. Robbins, "The Volume and Characteristics of Insanity Defense Pleas: An Eight-State Study," *Bulletin of the American Academy of Psychiatry and the Law* 19 (1991): 331–338.

3. Norval Morris, *Madness and Criminal Law.* Chicago: University of Chicago Press, 1982.

4. Anthony M. Platt, *The Child Savers; The Invention of Delinquency.* Chicago: University of Chicago Press, 1969.

5. David S. Tanenhaus, "The Evolution of Waiver in the Juvenile Court," in Jeffrey Fagan and Franklin Zimring, eds., *The Changing Borders of Juvenile Justice:*

Transfer of Adolescents to Criminal Court. Chicago: University of Chicago Press, 1999.

6. Patricia Tourbet and Linda Syzmanski, *State Legislative Responses to Violent Juvenile Crime: 1996–97 Update.* Washington, DC: Office of Juvenile Justice and Delinquency Prevention, 1998.

7. Howard N. Snyder and Melissa Sickmund, *Juvenile Offenders and Victims: 1999 National Report.* Washington, DC: Office of Juvenile Justice and Delinquency Prevention, 1999.

8. Kevin J. Strom, *Profile of State Prisoners Under Age 18, 1985–97.* Washington, DC: Bureau of Justice Statistics, February 2000.

9. Deborah Yurgelun-Todd, "Functional Brain Changes in Adolescents." Presentation at the Whitehead Institute for Bio-Medical Research, Massachusetts Institute of Technology, Cambridge, MA, June 1998.

10. Simon I. Singer and David McDowall, "Criminalizing Delinquency: The Deterrent Effects of the New York Juvenile Offender Law," *Law and Society Review* 22 (1988): 521–535.

11. Donna M. Bishop, Charles E. Frazier, Lonn Lanza-Kaduce, and Henry George White, *Juvenile Transfers to Criminal Court.* Washington, DC: Office of Juvenile Justice and Delinquency Prevention, 1998.

12. Jodi M. Brown and Patrick J. Langan, *Felony Sentences in the United States, 1996.* Washington, DC: Bureau of Justice Statistics, 1999.

13. James Alan Fox, Michael Radelet, and Julie Bonsteel, "Public Opinion on the Death Penalty in the Post-Furman Years," *New York University Review of Law and Social Change* 18 (1990–91): 499–528.

14. William J. Bowers, Margaret Vandiver, and Patricia H. Dugan, "A New Look at Public Opinion on Capital Punishment: What Citizens and Legislators Prefer," *American Journal of Criminal Law* 22 (1994): 77–150.

15. Thorsten J. Sellin, *Capital Punishment.* New York: Harper & Row, 1967.

16. Isaac Ehrlich, "The Deterrent Effect of Capital Punishment: A Question of Life and Death," *American Economic Review* 65 (1975): 397–417.

17. A. Gallup and F. Newport, "Death Penalty Support Remains Strong," *The Gallup Poll Monthly* 309 (June 1991): 40–45.

Suggested Readings

Abrahamsen, David, *The Murdering Mind*. New York: Harper Colophon Books, 1973.

Chester, Graham, *Berserk!: Motiveless Random Massacres*. New York: St. Martin's Press, 1995.

Daly, Martin and Margo Wilson, *Homicide*. New York: Aldine de Gruyter, 1988.

Egger, Steven A., *The Killers among Us: An Examination of Serial Murder and Its Investigation*. Upper Saddle River, NJ: Prentice Hall, 1998.

Elikann, Peter, *Superpredators: The Demonization of Our Children by the Law*. New York: Plenum Press, 1999.

Ewing, Charles Patrick, *Fatal Families: The Dynamics of Intrafamilial Homicide*. Thousand Oaks, CA: Sage Publications, 1997.

Fox, James Alan and Jack Levin, *Overkill: Mass Murder and Serial Killing Exposed*. New York: Plenum Press, 1994.

Garbarino, James, *Lost Boys: Why Our Sons Turn Violent and How We Can Save Them*. New York: The Free Press, 1999.

Gillespie, Cynthia K., *Justifiable Homicide: Battered Women, Self-Defense, and the Law*. Columbus, OH: Ohio State University Press, 1989.

Green, Edward, *The Intent to Kill: Making Sense of Murder*. Baltimore: Clevedon Books, 1993.

Godwin, John, *Murder USA: The Ways We Kill Each Other*. New York: Ballantine Books, 1978.

Hamilton, James T., *Channeling Violence: The Economic Market for Violent Television Programming*. Princeton, NJ: Princeton University Press, 1998.

Harries, Keith D., *Serious Violence: Patterns of Homicide and Assault in America*, Second Edition. Springfield, IL: Charles C. Thomas Publisher, 1997.

Heide, Kathleen M., *Why Kids Kill Parents: Child Abuse and Adolescent Homicide*. Thousand Oaks, CA: Sage Publications, 1995.

Heide, Kathleen M., *Young Killers: The Challenge of Juvenile Homicide*. Thousand Oaks, CA: Sage Publications, 1998.

Hickey, Eric W., *Serial Murderers and Their Victims*, Third Edition. Belmont, CA: Wadsworth Publishing Company, 2002.

Holmes, Ronald M. and Stephen T. Holmes, *Murder in America*. Thousand Oaks, CA: Sage Publications, 1993.

Holmes, Ronald M. and Stephen T. Holmes, *Mass Murder In the United States*. Upper Saddle River, NJ: Prentice Hall, 2001.

Jenkins, Philip, *Using Murder: The Social Construction of Serial Homicide*. Aldine de Gruyter, 1994.

Kelleher, Michael D., *When Good Kids Kill*. Westport, CT: Praeger, 1998.

Lane, Roger, *Murder in America: A History*. Columbus, OH: Ohio State University Press, 1997.

Lester, David, *Questions and Answers about Murder*. Philadelphia: Charles Press, 1991.

Levin, Jack and James Alan Fox, *Mass Murder: America's Growing Menace*. New York: Plenum Press, 1985.

Levin, Jack and Jack McDevitt, *Hate Crimes: The Rising Tide of Bigotry and Bloodshed*. New York: Plenum Press, 1993.

Leyton, Eliot, *Compulsive Killers: The Story of Modern Multiple Murderers*. New York: New York University Press, 1986.

Lundsguarde, Henry P., *Murder in Space City: A Cultural Analysis of Houston Homicide Patterns*. New York: Oxford University Press, 1977.

National Research Council Institute of Medicine, *Deadly Lessons: Understanding Lethal School Violence*. Washington, D.C.: The National Academies Press, 2003.

O'Reilly-Fleming, Thomas, ed., *Serial and Mass Murder: Theory, Research and Policy*. Toronto: Canadian Scholars' Press, 1996.

Patricia Pearson, *When She Was Bad*. New York: Penguin Books, 1998.

Prothrow-Stith, Deborah, *Deadly Consequences*. New York: Harper, 1993.

Ressler, Robert K., Ann W. Burgess, and John E. Douglas, *Sexual Homicide: Patterns and Motives*. Lexington, MA: Lexington Books, 1988.

Rhodes, Richard, *Why They Kill: The Discoveries of a Maverick Criminologist*. New York: Alfred A. Knopf, 1999.

Schreier, Herbert A. and Judith A. Libow, *Hurting for Love: Munchausen by Proxy Syndrome.* New York: The Guilford Press, 1993.

Smith, M. Dwayne and Margaret A. Zahn, *Homicide: A Sourcebook of Social Research.* Thousand Oaks, CA: Sage Publications, 1999.

Turvey, Brent, *Criminal Profiling: An Introduction to Behavioral Evidence Analysis.* United Kingdom: Elsevier Science Ltd., 2002.

Wilson, Anna Victoria, ed., *Homicide: The Victim/Offender Connection.* Cincinnati, OH: Anderson Publishing, 1993.

Wolfgang, Marvin E., *Patterns in Criminal Homicide.* Philadelphia: University of Pennsylvania Press, 1958.

A Note about Data Sources

Except for the few instances where a source note is indicated, the information for nearly all tables and charts was drawn from a cumulative data file of the FBI's Supplementary Homicide Reports (SHR) for the years 1976 through 2002, the most recent year available at publication time. Compiled and reformatted by one of the authors (Fox), the complete data file is available at the National Archive of Criminal Justice Data of the Inter-University Consortium of Political and Social Research at the University of Michigan.[1] In addition, many tabulations and charts are maintained and updated annually on the Website of the Bureau of Justice Statistics.[2]

The SHR provides incident-level details on location, victim, and offender characteristics for almost all homicides in the United States. Specifically, these data include information on the month and year of an offense, on the reporting agency and its residential population, county and Metropolitan Statistical Areas (MSA) codes, geographic division and population group, on the age, race, and sex of victims and offenders, and on the victim/offender relationship, weapon use, and circumstance of the crime. For the years 1976–2002, contributing agencies provided homicide reports for 492,672 of the estimated 544,909 murder victims, and for 545,720 of the estimated 603,826 offenders.

Although national coverage is quite high (about 92 percent of homicides are included in the SHR), missing reports have been corrected using weights to match national and state estimated counts prepared by the FBI. The most significant problem in using SHR data to analyze offender characteristics, however, is the sizable number of unsolved homicides contained in the data file. To the extent that the pattern of missing offender data is associated with certain offender characteristics, ignoring unsolved homicides would seriously underestimate rates of offending by particular sub-groups of the population, distort trends over time among these same sub-groups, and bias observed patterns of offending. To adjust for unsolved homicides, a method for offender imputation has been implemented, using available information about the victims murdered in both solved and unsolved homicides. Through this imputation procedure, the demographic characteristics of unidentified offenders are inferred on the basis of similar homicide cases—similar in terms of the victim profile, weapon, circumstances, region, and year of the offense—that had been solved. In other words, offender profiles for unsolved crimes are estimated based on the offender profiles in solved cases matched on victim age, sex, and race as well as weapon, circumstances, region, and year. This imputation strategy was particularly useful in tracking offending rates over time.

A number of terms and codes were used throughout the book, particularly in tables and graphs presented in Chapter 3. These are defined as follows:

Intimate homicide:	Killings involving spouses, ex-spouses, boyfriends/girlfriends, or homosexual couples
Family homicide:	Killings involving spouses, parents/children, siblings, other family members
Infanticide:	Victims under 5 years old
Eldercide:	Victims age 65 or over
Felony-murder:	Homicides involving rape, robbery, burglary, larceny, auto theft, arson, or vice law violations
Sex-related:	Homicides involving rape, prostitution, or other sex crimes
Drug-related:	Homicides involving narcotics law violations or arguments over narcotics
Gang-related:	Gangland or youth gang killing
Argument:	Homicides involving dispute over money, drugs/ alcohol, jealousy, etc.
Workplace:	Homicides by employers or employees

Finally, the following geographic divisions are use in regional analyses:

New England (NE):	Connecticut, Maine, Massachusetts, New Hampshire, Rhode Island, Vermont
Middle Atlantic (MA):	New Jersey, New York, Pennsylvania
East North Central (ENC):	Illinois, Indiana, Michigan, Ohio, Wisconsin
West North Central (WNC):	Iowa, Kansas, Minnesota, Missouri, Nebraska, North Dakota, South Dakota
South Atlantic (SA):	Delaware, District of Columbia, Florida, Georgia, Maryland, North Carolina, South Carolina, Virginia, West Virginia
East South Central (ESC):	Alabama, Kentucky, Mississippi, Tennessee
West South Central (WSC):	Arkansas, Louisiana, Oklahoma, Texas
Mountain (MT):	Arizona, Colorado, Idaho, Montana, Nevada, New Mexico, Utah, Wyoming
Pacific (PA):	Alaska, California, Hawaii, Oregon, Washington

Endnotes

1. James Alan Fox, *Uniform Crime Reports [United States]: Supplementary Homicide Reports, 1976–2002,* Ann Arbor, MI: Inter-University Consortium of Political and Social Research, 2004.

2. James Alan Fox and Marianne Zawitz, *Homicide trends in the United States,* Bureau of Justice Statistics Website, *www.ojp.usdoj.gov/bjs/homicide/homtrnd.htm,* January 2004.

Index